Talks on Pedagogics and Other Writings

Talks on Pedagogics:
An Outline of the Theory of Concentration
and Other Writings

Francis W. Parker

Originally edited by
Elise A. Wygant and Flora J. Cooke
Francis W. Parker School
Chicago

PUBLISHED BY THE

Francis W. Parker School

FRANCIS W. PARKER SCHOOL
1901-2001

A Centennial Celebration Publication
Edited by Daniel B. Frank

a

FOREWORD
To the Centennial
Celebration Edition

This is a book about passion. It is a book inspired by hope. It is a book of profound human ideals and a palpable, vital desire to create a great democratic society, comprised of citizens with strong character, cultivated through the imaginative thinking and courageous love of school teachers. It is a book for today. It is a book for tomorrow. It is a book for America.

The ideas contained in *Talks on Pedagogics* are those of Colonel Francis Wayland Parker, the pioneering 19th century educator. Named "the father of progressive education" by John Dewey, the renowned American philosopher of education, Parker was a man of no small vision.[1] He believed the promise of America rests in the quality of its public schools. He believed that America can be great only if its schools are free to be spirited and responsive places led by qualified teachers. These teachers would embrace their calling by seeking to understand how children think and feel and learn and by believing that children grow most thoroughly as individuals when they learn in the authentic context of a dynamic community life.

Colonel Parker understood that the school is an essential social institution necessary for the forward progress of the child and society. He dedicated his life to the conviction

[1]See Marie Kirchner Stone's book, *The Progressive Legacy: Chicago's Francis W. Parker School (1901-2001)*. New York: Peter Lang, 2001, for a fuller historical and philosophical treatment of Parker and Dewey's educational thinking and practice.

that the school holds the greatest potential for transforming both individual lives and the grander project of democratic life in America. He believed that a child's early educational experience not only shapes her development as a human being but also determines her long-term capacity to grow into an adult citizen with the empathy, disposition and intelligence to collaborate with others to promote freedom and equality for all Americans.

Colonel Parker's approach to education, human development and social transformation contains the attuned observations of a psychologist, the broad perspective of a sociologist and the moral convictions of a social reformer and activist. A man of his times, Parker was influenced by both creative and destructive forces. He embodied the transcendentalists' romance with the beauty of organic development and the grandeur that connects all living things, and he knew only too well the violent horrors of being a soldier in the Civil War. Colonel Parker was armed with the passionate belief that "... *the day would come when the teacher will lead society and mould opinion...*"[2] In this way, he forged the innocence of youth and the idealism of freedom with a battlefield pragmatism that drove him with a single, dedicated focus to create humane and excellent schools led by knowledgeable, empathic and inspirational teachers.

Parker said of himself: *"Fighting for four years in the Civil War, as best I could, for the preservation of the democratic ideal, a teacher of little children for nearly forty years, I believe four things: as I believe in God–that democracy is the one hope for the world; that democracy without efficient*

---

[2]Patridge, Lelila E. *Notes of Talks on Teaching, Given by Francis W. Parker, at the Martha's Vineyard Summer Institute, July 17 to August 19, 1882.* New York and Chicago: E.L. Kellogg & Co., (1889) p 5.

c

common (public) schools is impossible; that every school in the land should be made a home and a heaven for children; fourth, that when the ideal of the public school is realized, 'the blood shed by the blessed martyrs for freedom will not have been shed in vain.'"

In his career, Colonel Parker had commitments to both public and private education. Flora J. Cooke, a former student of Colonel Parker, and the first principal of the Francis W. Parker School in Chicago, describes this relationship in the final footnote to the 1937 edition of *Talks on Pedagogics*: *"While Colonel Parker believed that a private school for wealthy children only, had no place in a democracy–he thought that there was a definite need for private laboratory schools including children from all economic levels, all races and creeds who would live, work and play together through their growing years. In these laboratory schools educational experiments might be tried out for the benefit of public school practice, which would be impractical in an unwieldy large school system. Indeed, Colonel Parker himself more reluctantly left the Chicago Public School system in 1899. He had struggled valiantly and unremittingly for eighteen years against great odds and obstacles imposed by a politically controlled School Board. He believed he could work faster and most effectively for the children of the Chicago schools–for all children–in a private laboratory–a Normal and Demonstration School–where he could be free to put to the test the Social Philosophy of Education in which he ardently believed."*

d

For more than 100 years, Colonel Parker's thinking and actions have inspired generations of students, teachers and parents with a number of well-known and well-loved statements :

A school should be a model home, a complete community, an embryonic democracy.

What is the great word? Responsibility.

Everything to help and nothing to hinder.

The needs of society should determine the work of the school. The supreme need of society is ideal citizenship. Ideal citizenship demands for the individual the highest degree of knowledge, skill, power and service. Therefore, the one purpose of the school is to present conditions for growth toward ideal citizenship.

The highest duty of the individual is to contribute all in his power to the best good of all.

A fundamental principle of democracy is the responsibility of each for all, and all for each.

The primary concern of education is character.

The direction that I would give to all teachers is: Watch the child, watch his attitude of attention. Is it spontaneous? Is the light of pleasure in his eyes? Is interest the motive which controls him?

This book places these powerful and moving statements, and others, in the fuller context of Colonel Parker's thinking and teaching.

Talks on Pedagogics, first published in 1894, is comprised of essays Colonel Parker originally delivered in a series of public lectures to teachers. Parker was more a speaker than a writer. He was a man of action and teaching, and he chose to spend his time talking directly to teachers in lectures and seminars rather than reserving solitary time to write in the stillness of a quiet, reflective space.

It was his students who first began to create written texts of his ideas based on their notes from his lectures. Colonel Parker describes the making of *Talks on Pedagogics* in the preface to the original edition, which is reprinted in this volume. Also in this publication is the preface, written by Flora J. Cooke, to the 1937 edition, which she edited with Elise A. Wygant, another student of Colonel Parker. Many of the ideas articulated in this volume first appeared in another out-of-print book, *Notes of Talks on Teaching* (1883).[3] A teacher, Lelila E. Patridge, transformed the notes she had taken during Parker's 1882 Martha's Vineyard Summer Institute lectures into a set of essays, which Parker later read and approved for accuracy.

Talks on Pedagogics reappears now for two essential reasons. First, in honor of the Centennial Celebration of the Francis W. Parker School in Chicago, we believe that making the fuller body of the Colonel's thought available to students, educators and parents is indeed timely, if not long

---

[3]Patridge, Lelila E. *Notes of Talks on Teaching, Given by Francis W. Parker, at the Martha's Vineyard Summer Institute, July 17 to August 19, 1882.* New York and Chicago: E.L. Kellogg & Co., 1889.

f

overdue. Second, the current crisis in American public school education, especially in urban schools, calls for a renewed appreciation of the courage, strength and insight that Colonel Parker offered America more than a century ago–qualities of motivation for social action and social justice that may inspire each new generation of educators and citizens who read this book.

This Centennial Celebration reprint adds several writings to those included in the original edition. I have included these additions to give the reader both a fuller exposure to Colonel Parker's far-sighted, progressive thinking as well as a more vivid sense of the man and his passion for life, learning and democracy.

The first addition is an essay on examinations in education taken from Colonel Parker's lecture in the summer of 1882, which originally appeared in *Notes on Talks on Teaching*. The clarity of Colonel Parker's thinking and the logic of his argument seem astutely relevant in 2001, as public debate abounds concerning the pressure to expand the amount and influence of standardized testing in schools at the expense of creating and sustaining dynamic educational programs that engage students and teachers.

The second addition is Lelila E. Patridge's formerly out-of-print introduction to *Notes on Talks on Teaching*, in which she draws an impressive portrait of Colonel Parker as she encountered him in 1882.

g

And finally, there are four additional chapters that comprise a series of beautiful and moving eulogies delivered at Colonel Parker's funeral service on March 6, 1902, four days after his untimely death.[4] The eulogies originally were printed in *The Elementary School Teacher and Course of Study* in June 1902. Each of the four impressive speakers was a significant public figure in education, progressive politics and social justice activism in Chicago and nationally: William Rainey Harper, President of the University of Chicago; Albert G. Lane, District Superintendent, Chicago Public Schools; John Dewey, Professor of Education and Philosophy, the University of Chicago; and Rabbi Emil G. Hirsch, Rabbi of the Sinai Congregation and Chicago civic leader. Each of these eulogies gives the reader a vivid and stirring description of the man, his ideas and his passionate commitment to children and democracy.

Francis W. Parker's passion for life has inspired generations of educators and students to forward the progress of democracy and education. It is only fitting, then, to include in this republication of his work a few statements that he made, which, until now, had existed only in a well-documented, but now out-of-print, interpretive biographical essay by Ida Cassa Heffron (1930).[5] Each of these statements provides the reader with a rich and impressive sense of how Colonel Parker saw the world and the vast interrelationships that shape human life and the experience of learning. Each statement conveys the passionate connection Colonel Parker felt to the deeper meaning of his work and to his robust sense of purpose in life:

[4]"In Memoriam. Colonel Francis Wayland Parker." *The Elementary School Teacher and Course of Study* 2 (1902): 699-715.
[5]Heffron, Ida C. *Francis Wayland Parker: An Interpretive Biography.* Los Angeles: Ivan Deach Jr., 1934.

It seemed to me one of the most satisfying discoveries to myself of my life when I felt that there was only one study in the world, and that is the study of life, and all studies center in that–the study of the laws of life.

The great energy should center in the human being as a focus. Just what the human being can take into his soul of this All Life, and give it back again, is the function of the human being; to take the truth that comes in from all the universe and give it back being created and ever creative.

...the supreme joy of being is to take in this life and give it out to others.

The steps of progress that I can see are the concentration of this truth in an ideal school, in an ideal education. Mankind is lost upon anything else, because all forms of expression and all the so-called branches when seen under the light of one central thought of unity are all one. One cannot be known alone, and if all is known each study is only known as it is known in its relation to the great center. There is a perfect correlation and a perfect unity, and this all centers in God.

Colonel Parker was a man of substantial empathy and force, intelligence and spirituality, courage and character. But he would not want us to think that the future of education rests alone with his words and his understandings about how children learn and how democracy can thrive. He would want us to think hard and expansively for ourselves. He would want us to challenge his ideas, to test his assumptions against the reality of teaching today. He would want us to risk failure to grow, develop, to question tradition to understand the meaning of continuity and change, to confront and appreciate the past to make sense of the present and look forward to the future.

There is one statement, though, that Colonel Parker made more than 100 years ago that surely will have lasting meaning for future generations of educators, parents, students, citizens and policymakers:

The children of today are in our hands, whatever we do
for them will determine the future. Our lack of faith
in this direction is the greatest infidelity.

Colonel Parker's words provide wise direction for our reflection and action. The rest, however, is up to us.

Daniel B. Frank, Ph.D.'74
Associate Principal
Francis W. Parker School
Chicago, Illinois
August 2001

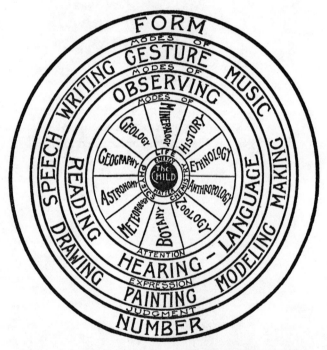

CHART ILLUSTRATING THE THEORY OF CONCENTRATION

FOREWORD

IN a special tribute prepared for the hundredth anniversary of Francis Parker's birth, Mrs. Anita McCormick Blaine draws the following pen portrait of Colonel Parker as she knew him:

On the path of life one day there beamed a great light.

One looked to see whence it came.

One saw a man—tall, massive, powerful; outgoing, yet reserved; forceful, direct and to the core in expression; genial; beaming kindness; and with the light of humor playing over all.

One forgot the setting at once in the eloquent incisive gifts, through the eyes, from the mind and soul.

This was Francis Wayland Parker.

Stepping on the path with him one found what the light was:

The gift to the children of all he had found of right principle to bring each of them, in the process and course of education, to his best self.

Found through the dedication of his life to the finding. And through devoted search at the feet of the masters of the world.

With the stern unyielding demand for all of this best, for all the children in the world, was the capstone of humility to yield all of his finding, if better could be found, for the children.

No pages nor words could express this light, this gift, fully.

Below and through the words one may glimpse and receive the gift of the spirit of Francis Wayland Parker.

Each age has its pioneers in education, and no one can read *Talks on Pedagogics* by Colonel Parker without realizing that its author was one of the real pioneers—one of those who left his impress by action. The book has long been out of print, and it is needed today more than ever to help those who struggle against superficiality and mechanization in education and in behalf of higher human values.

The Progressive Education Association is glad to make available this new edition of Francis Parker's most important work. We are particularly grateful to those devoted people who worked so carefully on the revision of the manuscript and made it available for publication.

W. CARSON RYAN, JR.

New York,
September 27, 1937.

TABLE OF CONTENTS

Talks On Pedagogics by Francis W. Parker

Other Writings

PREFACE
To Original Edition

THESE "Talks" were given at the Teachers' Retreat, Chautauqua Assembly, New York, July, 1891.* Their popular form has been changed to text for close study. Many repetitions have been omitted, but leaving, as the reader will find, a sufficient number to maintain the reputation of an average teacher. The experience of three years has naturally brought other changes, suggesting modifications and additions.

The discussion of the doctrine of Concentration presented in this book is the outcome of work done in the Cook County Normal School.

In 1883 I resigned my position as one of the supervisors of the Boston schools in order to come into closer range and contact with children's minds. The work done in Quincy was a slight beginning of something far better.

Of the special direction of progress, the ideal was value—not in the clear. One thing, however, appeared right—that the natural sciences and history should be put into the primary school, made an essential part of the course for eight years; and that reading and language lessons might spring from the thought aroused from the study of the central subjects. Another proposition presented itself with great force: that pupils under proper conditions could be led to govern themselves; that punishments, percents, and rewards were, to say the least, not necessary.

A corps of very earnest teachers went to work upon these

* They were also given at the New York Teachers' Training College, the University of Minnesota, and the Cook County Normal Summer School.

ideas. Whatever one teacher discovered was contributed to the general treasury. Every point was discussed in our weekly faculty meetings. My first intimation of Concentration came from the principles of Delsarte in his doctrine of the reaction of vocal and pantomimic expression upon the mind; these principles were applied to all the modes of expression.

The main purpose steadily developed itself. For methods of arousing and sustaining a body of educated thought, we looked in the direction of elementary science, geography, myth, and history.

Prof. and Mrs. H. H. Straight, of blessed memory, were enthusiastic believers in science for children. Prof. Straight had learned methods from Agassiz. A beginning in science teaching was made under his guidance, and it was soon found that reading, writing, indeed all language, could be profitably taught in connection with science lessons. The same discovery was made in regard to geography, myth, and history. The first idea of the unification of arithmetic and science came from Prof. Straight. Miss Mary E. Burt assisted very much in literature. Miss Ellen Montfort began modeling, painting, and drawing as a means of teaching science, geography, and history. Miss Harriet Iredell brought to light what I consider one of the most remarkable discoveries ever made in the School—the ability of little children to rapidly write words and sentences upon the blackboard under the impulse of thought.

I could not name one of the present faculty without naming them all; each one joins in the investigations with the utmost zeal and persistence. Most of them are well known to American teachers through their books and discussions of special subjects.

No one will misunderstand these lines by supposing that the School claims originality in either discoveries or methods. The rule is, that whatever any teacher *effectively* applies, he must discover for himself.

The psychology of Herbart, and the doctrine of Concentration enunciated and applied by his disciples, Ziller, Stoy, and Rein, have been a source of inspiration and a guide in the general direction of the work.

I must not fail to mention another never-failing source, the fundamental doctrine out of which, as a germ, the principles of Concentration are being developed; that is, the teachings of the founder of the Kindergarten—Froebel. From him we get the sublime idea of the unity of the human spirit; the unity of creation and the Creator; all life for one life, and each for all.

The faculty of the Cook County Normal School has had one great advantage: as one corps of teachers they have worked earnestly and honestly to find and apply the truth under the working hypothesis of Concentration; at every step, changes and modifications have been made, devices have been given up and new ones cheerfully accepted, materials and topics have been arranged and rearranged.

The initial steps in this work have been taken, and enough has been done to prove that the *direction is right*. The doctrine of Concentration in itself is a science of education that will absorb the attention of thoughtful teachers for centuries; it contains an ideal that is infinite in its possibilities.

The study of education as a science is imperatively demanded of all teachers who believe that the common school is the central means to preserve and perpetuate the true democracy. The teacher's profession is one day to stand at the head of all professions. It will take its true place when teachers exalt it by honest efficient study of the laws of being and a wise and courageous application of the truth found.

This book is a contribution to those of the profession who see an endless vista of better things for the children. The questions appended, the contents and marginal headings, are to lead students to a better understanding of the text, and above all, a just and righteous *criticism*.

I am more than willing to see every principle here enunciated fall to the ground under logical and convincing reason. Some one has said that the greatest invention of the nineteenth century is the "suspended judgment." I sincerely trust that in publishing this book I shall not in any way compromise my attitude towards truth by clinging to any statement here made when it is shown to be incorrect, or when something better is presented.

FRANCIS W. PARKER.

PREFACE

To Revised Edition

FRANCIS W. PARKER had absolute faith in democracy as the method of government under which the greatest possibilities for human welfare, progress, and happiness could be achieved. He believed that the success of democracy depends upon efficient public schools. Toward the improvement of public school education and to the training of teachers for this purpose, he dedicated his life, all his energy, force, and dynamic leadership.

Colonel Parker was an idealist who insisted that his educational philosophy should be tested by its effect upon individual growth, development, character, and daily living. He said: "The explanation of human life is that it *gives;* and just in proportion to the value of that which it gives, it grows." He exemplified this idea in his own life—he never stopped giving and growing. He profoundly influenced American education by what he gave to children, teachers, parents—to people everywhere in this country and abroad who came to see how his theories were applied in a school community.

Temperamentally, he was a man of action, and he left behind him few published articles to serve the uses of students of education. His best book was *Talks on Pedagogics,* a series of discussions held with teachers at a Chautauqua Assembly in 1891.

In these "talks" he discussed his "theory of concentration" which was largely the outcome of his work in the Cook County and Chicago Normal School. They represent the culmination of his life work up to the time of their publication in 1894. Colonel Parker lectured extensively throughout the United States, but his discussions on education were always informal in style, and characteristically subject to change at any moment as he sensed a sudden need, or met a challenging question from his audience.

When *Talks on Pedagogics* was published in book form, the material was not critically edited for a reading public. Many summaries and repetitions of points therefore appeared which were confusing to readers, although legitimate to lecture technique and clarifying to his audience through verbal emphasis.

The original book was for some years out of print. Since to many people its contents seem a legacy to modern education too valuable to be lost, the Francis W. Parker School decided to prepare for publication a revised edition of the book to be used by study classes and as a reference book on progressive education.

Both Miss Elsie A. Wygant, a graduate of Colonel Parker's Normal School and later a member of his faculty, and the writer, who as Principal for thirty-three years carried on Colonel Parker's work in the Francis W. Parker School of Chicago, had heard Colonel Parker explain his educational theories. They had participated in the faculty meetings where the principles of education enunciated in *Talks on Pedagogics* were weighed and discussed with his teachers. They saw these principles applied in the Cook County Normal School under Colonel Parker's supervision, and found in them inspiration for their own work in the teaching of children and the training of teachers. They were therefore willing to undertake the task of revision. As revising editors, they were conscious of their responsibility to keep unchanged, Colonel Parker's educational philosophy and used the utmost care in their work. In this edition no idea of Colonel Parker has been changed, and his statements and important sequences have been scrupulously retained. The work of the revising editors has been largely one of eliminating unnecessary repetition and of inserting such essential connections as omissions required. Colonel

Preface xvii

Parker's forward-looking educational philosophy anticipated much that is today the accepted basis of educational thought.[1] [2]

Mrs. Gudrun Thorne-Thomsen, Principal of the Ojai Valley School in California, was also a member of Colonel Parker's faculty and worked during a summer's vacation studying all revisions and checking them with the original copy. Therefore, all the omissions from the original text were made by consensus of people thoroughly familiar with Colonel Parker's ideas and work. On any controversial points, the revising editors had the help of interested advisers, including experts in various fields of education.[3]

Colonel Parker did not claim originality for discovery of educational principle or method, but he believed that enough had been done in the Quincy and Chicago schools under his guidance in applying his theory of concentration to demonstrate that the direction of his effort was right and to prove his contention that learning is an active rather than a passive process. Certainly this is a modest claim for one who has awakened hundreds of young teachers and convinced scores of parents of the vital importance of studying both the child and society.[4]

[1] Parallel readings given at the end of chapters give interesting proof of how far in advance of his day was Colonel Parker's educational philosophy. Modern education is now enunciating what sixty years ago he perceived. Many other parallels might be quoted. These quotations and references came to mind as appreciative side lights in the editing.——E. Wygant.

[2] Explanatory notes have been inserted to make clear certain points in the book. Like the parallel readings, these appear also at the end of the chapters. ——F. J. Cooke.

[3] In the original book Colonel Parker very carefully analyzed topically the content of each chapter. He placed also on each page marginal topics to index his points. At the back of the book there were thirty-eight pages of questions and suggestions to assist teachers in the study of the theory of concentration. Wisely or unwisely, all of these aids to teachers have been omitted from the revised edition.

[4] Colonel Parker was one of a group of educators who in the early 80's realized the importance of systematic child-study. He outlined study courses and led discussions with groups of parents and teachers.

The following is an excerpt from an article on Colonel Parker's work by

It was Colonel Parker's genius that he was able to reveal to his students the vast potentialities of education in the evolution of humanity; to spur them forward through their own daily experiences toward an understanding of what teaching means— its privileges and joys, its responsibilities and toil, its challenging difficulties and its compensating satisfactions and happiness—the sure rewards of the artist-teacher.

Colonel Parker believed that teachers and parents should be vigorously alive, with a zest for living and with absorbing interests of their own on a mature level, if they hoped to be fit in personality and power to live, guide, work, and play with growing children. Beyond self-education, or as a part of that, he assumed that teachers who deserve the name would search everlastingly for the conditions most favorable to the full development of the child.

In Colonel Parker's conception, the social factor in education stood above all others in its influence. "What children learn from each other is all-important." He considered the school as a simplified form of community life in which each child had his rights and privileges, each his duties and responsibilities. The child and society were parts of a related whole in an education for democracy.

Mrs. W. D. Hefferan, long a member of the Chicago School Board and once a member of Colonel Parker's Normal School faculty. (See *Chicago School Journal,* September, 1936.)
    "Colonel Parker believed that the welfare of children demanded the fullest coöperation between the home and the school. Interested parents gathered frequently to hear Colonel Parker and his teachers explain what the school was trying to do, and its objective—which at that time was a startling new idea—the education of the whole child—head, hand, heart, and spirit. In 1887 he organized a Parent-Teacher Association which was one of the first in the Middle West. When in 1892 the Englewood Normal Park territory was annexed to Chicago, Colonel Parker's activities were promptly adopted by city schools and between 1892-1900 when the Illinois Congress of P. T. A. was organized—20 schools on the south side had Parent-Teacher Associations patterned after the one established by Colonel Parker in 1887."

I insert here an illustrative quotation on this point, not found in *Talks on Pedagogics:*

The needs of society should determine the work of the school. The supreme need of society is ideal citizenship. Ideal citizenship demands for the individual the highest degree of knowledge, power, skill, and service. Therefore, the one purpose of the school is to present conditions for growth toward ideal citizenship.

The following quotation which appears in the original Preface is used here because it contains the idea used chiefly in argument by the Advisory Committee in helping the revising editors decide upon the content and arrangement of material for this edition. It is also particularly important in portraying Colonel Parker's open-minded attitude toward truth, and gives the key to his life-long struggle for the better education of children and teachers.

I am more than willing to see every principle here enunciated fall to the ground under logical and convincing reason. Some one has said that the greatest invention of the nineteenth century is the "suspended judgment." I sincerely trust that in publishing this book I shall not in any way compromise my attitude towards truth by clinging to any statement here made when it is shown to be incorrect, or when something better is presented.

It was in the light of this attitude that the revising editors had considered putting into an appendix, as historical data, certain matters of theory or practice which Colonel Parker enthusiastically approved and used in his school, but which are not accepted by educators today—notably his arguments for "Partition" in arithmetic, "arm movement" in the teaching of penmanship to young children; and certain psychological discussions which appeared in Chapter VI on "Attention" and in Chapter VII on "Observation," in which the terminology is not that now in use. However, it was the judgment of a large group of interested critics that all such material should remain in the body of the text.

It may be enlightening to quote the comment of Thomas E. Benner, Dean of the College of Education of the University of Illinois, as representative of the spirit of a majority of the committee which made the final decision to keep the original text of the book intact.

It seems to me that such omissions would impair the usefulness of the book to students of education in universities who wish to understand Colonel Parker's theory and practice. No one would think of tampering with Plato's *Republic*. Why should anyone feel free to omit topics here and there from a unified statement of educational philosophy by a far-visioned educator of our own time?

The revising editors decided to include also Colonel Parker's original preface in the new edition in order to give his own interpretation of his work.

It seems an amazing thing that this book, written nearly a half-century ago, should be, on the whole, so modern in its point of view. There are many instances where Colonel Parker's prophetic vision not only predicted the best current educational practice, but passed beyond that to objectives not yet achieved in the most progressive schools. A study of society today indicates that he was right in his insistence that the purpose of all education should be the development of character and intelligent social coöperation. He believed that we "learn to do by doing" and that only by experience and daily exercise in work and play can growing human beings develop the physical, intellectual, and spiritual qualities, the habits and attitudes necessary for ideal citizenship. He was at one with Froebel in his democratic philosophy of "each for all and all for each." He believed, as he states in the last paragraph in *Talks on Pedagogics,* "that every school in the land should be made a home and a heaven for children and that when the ideal of the public school is realized the blood shed by the blessed martyrs for freedom will not have been shed in vain."

FLORA J. COOKE.

Talks on Pedagogics

I

THE CHILD

I PROPOSE in this and in the following chapters to present a general exposition of the theory of concentration. It presents an outline of an educational doctrine for the study and criticism of teachers.

In the beginning of these discussions on education, the question of all questions, the everlasting question is: What is the being to be educated? What is the child? What is this little lump of flesh, breathing life and singing the song of immortality? The wisdom and philosophy of ages upon ages have asked this question, and still it remains unanswered. It is the central problem of the universe. The child is the climax and culmination of all God's creations, and to answer the question, "What is the child?" is to approach nearer the still greater question, What is the Creator and Giver of Life?

I can answer the question tentatively.[1, 2] It is a question for you and for me, for the teachers of the present and the future, to answer; and still it will ever remain the unanswered question. We should study the child by his actions, and by his tendencies

Editor's Note: Parallel readings given at the end of chapters are interesting proof of how far in advance of his day was Colonel Parker's educational philosophy. Modern education is now enunciating what sixty years ago he perceived. Many other parallels might be quoted. These notations and references came to mind as appreciative side lights in the editing. Explanatory notes have been inserted to make clear certain points in the book. These also appear at the ends of the chapters containing the points to which they refer.

to act. The child is born, we are told by scientists, deaf, dumb, and blind; yet, in design, possessing marvelous possibilities for development. It is well for us as teachers to stand by the cradle of a child who has drawn his first breath and is ready to be acted upon by the external energies which surround him.

One hypothesis we can accept as true: the inherited organism of bone, muscle, and brain determines exactly the limits or boundaries of the baby's development. Each nerve fiber or convolution of the brain says: "Thus far shalt thou go and no farther"; and it is well to say in the same breath that no human being ever had the external conditions for growth by which the full possibilities, predetermined and fixed by the organism, have been realized.[3] The organism itself determines the external conditions for development.[4] Every muscle, every nerve, every fiber, every convolution of the brain, their nature and power, are in themselves possibilities for the reception of those external energies which act upon the body of the child, and make their way to the brain through the sensorium.[5] The child itself is a central energy, or complex of energies, upon which and through which certain external energies act. No simple energy can enter a child's brain except by first touching the child's body (the end-organs), and countless energies touch the child's body which do not enter the brain at all.[6] Others enter, but lie below the plane of consciousness.

Waves of light touch the eye and create elementary ideas of color in the brain, but just what colors there shall be in the brain is determined by the passive power and delicacy of the organism itself. Vibrations of air touch and enter the brain through the ear. Strongest and most effective of all is the contact and resistance of the body to objects more dense than waves of air or waves of ether. The giant sense of touch begins its creative power in the brain at the birth of the child, and even before birth. It is well for us to understand thoroughly that the child, an organic complex of energies, is acted upon and through by external energies; and, whatever matter may be in itself, the mind is conscious of nothing but pure energy and is primarily developed by external energies which we infer, not through forms and qualities of matter. Stimuli come from all the surroundings of the child. The products of the stimuli create in the child's mind concepts corresponding to external objects. These concepts are activities in themselves, or phases of differentiated energy. Units of elementary ideas, individual concepts, enable the mind to react upon externality. The child begins to move under the stimulus created by external activities, to smile, to laugh, to stretch out his hands, to see, to hear, to touch, to taste, and to smell.[7]

It is not possible for me to state the exact order of the succession of the arousing to action of the different senses. Our question here is: What are the spontaneous activities of the child? In other words, what must the child do from the nature of its being, the nature of the stimulus acting through its body and in its mind, and the potentialities of the ego?

What are the tendencies of these spontaneous activities? The child's consciousness begins in obscurity, weakness, and vagueness, and still in this very obscurity and vagueness there is great activity. The very few weak and obscure ideas of color, sound, and form set the whole being into motion. Before there is any consciousness, before the child has the most obscure feeling of self, music affects it in a wonderful way. Lullaby songs can soothe the baby to sleep, changing vague pain into vague pleasure. The whole being is sensitive to the rhythm of music. Not only can the child be soothed and lulled to sleep with music, but often the first dawning consciousness of life is marked by a smile aroused by a song. The first spiritual breath of external life comes with musical cadences. One of the first sounds that a child makes is an imitation of rhythm. What is this marvelous

gift that makes him so sensitive to musical cadence? The whole
universe moves in rhythm: the avalanche thunders from the
mountainside in deep cadences; the ocean surf roars in musical
cadence. The rippling of the brook and the soughing of the
breeze in the foliage are the simple music of nature. The little
child is the center of all this rhythm, and the feeling of this
rhythm is the truth of the universe whispering its sweet songs
to the child's soul.

Perhaps the most marked mental action of the little child
is the fanciful creation of new ideas and images. A little vague
color and sound, and a few percepts of touch, are sufficient
to set his being into vigorous action. External objects act upon
the child and produce their correspondences, individual concepts,
in his mind. As I have already said, these concepts are very
vague, obscure, and indistinct.

Notwithstanding all this, creation is the moving central
power and delight of the child. The baby creates out of his
meager store of ideas a new world, his own world, in which
he lives and moves and has his being. Let us pause a moment
and look at the marvelous meaning of this power of the child
in the creations of fancy. If he were limited to actuality (that is,
to the vague reflex of external objects), if he were bound by
his own meager store of so-called facts, he would indeed live
in a dark and dismal prison; but he bursts the bonds of reality
and goes into a higher world of invisible life. He lives over
again the childhood of the race in the myth. He revels in fanciful forms of his own vivid creations; he spontaneously seeks
the invisible.

Next to the cradle song is the cradle story. You know well
how eager a child is for stories that arouse his love for rhythm
and excite his fancy. The child delights in fairy tales, the mythical treasures of the ages. The cruel bonds of stern reality are
broken and he enters a beautiful and invisible world, peopled

by creations of his own fancy. If a child were limited in his early stages to the world of reality, if he could not go out into the unknown world, the invisible world, he would lead the life of a brute. The human animal differs from the brute in its faith in an invisible world. The self-created, invisible world to the child is the chaos that precedes his spiritual life. Banish myth from the child, and you take away that beauty which is the essence of truth. Parents who forbid the myth because they conceive it is not the truth, limit the child to the baldest materialism.

What is the myth? The record of the human race is full of myths. Myth comes from the imperfect answer which nature gives to the childish soul of man. The answers are not false, but they are imperfect and partial, and are, to childish souls, the solution of their great problems. Every such answer given to a spontaneous and innocent question contains a kernel of intrinsic truth. It is that truth which a child can bear in his early years. He cannot grasp precepts and logic, but he can understand the truth, like those who crowded around the Savior—in parables. The myth is common to all tribes and nations on the face of the earth. All myths have a wonderful similarity, proving that the human spirit in every stage of growth, and in every clime and under all environments, has the same strong everlasting tendency upward. Every myth contains a lesson to man. Out of ignorance of the nature of the child, and from a spirit of dogmatism and bigotry, there has come the falsehood that says that the myth does not contain the whole truth and, therefore, must be rejected. Who knows the whole truth? Shall the child be robbed of that which delights his soul and lays the foundation of true religious life? No greater mistake can be made in regard to the spontaneous activities of the child, for the myth is the true fire-mist of character, it contains symbols which point upward to God and to heaven.

The myth is the foundation of faith in the future life, the foundation of all spiritual growth. The fairies and trolls change, as the soul changes to corresponding actuality.

The myth is the beginning of history. The creatures of fancy foreshadow the real people with whom the child must live. The myth offers to the child, who indeed sees through a glass darkly, that suggestion of truth and tendency toward which are absolutely essential to his growth.

The myth is the beginning of science. The human race began, we are told, with a firm belief that every object in the universe was animated, lifelike, human-like. This was the childish study of science, but it sustained a great truth. The stone and the mountain are not organisms for life, it is true, but there breathes through them an irresistible energy which comes from the Giver of all life. The myth of the early ages points toward the marvelous revelations of the scientific truth of the present. The myth is an imperfect and partial apprenhension of truth. The myth clears away under the steady light of the ever-moving mind; it is essential to the understanding of the child. "The night veileth the morning."

Just as the human race arose in its developments from the myths of antiquity, so the child must rise from the myths of childhood. The lack of ideality, the failure in spiritual growth, in true religious life, are caused more by the failure of the parents to recognize the true nature of the child and his inborn love for myth than from any other cause whatever. The rankest materialism in its worst form has never struck harder blows at true spiritual life than the ignorance of misguided parents who keep their child from fairy life and fairy land. Fairy land is over the border of the present into the future; and the truest tendency of human life is to live in the ideal of the future, to reach forward toward the invisible and the unknown. Slowly human beings have arisen—guided by a glimmering light—and have climbed spiritually from the earth and the clod, from the shrub and tree, up the broad walls of the arched sky to stars, and moon, and sun—and then beyond the sun, toward divinity. Seeking divinity, imagination stretches away to the invisible, all-controlling One who permeates the universe and breathes His eternal Life through it to be taken into the human soul. The myth is the obscure image, in the child's soul, of God Himself. There are many parents who shudder at the myth of Santa Claus, an invisible being who brings the child gifts; but that invisible being, to the child's weak apprehension, is the fore-shadowing of the All-Giver, the forerunner of Christ who came to man on that blessed Christmas night. No rough voice and no ignorant soul should ever tell the little child that Santa Claus does not exist, for Santa Claus is the foreshadowing of the All-Lover, the One who gives because He Loves.

It is impossible to take a child into history, science, ethics, and religion without the continued exercise of these spontaneous fanciful tendencies. You may reply that a child may live in myth and fancy all his life. I admit that this is possible. Many people do live in fancy all their lives just because fancy is not put into the crucible of reason; just because the conditions are not pre-sented for myth to change to history, to science, to ethics, and to religion. This is no proof that the strongest spontaneous tendency of the child is wrong; it is only a proof of neglect to build upon it. I think we can take it for granted that, as God made the child His highest creation, He put into that child His divinity, and that this divinity manifests itself in the seeking for truth through the visible and tangible.

The child is brought into direct contact with its mother, its father, and the whole family; and who will dare to say that the child is not, above all, a student of human nature? Who will say that a child's eyes, when they look into one's face, cannot read the soul better than older people? The child looks at you with the innocence and purity of childhood, and no hypocrisy, no dissimulation, though it may veil the truth from older eyes, can keep it from the child. He studies the relation of being to being, father to mother, parents to children. It may be that I use too strong a word when I say he "studies," but still it is something very like study. The study of family life is the child's beginning of the study of anthropology and of history. The child is not only a student of individual life, but of community life, of the life of the family, the life of the neighbors, of the children he meets at play, in the house, in the yard, in the street; and this measure of the child's judgment of community life is the measure he later applies in his study of history. He may study history in school or in the university, but in all life the judgments formed at home, in the nursery, in the parlor, in the kitchen, in the street, are the strongest, ever-enduring measures in all his after-judgments of the record of human life taught by experience and history. Every human being with whom he comes in contact is a new object of study to him.[8] The looks, the manners, the dress, the attitude, and the facial expression lead him to make his childish inferences. Then comes the kindergarten and the school, the first step in a broader community life than that which home furnishes. Here the study of civics begins. The true foundation of civics is community life. The child's home-measures of life, the government of his home, give him democratic, monarchical, or socialistic principles. Whatever the rule of the home or school may be, that rule is ever afterwards either loved or hated by the child. Thus the child spontaneously begins the study of anthropology, ethnology, and history. In these studies he has a profound, abiding interest. In these studies he forms habits of judgment which too often remain fixed and permanent.

It needs no argument to prove that the child studies, or, at least, is exceedingly interested in, zoölogy. Few beings, except perhaps the father and mother, can interest a child more deeply than the brute life which surrounds him. The cat is "a joy forever"; the dog is his particular friend. The child stretches out his little hands before he can speak, and his first utterances follow the attempts of his original ancestors in imitating the voice of the dog. The child delights in birds, butterflies, and bees. Place any moving, living thing before the child, and he moves toward it with an excited interest. He wants to touch it, to stroke it, to know more about it. Endowed with the original idea of animism, he no doubt believes every animal that he sees has a mind like his own. He will imitate the dog, the cat, and the birds; and he will talk to them as to his own companions. Thus he studies zoölogy in becoming acquainted with the animal life he sees. Every animal wild or tame, every insect—the grasshopper, the locust, bugs that scurry away when he lifts a stone, the fishworms which he digs for bait—are objects of intense interest. He knows the difference between the white grub and the common earthworm. The animals in the woods are his friends. The birds—their habits, their nests, their young, and their songs—fill him with joy. He knows the sly habits of the crows, studies the psychology of their reasoning. The horses, and oxen, and sheep are all his friends. What farm-boy has not cried over the loss of a favorite sheep taken away by the butcher?

The child has a great love for vegetable life. Was there ever a child who did not love flowers, reach out for them, desire to hold them in his hands, gaze at them, and smell them? Of course, the spontaneous activities of the child are governed to a great degree by his environment. Take a little boy with the environment of a farm—such an instance comes to me—a boy upon a rocky farm in New England. He studies spontaneously his entire environment. It is safe to say that he knows every plant upon the farm, every kind of grass, every weed. He comes in direct contact with wormwood, sorrel, rag-weed. He can tell all the kinds of grasses from the graceful silver grass to the stately timothy. He knows the mosses and lichens that cling to the rocks and carpet the marshy land. He knows the shrubs and bushes; the huckleberry bush is his delight. The strawberry in the rich meadow he watches from blossom to fruit with a keen sense of the joy which is to follow. Every tree he knows—the magnificent pine, the stately maple, the spreading chestnut in the pasture. He can tell you the shape of the tree—its trunk, its foliage; its fruit he spontaneously classifies. Thus, every child is an earnest, indefatigable lover of botany. In his future life, the rural child carries his botany of the farm with him wherever he goes. He compares all other plants and classifies them according to the spontaneous classifications made on the farm. He says: "This was on the old farm; this was not." "This is something new." "This is like something I've seen before." "This bush is like the lilac; this rose is like the rose in the old garden."

Not only is the boy on the farm a student of life, but he extends his study to the forces of earth, air, and water. The earth touches him, heaven bends down to him and asks him questions. The clouds he knows from the rounded thunderhead to the mackerel sky. He knows also the winds; he can foretell the weather. He looks with intense joy to the next rainy day; that will bring him rest, or something better, fishing. He watches the sun with a deep interest. It would be a very stupid boy who could not tell exactly the noon hour by the sun, aided by that internal monitor, his stomach. Winds, clouds, air, and heat—everything that influences vegetation comes within the mental range of the farm-boy.

Mineralogy, especially upon a rocky farm, comes very close to the boy in clearing the ground, in picking stones, in building stone walls, in quarrying ledges. Watch a crowd of children upon the beach gathering pebbles and curious stones. They are interested in the color and form of the pebbles, and may be made exceedingly interested in the origin of the different forms if some observant friend is there to continue the questions which the stones themselves ask. Children take to playing in the dirt as naturally as ducks to water. The different kinds of soils attract their attention—sand, gravel, and clay. They never tire of playing in sand, or expressing crude fancies by modeling in clay. The changes which natural forces bring about on the earth's surface are of deep interest to children, especially the changes brought about by running water after a rain, or the wind swirling the sand into piles. They never tire of damming up a temporary stream or changing its current, and of watching its effects when it spreads out silt, or makes cuts in the soft earth. The brooks and rivers are never ceasing sources of delight to children; they watch them at flood-time, when the water spreads out over the meadows; they notice the caving-in of banks, the carrying of earth by water and its deposition on the shelving shores.

Real geography, or the appearance of the earth's surface, is a subject of intense, though unconscious, interest on the part of the child. Let a boy hunt stray cows or sheep over a large farm; he soon learns to know every crook, every turn and corner on the whole farm, every hiding place. He knows the hills, valleys, springs, and meadows. Of all the mental pictures that remain vivid through life and are recalled with ever-renewed pleasure, the most vivid and pleasurable are the pictures of the country surrounding one's birthplace, or the house in which we lived when children. The house itself, the fireplace, paper on the wall, furniture—everything is distinct in our minds when other pictures fade or are blurred by time. All the country round about, every hillock, every depression, brook, and rivulet are never-fading images in the brain.

To sum up, the subjects of the child's spontaneous study and persistent interest include all the central subjects of study—geography, geology, mineralogy, botany, zoölogy, anthropology, etc. In fact, the child begins every subject spontaneously and unconsciously. He must begin these subjects, because he lives, and because his environment acts upon him and educates him. Of course, difference in environment makes a great difference in the child's mental imagery and in his individual concepts; still, in all children there are the same spontaneous tendencies. For instance, the boy on a farm has a vastly larger range of vegetation to study than the child of the city. But even the city child may study the clouds, the sky, the stars, the earth, vegetation, animal life, history, every hour of the day. To be sure, interests vary; but to a child all these subjects are related one to the other, as the cloud is related to rain, and the rain is related to vegetation and soil. It is the tendency of pedantry to search in the far distance for facts and mysteries, but the truth is that the marvelous is close to us, that miracles are of the most common occurrence.[9]

I wish to call your attention to the wonderful powers acquired by the child in the first three years of life, and the wonderful persistence there is in such acquirement.[10] Take, for instance, the art of locomotion, creeping and walking. Watch the face of the child standing for the first time upon his little legs, attracted by the outstretched arms of his mother, who stands across the room; look at the mingled courage and fear in the baby's face. He has a great ambition to move, as he has seen others move, upon his two feet. He stretches out his arms; he fears, he takes courage; he moves one foot and is successful, and then the other; he looks at his mother's encouraging smile, takes another step, and then another, until the great fear of walking across the room is accomplished. From the time he first stands upon his feet until the time he runs with perfect unconsciousness of his power of movement, there takes place a succession of experiments, of trials, failures, and successes—all guided and controlled by his desire to walk.

More wonderful than learning to walk is learning to understand language and to talk. In the beginning the child creates his own language of gesture, by means of his own body. He hears language, words that are in themselves complex. Oral words act upon his consciousness and are associated by a fixed and everlasting law of the mind. Idioms are acquired by hearing and association; and, with this hearing receptivity, there comes an intense desire to express thought. With his voice he creates at first his own language, which consists of crudely articulate sounds, and then follows the acquisition of the vernacular which he hears. It is well for us to consider carefully the processes of learning to talk. The child must learn to hear first; that is, the words must act upon consciousness and their correspondences must be associated with the appropriate activities in consciousness. The idioms must act in the same way and be associated with their appropriate activities or relations of · ideas. Then follows the making of oral words. He learns enunciation, or the utterance of single sounds. He learns articulation, or the unity of sounds in words. He learns accent, pronunciation, and syntax, all by hearing language and under the one controlling motive of expressing his own thought. He begins, it is true, with crude utterances, but these utterances are to him the best possible expression of his thought. He learns any language and every language that he hears. If we could understand the psychological mechanical process by which a child learns his own vernacular from the first step of hearing to the last step by which the sentence is in his power, we should understand the whole theory of learning any language. Those who have tried to speak a foreign language will readily understand something of the struggle the child goes through in order to master one single phonic element. You see that he does all this unconsciously, that all these efforts are natural and to a great degree automatic. He never for a moment thinks of a single sound by itself unless that sound is a whole word. He knows nothing at all of the complex elements of a language, nothing of slow pronunciation, nothing of syntax; yet, he masters the language by a natural process. This word "natural" is variously interpreted and is exceedingly ambiguous, almost as ambiguous as the word "abstract." Still I believe that we can find a scientific definition of the word *natural*. If the word natural means anything, it means strict conformity to God's laws. That is, a child learns every oral word by the same law under which every oral or written word in any and every language must be learned. The child does not know the law, but he obeys it by instinct. If the child makes these marvelous acquisitions naturally, in conformity to law, why not have him continue that conformity to law in all his later learnings?

If we follow this natural law, learning to write is far easier in itself than learning to hear language or learning to speak. The great lesson to teachers is: find the law, follow the law; give the child conditions in learning to write similar to those he has had in learning to speak. Indeed, the conditions can be made far better, for learning to speak is left very much to accident and to desultory instruction, while learning to write may be under the most careful guidance.

It goes without saying that the child is a student of form and color. Everything that enters his brain, as I have already said, must touch the end-organs, and these attributes or objects which touch the end-organs are forms of matter. Froebel, who had such divine insight, understood the great value of the tactual sense. This sense preëminently brings into consciousness the forms of external objects.

Not only does the child study form, but he makes intuitively a systematic preparation for the study of number. The child begins with no idea of distance. He grasps for the moon with the same confidence as for an object near at hand. Ideas of distance, size, weight, are preparations for number. The child first learns to measure by constantly reaching out his hands, creeping and walking, and after that measures distance by sight. Not only does the child begin to measure and estimate distances, but he also begins to judge area and bulk, and compare different sizes, areas, weights, and bulks. The study of weight to him is the measure of the difference of pressure of objects upon his hands, his own weight in the effort of other children to lift him. He measures force and also time in the same unconscious way—the time of sleeping, the time between a promised pleasure and its anticipated realization—and soon he learns to look at the clock to help him out in his judgment. He estimates very carefully the value of a cent and a stick of candy. All these spontaneous activities in the direction of number study are mingled with all his activities, and are absolutely necessary to his mental and physical action. It is true these measures are very crude and imperfect; but they are the beginnings of the power of accurate measuring, that mode of judgment which will end, if he continues to have the right conditions, in exact measuring and weighing, and in accurate knowledge of values.

A precious possession of early childhood is a perfect unity of thought and action. Hear the voice and watch the movements of a little child. No dancing teacher, no teacher of elocution, no actor, can ever successfully imitiate the voice of a child, or the perfectly unconscious beauty and grace of his movements. Indeed, it is the highest aim of artists in acting and elocution to acquire the unconscious grace and power of a child. Listen to the voice of the child—melodious, harmonious, perfect in emphasis; it is the immediate pulsation of his soul, the instantaneous reflex of his consciousness, but with complete unconsciousness of his body, his organs of expression, his forms of speech. The child, until education intervenes, is a unit of action and expression, and that unity is acquired and maintained because action is controlled by a motive with no overpowering consciousness of the means or forms of expression. Must that beautiful unity be broken or can it be perpetuated and strengthened?

There never was such a thing as a lazy child born on earth. Childhood is full of activities of every kind, stimulated by external energies and shaped by internal power. The child experiments continually until it gains its ends. It will reach hundreds of times for an object, and at last succeed.

What modes of expression, excepting speech, does a child acquire in the first years of its life? I should say that all children love music, though there is a vast difference in individual organisms in this as in all other modes of expression. Most children strive to imitate that which they hear in rhythm. Making, or manual work, is really the natural element of the child. I think I can say, without fear of dispute, that a child tries to make everything that he sees made. The little girl wishes to use the scissors, needle, and thread. In the kitchen, unless repressed by the mother, she makes cakes and bread. In fact, the whole round of housekeeping in the beginning furnishes countless objects for activity and a desire to imitate. Children in the shop or on the farm strive to do what they see done. They harness each other in teams, they drive the dog and the goat, they make millwheels and dams. The tendency to imitate, the desire to make the objects they see made, is intensely strong in every child.

Every child has the artist element born in him; he loves to model objects out of sand and clay. Paint is a perfect delight to children, bright colors charm them. Give the child a paintbrush, and though his expression of thought will be exceedingly crude, it will be very satisfactory to him; he will paint any object with the greatest confidence.

It has been very interesting this summer to watch the crowd of little children near Lake Chautauqua, as busy as bees and as happy as angels. Let us look at the forms the children mold out of the sand. Here are caves where the fairies dwell; mountains, volcanoes, houses where the giants live. All these fantastic forms spring from the brain of the child and are expressed by means of this plastic material. See that little three-year-old girl with the model of a house in her brain; she is now wheeling a wheelbarrow, assisted by a little companion; in the barrow is the wood, and in her brain is the house. Energetic, persistent, happy—in what direction? In the direction of true growth! The little girl in the kitchen is not happy until she can mold and change the flour into dough, and dough into forms for baking; and here begins her first lessons in chemistry, the wonderful changes which heat brings about. She will dress her doll, working patiently for hours. Inexpert beholders may not know what the crude form means, but the child knows and is satisfied—nay, delighted. Give a child a piece of chalk and his fancy runs riot; people, horses, houses, sheep, trees, birds, spring up in the brave confidence of childhood. In fact, except writing, all the modes of expression are spontaneously and persistently exercised by the child from the beginning. He sings, he makes, he molds, he paints, he draws, he expresses thought in all these, his creations.

I have very imperfectly presented some of the spontaneous activities of the little child. The more I strive to present them, the more imperfect seems the result, so much lies beyond in the interpretation of the child's instinctive activities, so much seems to exceed all present discovery. The question, my fellow teachers, is: What should these activities teach us? The child instinctively begins all subjects known in the curriculum of the university. He begins them because he cannot help it; his very nature impels him. These tendencies, these spontaneous activities of the child, spring from the depths of being, spring from all the past, for the child is the fruit of all the past, and the seed of all the future. These quiet, persistent, powerful tendencies we, as teachers, must examine and continue with the greatest care. The child overcomes great obstacles by persistent energy, always acting with great confidence in himself and his powers. He overcomes these obstacles because his whole being is a unit of action, controlled by one motive. The spontaneous tendencies of the child are the records of inborn divinity; we are here, my fellow teachers, for one purpose, and that purpose is to understand these tendencies and continue them in all these directions, following nature. First of all, we should recognize the great dignity of the child, the child's divine power and divine possibilities, and then present the conditions for their complete outworking. We are here that the child may take one step higher; we are here to find and present the conditions adapted to the divine nature of the child.

I have tried to show that the whole round of knowledge is begun by the child, and begun because he breathes, because he lives. If the child loves science and history and studies them instinctively, then he should go on, and we must know the conditions and subjects which should be presented to him for each new demand of his growth.

In the past, education has been directed too much to dead forms of thought, and for one good reason at least. The sciences are a relatively modern achievement of man's creative genius and have not yet reached the child. Now we have these marvelous subjects presented to us, worked out by great thinkers of the present, and we are to choose whether we will continue the dead formalism that too often leads to pedantry and bigotry, or whether we are to lead the child's soul in that direction which God designed in His creation of the human being.

In conclusion I commend to you, in the words of our greatest American philosopher:

> A babe by its mother lies bathed in joy;
> Glide the hours uncounted; the sun is its toy;
> Shines the peace of all being without cloud in its eyes,
> And the sum of the world in soft miniature lies.

I commend to you the "sum of the world" for your study, for in this direction lies all the future progress of humanity.

---

[1] Gertrude Hartman, *The Child and the School* (Dutton), pp. 9-22.

[2] Froebel, *Education of Man* (Appleton), p. 15, paragraphs 14-36.

[3] H. S. Jennings, *Suggestions of Modern Science Concerning Education,* pp. 3-50.

[4] Blanton and Blanton, *Child Guidance* (Century Co.), Chap. 11, "The Original Endowment."

[5] Sherman and Sherman, *The Process of Human Behavior* (W. W. Norton & Co.), Chap. 11, "The Functional Significance of the Human Nervous System."

[6] Woodworth, *Psychology* (Holt), p. 415.

[7] Blanton and Blanton, *Child Guidance* (Century Co.), Chap. VI, "Sensory Training."

[8] John Dewey, *My Pedagogic Creed* (Progressive Education Assn.), Article I.

[9] Lucy Sprague Mitchell, *Here and Now Story Book* (Dutton), pp. 14-17.

[10] E. A. Kirkpatrick, *The Individual in the Making* (Houghton Mifflin Co.), Chap. 5.

II

THE CENTRAL SUBJECTS OF STUDY

DESIGN is a fundamental premise in all that exists. There is a design in each individual being. Another term for design is possibilities to be realized. The working out of the design of a human being into character is education; the realization of all the possibilities of human growth and development is education. In the presentation of conditions for the working out of that design, consists the art of educating. All mental and moral development is by self-activity. Education is the economizing of self-effort in the direction of all-sided development.

Economy of energy is the intrinsic mark and sign of all progress in nature and in art. Apply this fact to education: the individual being is developed by immutable laws, the fundamental law of which is self-activity. Better conditions for human growth and a better knowledge of the adaptation of those conditions to each stage of development is the preëminent need of education to-day. The study of the science of education gives us a higher knowledge of the human being, and a better knowledge of the conditions to be applied. The art of teaching is the scientific, economical adaptation of conditions for educative effort.

In this connection, it must be admitted that there is much studying, much toiling and moiling, much persistent effort and protracted mental struggle that is not educative, because the

conditions presented for self-effort are not adapted to the immediate needs of the individual. Our motive, then, my fellow
teachers, should be to economize educative effort, and with this
guide we should seek earnestly for that doctrine of education
by the application of which this central aim of education can
be best attained.

The present trend in the science of education is toward the
correlation and unification of educative subjects, and their concentration upon human development. All subjects, means, and
modes of study are concentrated under this doctrine upon
economy of educative efforts. In the unification and correlation
of subjects of thought and expression, each subject finds its
absolute and relative educational value in the conditions for
self-activity and self-effort.

The unification of subjects takes for its hypotheses, first, the
unity of the human being in design; second, the unity of the
Creator and His creations; and third, that the approximating
unity of the human being to his Creator is the sublime destiny
of man. "For He made man in His own image." "He has
crowned him with glory and honor." Unity of body, mind, and
soul, unity of educative effort, unity of action, unity of thought,
and unity of thought and expression are the aims of the theory
of concentration.

The central subjects of study, which are the main consideration of this chapter, are those which lie nearest the truth. All
true study is the study of the Creator through the manifestation
of His thought, in the universe and man. The central subjects
of study are but the main branches of one subject, and that
subject is creation. Creation is eternal; it is the manifestation
of invisible, all-efficient power; therefore all study has for its sole
aim the knowledge of the invisible. The highest and at the same
time the most economical effort of the mind is the effective striving after the truth of creation. This action of the mind may be

called intrinsic; it is the line of least resistance between the soul and truth. The central subjects of study represent that line and point in that direction.

As the basis of my discussion of the central subjects of study, I shall take the subject of *geography*. You will readily grant that, in order to understand the relations of one study to another, it is absolutely necessary to define with accuracy each branch of study in itself. Through the accurate definition of one branch, it may be separated in theory, in this discussion, from all other branches, and through this separation its relations to all other studies may be understood.

The first definition of geography that I give is: "Geography is the knowledge or science of the present appearance of the earth's surface." This definition premises that there have been countless other appearances of the earth's surface in past æons, that constant changes have been going on in the crust of the earth, and that changes will be continually made in the future. The present appearance of the earth's surface is the result, or present effect, of countless changes in the earth's crust. Geologists teach us that the creation of the earth is going on to-day in precisely the same way and by the same causes as it has been going on for countless ages. To know geography is to know the present appearance of the earth's surface. This definition gives geography a place as a branch of study and shows its relations to other studies. Any definition more comprehensive than this would include other subjects. Thus the study of the surface forms of the earth is a subject by itself, excluding, by its definition, all other branches.

Geology, in its relation to geography, may be defined as the history of the present appearance of the earth's surface, from fire-mist up through the long stages of development to the present modeled continents, ocean beds, and islands. Present geography is but one form or phase of countless other forms and phases of the earth's surface. Thus, the unification of geology and geography is not far to seek. It is the relation of effect to cause, or of present effects to a countless succession of causes. Geology is the causal nexus of geography. Each characteristic area of the earth's surface, with its arrangements of slopes, counter-slopes, its river basins, plains, and mountain masses, is the product of a particular succession of changes of conditions under law, and therefore has a definite geological history. Professor Thomas C. Chamberlin, an eminent geologist, presents this truth in a striking and beautiful way. He says (I may not give his exact words) that each special characteristic area of surface has its prenatal conditions, its birth, babyhood, adolescence, maturity, old age, decay, and death. Thus, the eye of a trained geologist reads as in an open book the stage of development of any given unit of surface and, also, the long chain of changes and causes which have led up to its present appearance. Geography is one phase in the history of geology. Effects may be traced to causes—causes of upheaval, subsidence, folding, extrusion, intrusion, erosion, abrasion, the removal and building up of eroded material. What book of man is like the book of the Eternal? The child may read it, the learned may read it, and still the thought of the invisible in creation can never be exhausted.

It may be positively stated that geography can be in no way profitably studied without the immediate study of geology. The human mind in its healthy normal condition must go, if it goes at all, in the search for truth, from effect to cause. The child who sees the cutting in of the banks of a brook, and the rippling, rushing water making its way over a pebbly bed, must, by the tendency of his own mind, ask for the causes of the observed effects. The present effects, which his eye sees, are geography; the cause of the effects leads him to study geology. The child will see the crumbling bank, the carrying down of silt by the water, its deposition and spreading out on surfaces below, thus making new forms. He will not, it is true, ask at first, as he stands in the valley, what forces carved out the whole valley. To rouse that dormant curiosity which is the basis of normal intellectual life is the art of the teacher. One wise answer will open another question. Through the answer the child may be led to discover for himself the mighty work of erosion and building, of sculpturing and constructing, in which every stream since its beginning has been unceasingly engaged. The result or effect is the valley itself, with its rounded hills and intervals of plains. This is only an illustration of the trend of all observation of surfaces. He picks up a shell far inland. To the alert mind the inevitable question comes from the shell itself, "How came this here?" In fact, every surface and all units of the surface are full of questions.

It may be asked here very pertinently, which should come first pedagogically, geology or geography? The effect must always be studied before the cause. Geography, under this definition, is a phase of geology. To study a surface form without studying the causes which led to its formation is superficial study of the surface.

The fundamental product of the study of geography is an individual concept, acquired through observation and imagination, of a part of the earth's surface.

Mere observation would generally have for its results a vague individual concept; but as the mind searches for causes its action becomes more intense, the observation and imagination of surfaces move toward adequacy, for the good reason that the search for causes must necessarily enhance the clearness and distinctness of the effects. Thus, the study of geology from the standpoint of geography intensifies in a very marked degree the clearness of the individual geographic concept. So the study of geography finds its highest and best results in the study of geology. On the other hand, the study of geography is absolutely necessary to the study of geology. The field geologist marks with critical eye every appearance of surface: slope, elevation, or depression, in order to ascertain the history of the surface.

The relation of *mineralogy* to geology is the relation of matter to motion. Mineralogy is the study of the rock material; geology, the study of the changes in the rock material. The nature of these changes is determined very largely by the nature of the rock itself. Thus, in the study of geology, the first question is: "What is the kind of material that is acted upon by physical forces? Is it archaic? Is it sedimentary rock, sandstone, limestone?" and so on to the end of the great chapter. We take up a rounded pebble from the beach and ask of what kind of material is it composed, whence it came, what produced the changes in it, and then we classify the pebble itself. The earth may be called with truthfulness one great rock. This rock appears in a solid or ground-up state. Ground-up rock is superimposed and forms the soil of the earth, from the coarsest gravel to the finest clay. The study of soils is the study of mineralogy. The true study of mineralogy is the study of that which is right under our feet—the clays, gravels, sands, and vegetable mold over which we walk—the things with which a child comes in contact every day.

Thus we see that geology cannot be studied without a study of mineralogy. What the study of timber, brick, iron, and stone is to the construction of buildings, the science of mineralogy is to the science of geology. Pure geography is the study of form alone. The character of the surface, the nature of meeting slopes, river basins, valleys, etc., is determined by the kinds of minerals of which the surfaces consist and the nature of the forces which have acted upon them. Enough has been said to show the organic unity of the three subjects, geography, geology and mineralogy;

they exist in the closest relationship, they cannot be severed in thought, except by unscientific teaching.

The thought that everything changes in this universe of ours, that there is no such thing as absolute quiescence, that differences in effects are only differences in time and differences in forces and resistance, that the planets move in their orbits, that the earth moves around the sun, that the whole earth is changing at every moment under immutable laws, that the mountains are lifted up and are ground down by ever-acting energies, is overwhelming. All is change and motion. The crust of the earth we walk on floats, we are told by geologists, upon a wavering mass. Geology is the science of everlasting change written in the earth's crust; geography is one phase of that change.

It goes without saying that the opportunities for the study of these subjects are countless. There is no bit of the earth's surface that is not full of the deepest interest to every child if the true teacher is there to make him aware of the questions of nature. Yet in the usual textbook of science there is a studied attempt at the distant, the marvelous—such as volcanoes, earthquakes—as if these subjects would excite the child's curiosity more than the marvels of clay and gravel, vegetable mold, and wonderfully modeled forms right under his feet. The real miracles are closest at hand.

There are two great sciences of change and motion. The science of direct force we call *physics;* the science of the more subtle changes which modify the physical properties of matter in the rock, in the water, and in the air we call *chemistry*. No argument is required to show that the studies of geography, geology, and mineralogy are impossible without the essentially correlative studies of physics and chemistry.

The crust of the earth floats on plastic material like a raft upon water, yielding to its movements either in upheaval, subsidence, or folding by lateral pressure. Water forms a partial envelope of the surface of the crust, changing under heat to vapor, and condensing for lack of heat. The atmosphere is a complete envelope of the earth. That mode of motion called "heat" acts through air, causes its movements, fills it with invisible and visible forms of water, determines condensation into clouds and rain, moves by air-currents the great rivers of the ocean. The atmosphere, with its suspended moisture, is the great medium through which heat acts and reacts upon the crust of the earth, changing it, modeling it, creating new surface forms. The science of heat, that physical life-giving energy, acting through air, water, and rock is *meteorology*. Meteorology is the physics and chemistry of heat, manifested in air and vapor. It is the science of the distribution of sunshine. The unity of these sciences of inorganic matter seems self-evident. The main point in geology is to discover the climatic conditions under which the different rock formations had their origin. Coal is stored-up sunshine. The observation of the effects of air and of water in all its forms in modeling surfaces makes meteorology, geology, mineralogy, geography, physics, and chemistry inseparable in the economical acquisition of knowledge.

We have then the central subjects of thought that relates to inorganic matter:

Central Subjects	Modes of Motion or Laws of Change
Meteorology	
Geography	Physics
Geology	and
Mineralogy	Chemistry

I beg leave to say that I am not trying to unfold a philosophy of the natural sciences, but to show the unity of these sciences in their relations to the action of the child's mind and to his education.

It is now our purpose to show the relation of the sciences of inorganic matter to the sciences pertaining to organic matter, or to life. These subjects present the studies of the physical basis, the environment, the support, and the nourishment of living organisms. The study of environment then consists in observations and investigations of the energies which act through inorganic matter and influence the germination, growth, and development of living organisms.

Botany is the science of the lowest forms of life. How can one plant be observed without first learning its structural environment, its relations to climate, to air, to water, and to heat? Pull it up by the roots, and the questions of mineralogy meet the eye. Geology and geography are studies of the forms of rock material; anatomy is the study of the forms of life; physics and chemistry of inorganic matter are called "physiology" in its relation to living organisms. The relations of inorganic matter to living organisms are of the closest nature. That knowledge of a plant which does not include its physical basis, support, nourishment, and function, is of little use. Thus any efficient knowledge of plant life and the distribution of vegetation depends absolutely upon the knowledge of the structure of the surface and of meteorology.

Each living organism is a focus of external energies which concenter upon it. The number and qualities of the energies which act upon a living organism are determined by the organism itself. The more developed an organism is, the more complex its life, the more energies concentrate upon and develop it. In this sense, the higher the ascent in the scale of life the more dependent life becomes upon its environment, and the more it derives from its surroundings. Thus living beings, no matter how high their development, can never be freed in this world, at least from their environment. The artist who stands on the beetling crag receives far more from the earth and air than the chamois;

the traveler who is now drawn over the Rocky Mountains by a locomotive is more dependent upon physical force than the early pioneer who wheeled his barrow over the trackless plains. Human progress needs more, demands more and takes more from nature, and in this sense is more dependent upon environment.

The limit of the line of absolute dependence of animal life upon its surroundings can hardly be drawn; it is indeed of the closest nature. The best illustration of the dependence of the evolution of animal life upon geography and climate is shown by *paleontology*. From the archaic rock up to the latest drift, the record of geological periods is kept by the mineral molds, and the remains of plants and animals found in each evolved formation. From the record of a geological period thus kept, the geologist constructs in imagination the surface structure and climate of the earth then adapted as a physical basis and environment of the living creatures of that period.

The hypothesis is doubtless true of all geological periods, that the structure and climate of the earth had a tremendous influence upon both the animal and vegetable life which they sustained. As that is true of the past, so the present structure of the earth is the result of all the former geological changes; its varied climate and conditions hold the same powerful influence in developing the animal life to-day.

No fact is more evident than the dependence of animal life upon structural and climatic environment, and also upon vegetation. Animal life, or *zoölogy*, therefore, cannot be economically studied without studying all the subjects comprised in the environment of life: i.e., the sciences of inorganic life and the science of botany. We study, for instance, the skin and other coverings of animals, and the protections which they afford. The question of animal covering leads directly to the study of climate. Again, animals of the plains differ from animals whose abode is in the mountains. The camel adapts himself to the life of the desert. There can be no study of zoölogy, worthy of the name, without the study of the relations of animal life to its physical basis, environment, nourishment, and support.

The primary study of zoölogy should consist in investigating the habits and habitats of the little folks in feathers and in fur. What animals eat, how they procure their food, the houses they live in, the homes they make for themselves, and the surroundings of their homes, are subjects of intense interest to children. These not only serve to arouse the keenest pleasure, but they give, at the same time, part of this essential realization of the unity of creation.

The study of zoölogy, with all that it implies in the unification of studies, is in every step a preparation for the study of the zoölogy of the highest animal—man. The zoölogical study of man is *anthropology,* and should be pursued by exactly the same methods by which the lower animals are studied. Man is far more under the influence of climate and structure, and therefore more dependent upon them, than less complex or less developed beings. Man, it is true, overcomes, commands, controls, and uses his environment. Just so far as he does this is he developed into higher stages of being. To know, then, the history of the evolution of man, we must know the environment, the circumstances, the energies, which have influenced his acts. Did he live upon grassy plains? In forests? Was he protected by mountains? Was he under the influence of burning heat or the cold of the extreme zones? What was his food, his clothing, his means of shelter? What obstacles had he to overcome? All these questions, intrinsic to the study of anthropology, lead directly to the study of all the central subjects.

The living environment of individual life or community influence, all upon each, and each upon all, is coördinate with the study of structural and climate environment. The relative

influence of masses of vegetation upon the individual plant is
of the closest nature. The tree in the pasture spreads its broad
branches over a large space; the tree in the forest shoots up into
the air with its long trunk. Thus each individual is influenced
by the mass. There is also the study of assembled brute life;
indeed, the knowledge of the relations of flocks, coveys, and
herds to each other is part of the study of the individual.

The mutual relations of human beings, and their potent
influences upon each other in families, gens, phratries, clans,
tribes, and nations, opens the intensely interesting subject of
ethnology, so rich in recent investigations.[1] Anthropology is allied
to ethnology by the intimate notions of the particular and the
general, the individual and the mass. Ethnology is, then, the
science of the influence of a community upon its members.
Mutual influence is far stronger in its determination of character than structural and climate environment; human life in
itself is far more potent in its possibilities than all that lies below
it and supports it. Material environment, so-called, is a powerful
factor in shaping human life, but life itself transcends all other
influences. Like myths, like fetishes, totems, religions, forms
of government appear and reappear in all tribes and all peoples
from the beginning of history without the slightest mark of
collusion or mutual influences.

Nevertheless, the stages of human evolution are in a great
degree determined by the nature of countries, their surface forms,
climate, flora, and fauna. The vexing question of the origin of
the Aryan race, of which there are at least one hundred and
fifty theories, has led to the closest study of geography and its
kindred sciences, for without such knowledge the most protracted researches cannot arrive at a stable hypothesis. Grassy
plains have one easily determined influence, forest plains another;
mountain walls have served as refuges for peoples too far-ad-
vanced for constant wars. A seacoast with protecting walls gave

the Phoenicians the conditions for commerce; the Syrian desert
and the natural moat of the Jordan shut in a race long enough
to develop stable homes and consequent progress; embraced by
the sands of two deserts the ribbon plain and fan-like delta of
Egypt gave the world a mighty civilization.

Ethnology in its broadest meaning comprehends *history:* the
former has as its means of investigation language, literature,
buildings, tools, inventions, and the results of anthropological
study; history adds the written and printed records of mankind.
Although history is the most prominent factor in acquiring a
knowledge of the eternal laws which have controlled the spirit
of man in his evolution, the real truth of printed records is
hidden in a mass of prejudices, flattery of authorities, misrep-
resentations, superstitions, and even rank falsehoods. The subjects peculiar to ethnology interpret and explain obscure points in
history.

The earth is the home of man; vegetation and animal life
comprise its furniture and furnishings. Each characteristic area
of surface may be called an apartment in this home. It has a
definite shape consisting of meeting slopes, of valleys, hills, and
mountains, of rivers and seas. The tremendous influence of
natural environment upon the evolution of tribes and nations,
I have already briefly discussed. One river (the Nile), one
alluvial plain fertilized by floods, gave us, says Ranke, monothe-
ism and monarchy. The Pindus, with its mountain spurs enclos-
ing valleys and opening upon the sea, gave us polytheism and
democracy. There can be no efficient explanation of countless
differences in beings of one species without a thorough knowledge of geography and meteorology.

But geography has a close psychological relation to history.
The initial mental action in the study of history is that of the
imagination: events, architecture, cities, the composition and
march of armies, points of strategy, the prominent characters,

must be clearly pictured in the mind; but such pictures are ever changing with kaleidoscopic rapidity in the onward-moving tide of time. Forests spring up and are destroyed; nations rise and perish; wars succeed wars; and conquests, conquests: one factor remains comparatively fixed and stable, and that is the great background of events, the stage of human comedies and tragedies, the land itself. A vivid concept of the structure of a country is the main means of binding historical knowledge into a more complete concept. Events, dates, narrations, characters, are facts mingled in hopeless confusion without an adequate knowledge of geography. No system of mnemonics can be compared for a moment with the assistance a clear concept of structure affords to the memory of historical facts. We are thus able to follow the march of armies, migrations, the extension of empires by conquest and colonization, and retain in the mind all the intrinsic features. The study of history without the continual use of the best maps is an extravagant use of time and waste of power. I hold then, in this brief outline of a vast subject, that all these central subjects of study are in fact one subject. The child begins all these subjects spontaneously; and these tendencies, these spontaneous activities, are the indications, positive, of that which should afterwards follow in education.[2]

These subjects can be considered as one in *several* relations. First, they are related in the *study of form*. The universe is filled with matter. The human mind has the power to differentiate by inference one object from all other objects. Form may be called the surface limitations of a body of matter or an object. Even the forms of invisible bodies of matter must be known in order to make any rational deduction as to cause and effect. We began to know what colors are when the shape and rapidity of waves of ether were discovered. We took our first lesson in sound when we measured the shape and extent of an air-wave. We shall know electricity when we can measure the form of each vibra tion and time of its continuance. In fact, the study of form is intrinsic to all the central subjects of study. Geography is the pure study of form, form of the earth's surface. Geology is no less a study of form, but has to do more with the direct forces which produce the form. Mineralogy is properly a study of form. Anatomy is the study of the structure of living organisms from the lowest to the highest. The form of an object is the product of energy which acted through the form of the object which preceded it and out of which it was produced. Form is the product of energy.

There is another relation which binds all study together, and that is the *study of number*. We can have no accurate knowledge of matter unless we know the exact size of material bodies. We must know length, breadth, and thickness; we must know weight; we must measure the force which acts through it, and know the time of its duration. Therefore number, as a mode of judgment, is common to the study of all the central subjects.

There is still a closer unity in the study of the central subjects, and that is the *unity of function,* the dependent interrelation of the subject of one study upon the subjects of all studies. Leave out the subject of one study, and none of the others could exist. Each subject exists because the other exists.[8] The function of minerals, the function of air, and of heat acting through air, the function of the physical basis of life to the life which it supports and nourishes, are all interdependent. Thus a knowledge of plant life is utterly dependent upon all of the other subjects of study. The same can be said of brute life and of the highest animal— man. So we can say that these subjects are bound together in function, and we can take it for granted that there is no atom in this universe, no form or body of matter, that has not its specific use, and infer that this use is the highest when it serves to develop the highest creation of God—man.

Initial study is always the study of effects. We study effects directly; we observe and investigate effects, the form and quality of the mineral, each stage of geology, each phase of geography. But an effect presupposes a cause; indeed, a knowledge of effects is useless in education unless it leads directly to the investigation of causes. All educative study since man breathed has been the study of causes. Causes cannot be exactly known unless effects are exactly known. As is the knowledge of effects, so will be the judgments of causes. Effects are presented to the ego through the senses and by the imagination; just as they are known so can their causes be known. All these subjects are bound together by the observation and investigation of effects, and the inferences of causes.

But there is another name for the study of cause and effect, and that is the *study of law,* immutable, unchangeable law. A law of nature can be defined as the direction of energy acting through bodies of matter. The quality of the object through which energy acts determines the quality of the energy which acts through it. We can take it as a sound hypothesis that there is one all-efficient energy which acts through matter. This matter is differentiated into bodies and objects by energy itself, and energy in turn is differentiated in its action through different qualities of matter. Thus we study force, and only force as an end, in the studies of geography, geology, and mineralogy. We call these studies of the laws of force "physics" and "chemistry." When we come to organic life, we call the laws of energy the "laws of life" the "chemistry and physics of life," physiology or, more comprehensively, *biology.*

I would present, then, the study of law as the end and aim of all these central subjects of study. I would lay down the hypothesis (which can scarcely be called a working hypothesis) that there is only one study, and that study is the study of the Infinite, differentiated in its action through the bodies of matter of different qualities and properties: first, the non-sensient, inorganic matter; and, second, the sensient, organic matter. The study of law, or the study of differentiated energies acting through matter, is the one unit of investigation. I can assert that, from the beginning, man's growth and development have utterly depended, without variation or shadow of turning, upon his search for God's laws, and his application of them when found, and that there is no other study and no other work of man. We are made in His image, and through the knowledge of His laws and their application we manifest our likeness to Him, we approach His image.

All study is a unit; the focus of all efficient energy is the human soul, endowed with reason to know that energy, and the motives to apply it. All acts of consciousness are non-spacial, non-ponderable energy, pure energy, and the human ego infers from the presence of differentiated energies in consciousness, the nature of the matter external to consciousness, the matter through which these energies act. I repeat, my fellow teachers, that there is but one study in this world of ours, and I can call it in one breath, the study of law, and the study of God.[4]

[1] Edward Yoemans, *Shackled Youth* (Atlantic Monthly Press), pp. 13-25.

[2] John Dewey, *My Pedagogic Creed* (Progressive Education Assn.), Article III, "No succession of studies . . . "

[3] John Dewey, *My Pedagogic Creed* (Progressive Education Assn.), Articles III and IV.

[4] Froebel, *Education of Man* (Appleton), pp. 1-3.

III

FORM AS A MODE OF JUDGMENT

THE two modes of judgment, form and number, are indispensable factors of mental action in the acquisition of knowledge, and in the development of mental power.

All space known to man is filled with matter—earth, air, water, and ether.

We are apt to limit objects to portions of solid matter. Every object, for instance, has length, breadth, and thickness. An oral word, a wave of air or ether, a sound, a note in music, a written word and a numerical figure, are just as much objects as a tree, a stone, or a mountain. A wave of air has length, breadth, and thickness; it has a definite shape, it occupies space, and it consists of matter. Any defined portion of matter, therefore, occupying space, and having a fixed boundary in space, is an object. It is true that, so far as we know, each object is indefinitely divisible, and therefore each part of an object may be called an object itself. This gives the word object a very broad significance. Each successive wave of ether that touches the eye stimulates and arouses elementary ideas in consciousness, each vibration that touches the ear and makes the mind conscious of a corresponding sound, is an object. They are definite portions of matter and have definite shapes. Each vibration of heat, sound, or electricity is an object. A wave of ether one eight-hundred-trillionth of a second in duration is as much an

object as is a mountain mass. A wave upon the surface of the
ocean is an object, and just as much an object as its corresponding form in land surface, on the prairie. Each and every object
has a definite form. The form of an object is the surface boundaries of that object, or its superficial limitations. Each object is
limited by a surface or surfaces.

All objects change. They are continually becoming other
objects. It is perfectly safe to say that no object in the universe
remains identical with itself in any two successive moments of
time. The differences in changes of different objects are marked
by differences in time. A wave of ether exists in one form—as
I have already said, one eight-hundred-trillionth of a second.
Changes in solid material are far slower, but everything changes;
every portion of matter is becoming something else at every
moment; in fact, all there is for man to study is the phenomena
of everlasting change.

Matter does not change itself. I think it safe to hold the
hypothesis that there is no energy inherent in matter. Matter
is a condition of change, but not the means of changing. We
can give the cause of all changes in matter one general term—
energy. Physical energy acts through inorganic matter; life, the
higher form of energy, acts through organic matter; and the
result of these energies is a continual and continuous becoming.
As previously stated, "The qualities of an object through which
energy acts determine the direction of the energy or the law of
the energy." Any one act of energy causes a change in the
object; that is, it becomes another object with another form and
other qualities. Supposing energy to be one unchangeable, all-
efficient, complete unit, we can then suppose that this unit of
energy is differentiated through and by means of the qualities of
matter through which it acts. Without qualities of matter, we
may infer that there would be no differentiation of energy, and
therefore no knowledge of energy, or inferences in regard to

matter through which energy acts, possible to the human mind. The quality of an object, I repeat, through which energy acts—and energy acts through all objects—determines the direction of that energy. This differentiated energy acts upon and manifests itself in consciousness if the organism is capable of receiving it.

All objects are being changed, we can say, continually, by physical and life forces. Each and every change in an object causes a change in the form of that object.

The qualities of an object at one moment determines the qualities of the object into which it is changed the next moment. We study, for instance, the development of the earth's surface. This development is manifested to us in forms and in the successive changes in form, from the old archaic rock, up through all the changes to the geographical forms of the present. We seek for the forces and the laws of those forces which brought about the changes. We trace the change of each successive formation, the present effect and the present form, giving us a clew to the causes of that form. This is only an illustration of the study of all objects. All changes in matter result in changes in form. We follow the acorn from its planting to its becoming a mighty tree. It exists in one form, that of the acorn; then changes into another form, and then into others, each successive change demanding a new direction of energy, resulting in a new form. Thus form is the product of energy.[1]

Every quality or property of matter is known first of all by its form. I am not here saying that there are no other intrinsic qualities in matter except form; but I think we can truly say that form is the supreme manifestation of energy, and that educative knowledge is dependent upon the power of judging form with some degree of accuracy. By divine intuitions Froebel, in his great plan of educating little children, recognized the importance of a knowledge of form. He taught us that the great intellectual sense of touch, and the products of this sense, form, lie at the basis of all intellectual development.

An object is known to the mind, and known only, by an individual concept which corresponds to that object. If, then, all knowledge depends primarily upon a knowledge of form, it becomes a question of vast importance for us, as teachers, to know how this knowledge of form is acquired by the mind. The bases of all mental action are acquired through the sense, by the action of external energy, through the sensorium. There are five great avenues for this action of external stimuli: *the five senses*—touch, taste, hearing, sight, and smell.

The development of the knowledge of form is left fundamentally to the greatest intellectual sense, that of touch. Knowledge of form is the direct product of the action of the tactual sense. Although touch may in a certain degree be a substitute for the products of the other senses, one or all of the products of the other senses cannot in any way be a substitute for the effects of touch. The continued action of the sense of sight in observation cannot intrinsically enhance a knowledge of form. It is true, classification of forms and reasoning in regard to forms are brought about by all the senses, and probably that of sight plays a most active part; but any approximation to adequacy in form concepts can only be brought about by the direct exercise of the sense of touch.

All energies which act through matter must first touch, or come in contact with, the end-organs of the senses before they can enter the brain over the sensory tracts. Therefore, all the senses may be truly called tactual; and, if we take the hypothesis of evolution, that all the senses were evolved out of, and differentiated from, the fundamental sense of touch, we get a clearer idea of the vital importance of the development of the tactual sense in education. The actions of the other senses are over special sensory tracts; but the tactual sense, *per se,* is distributed over all the end-organs of the body.

The lessons derived from children who have had the great misfortune to have been born without, or to have early lost, one or more senses are invaluable. Laura Bridgman taught us the immense importance of the tactual sense, but the most striking, and indeed the most beautiful, of all the examples is found in the case of Helen Keller; as a little girl of ten years of age (1891), she evidenced what may be called genius; her knowledge was phenomenal, her power of thought and expression marvelous. The first few years of this child's life, after she lost the senses of hearing and sight, were spent in a blind, unreasoning desire to have some knowledge of and contact with the outer world. The first, futile, passionate attempts to know without any guidance made Helen Keller exhibit the traits of a brute; then came the marvelous teacher, Miss Sullivan, who simply presented the conditions for the natural, and therefore best, action of this wonderful being. The result was as I have already said. I have never known a child of ten years of age who had the intellectual power of this deaf and blind girl. It cannot be denied that there were still traces in her mind of color and sound; but these must have been necessarily faint, and have had very little intellectual influence over her development. The lives of Laura Bridgman and Helen Keller prove beyond all doubt that great intellectual power may be attained through the normal exercise of the sense of touch; that the products of touch offer the basis of all intellectual action. It follows then that the sense by which form is conceived or judged in the mind must therefore stand first and in a better method of education, "The stone which the builders rejected" will become "the head of the corner."

All conscious activities, states of consciousness, all mental action directly known to the ego, are non-spacial and non-ponderable. They consist wholly and entirely of pure energy. This energy acts through matter, and finally through the highest form and quality of matter, the human brain, and is known to the ego only as pure energy differentiated into elementary ideas or specific activities.

A knowledge of form is absolutely indispensable to a knowledge of the energy which acts through matter, and the laws of that energy. The more nearly adequate the concept corresponding to an external form, the greater is the mind's power to know the object of which the form is a superficial boundary. A knowledge of form, then, is the great entrance hall to all knowledge; without knowledge of form, other knowledge is not possible.

Later I shall discuss to some length the obscurity and crudeness of individual concepts. The concepts produced by the spontaneous activities of the mind are exceedingly vague. It follows, therefore, that out of such crude concepts spontaneous comparison and subsequent classification must also be exceedingly imperfect. There is no education in such comparisons and classifications. These crude concepts are, it is true, the beginnings or the germs of education; but if they remain obscure and vague, the being will remain undeveloped and mentally weak.

The problem is, then, by what mental action and by what conditions may these concepts corresponding to external forms be developed? [2]

There are no external forms in the mind. The knowledge of a form is a product of mental action entirely dependent upon the nature of the brain and upon external attributes of form acting through the sense of touch. The external attributes of touch create in the brain their corresponding elementary ideas or percepts. The elementary ideas are united into individual concepts by the action of objects through all the senses, notably that of sight. The individual concepts are united in consciousness through analysis, comparison, classification, and consequent processes of reasoning. Upon their approximation to adequacy depends the educational value of the analysis, inference, and generalization. Defective and crude analysis, comparison, classification, inference, and generalization are the inevitable results of crude and obscure individual concepts. This fact cannot be impressed too strongly upon the attention of teachers. By the ordinary action of objects through the senses elementary ideas arise above the plane of consciousness and are united or synthesized into wholes. Observation is the elaboration and intensification of these individual concepts by the continued action of external objects upon consciousness.

The mind has the power to construct new unities out of senses products, new individual concepts, which are not the direct result of the action of objects. This power of the mind is called imagination. The mental process, so far as the synthesis of ideas is concerned, is precisely the same as in the ordinary action of the senses in observation. In seeing, hearing, and touching the object itself is the cause of the synthesis. Imagination is the power to synthesize or unite elementary ideas into wholes, without the direct action of external objects. The relations of sense products and of individual concepts acquired by observation, to the products of the imagination, are exceedingly close. The vividness, distinctness, and intensity of the individual concepts, constructed by the imagination, depend fundamentally upon the vividness, distinctness, and intensity of the elementary ideas which form individual concepts created by external attributes and objects through the senses; the relation, if I may use the illustration, is of material to construction. The psychic elements and the unities of elements are the materials out of which are constructed or synthesized the products of the imagination. As the former are in clearness and distinctness, so will the latter be. A person with crude ideas of form can never by the imagination construct anything but crude forms. The only educational

value that crude or obscure elementary ideas and imperfect
individual concepts have, consists in the fact that they are the
germs or potentialities for development. They will never reach
an educational value until they are developed into clearness and
distinctness. On the other hand, a good observer may not have
a highly trained imagination; because for this the psychic material in the brain must be exercised; this does not lessen, however,
the proof of the relation of the products of the senses to the
products of imagination.

Through imagination we are able to go beyond the limited
horizon of the senses.[8] Sense training and sense development
are the preparatory steps to this great journey into the unseen.
Observation produces individual conception when the objects
are within the sense grasp; imagination produces the mental
concept, beyond the realm of sense. In all the creations of the
imagination, form is the primary, fundamental, and indispensable factor to mental action and mental power. There can be no
reasoning, no effective study of cause, in geography, geology,
mineralogy, or any of the central subjects, there can be no effective hearing of language, no educative reasoning, unless the
mind has the power to construct clear images. I repeat, all these
images or creations of the mind are utterly dependent upon the
sense products out of which they are formed.

As form study is the construction of individual concepts of
form by the immediate action of objects upon consciousness, so
geometry is the science of imaging forms that lie beyond the
limits of the senses. Geometry is the great means by which the
imagination is aided in the construction and relation of forms
not directly called into being by external objects. This gives
geometry a commanding position in all the central subjects of
study. For instance, geography in itself is a science of the surface forms of the earth; the initial steps in geology are through
form, and the same can be positively said of mineralogy.

The study of mathematical geography is perhaps the best illustration of the use of geometry in the acquisition of that knowledge which has for its aim the distribution of sunshine over the earth's surface, and the causes of that distribution. No one step in reasoning, in this direction, can be taken without, first, the study of forms by observation, and, second, the imagination of forms which lie beyond the reach of observation. The tendency of the mind is to relate all irregular forms of objects to conventional or typical forms. Geometry gives us the typical form, as the basis of imaging the real form. Thus a river-basin may be first pictured as two slopes meeting at their lower edges. The imaging of the two slopes thus meeting is the initial step to the mental construction of any and all river-basins.

Teachers need to ask themselves, what opportunities does the school offer to the child for form study? We, as teachers, have wandered far away from the essential subjects of study. Our mental vision has been fixed too much upon dead forms and formalism, and not upon the thought to be expressed. When we turn our eyes upon the central subjects of study, and their intrinsic value in human development, the opportunities for form study become to us endless and infinite; and we realize that the value of all true study depends upon the distinctness of concepts corresponding to external forms.[4]

Geography is fundamentally a study of form, forms of the earth's surface, forms of meeting and parting slopes, of which all the characteristic areas of the earth's surface consist. For years I have endeavored to lead graduates of high schools and colleges into the rich and beautiful fields of imagination, which in geography lie beyond the sense grasp. I find continual and fundamental weakness in the action of the imagination. I seek for its cause and find it in the reliance upon dead forms of expression, rather than direct observation. Observation of surface forms is the indispensable foundation of all attempts to image the

continental structure; thus, field excursions in geography are
of the first importance. Under the direction of these teachers
who are keen observers, field excursions are never-failing sources
of delight and economical instruction to the child.

You will recall the discussion in regard to the organic relation of geography to geology. Although in the study of geology
and mineralogy, color, density, and weight are of great importance, still form always stands first. When we rise from the subjects that pertain to inorganic matter to those that pertain to
organic matter, we have a continuous study of form; in plant-
life we have the form of the leaf, the stem, the flower, and the
root. Form is the principal environment of the child, and the
teacher's main purpose should be that the forms studied should
continually enhance the conscious activities corresponding to
the forms of external objects. The innumerable forms in nature
and art may be reduced conventionally to a few types; for
instance, the sphere, the cylinder, and the cube. There are no
typical forms in nature. All the forms in nature are irregular.
They depart in every line and surface from the conventional
or typical forms. Therefore it seems logical that real or natural
form should be studied first, that they are more adapted to the
crude concepts of the child, and that typical forms should be
slowly approximated. When geometry becomes a necessity in
education, as it should very early, probably in the sixth, seventh,
or eighth grades, then the direct study of typical forms becomes
necessary in order to imagine the real forms which lie beyond
the sense grasp.

The conclusions that may be reached from this imperfect
presentation of the subject of form and geometry study are
these: first, the study of form and geometry are of fundamental,
intrinsic importance in education; second, all study of form may
be confined to observation and the study of all the central subjects, that is, there is no necessity for form lessons in themselves,

or form study, *per se;* third, that in the study of the central subjects which require the action of the imagination, the principles and propositions of elementary geometry may be fully acquired in direct relation to the study of the central subjects; fourth, the immediate and the highest aim of the study of form and geometry is to know the laws of energy acting through matter.

[1] Froebel, *Education of Man* (Appelton), pp. 167-171.

[2] John Dewey, *My Pedagogic Creed* (Progressive Education Assn.), Article IV, 1, 2.

[3] Porter Lander MacClintock, *Literature in the Elementary School,* pp. 18-26; *also see* Caroline Pratt, *Experimental Practice in the City and Country School* (Dutton), pp. 39-44.

[4] John Dewey, *My Pedagogic Creed* (Progressive Education Assn.), Article IV, 2.

IV

NUMBER AND ITS RELATION TO THE CENTRAL SUBJECTS

ARITHMETIC was one of the first subjects to be taught after the classics had resigned their almost universal sway; it was indeed the successor of classics in public schools. The cause of its popularity and universal use is not far to seek. It presented an immense amount of practice for both pupils and teachers, and it filled school-hours with definite exercises. The solving of problems, or, as it used to be called, "doing of sums," was something that every teacher no matter how uneducated or untrained could give his pupils for tasks, and the people readily acknowledged the practicality of arithmetic. Long before geography was thought of, or English grammar came into the schools, arithmetic had taken a firm hold; and to-day it is probably true that one-fourth of all the time in schools of English-speaking people is taken up by the study of this subject.

Some progress was made in the methods of teaching number through German educators, notably Grube and Bohme, who called particular attention to the use of objects as a means of teaching number, and to the fact that the five operations should be taught in immediate relation. With the exception of these improvements, arithmetic as a study remains practically the same as it has been for years—the solution of problems, the memorizing of figures, and the learning of rules.

The science of numbers was discovered in the remote past,

out of the reach of recorded history, and, in common with all other sciences, it had its birth in mythology, as had chemistry in alchemy and astronomy in astrology. Number was born in superstition and reared in mystery. We know that numbers were once made the foundation of religion and philosophy, and that the tricks of figures have had a marvelous effect on credulous peoples.

Arithmetic is an essential factor in every step of human progress; still, the subject as a school study has been held until to-day almost entirely apart from anything like practical education. That which is most deeply rooted in tradition has a sort of benumbing effect upon the intellect; the profound reverence of the average scholar for the past making him accept the logic of his ancestors without question.

Mathematics is called the exact science. The science of arithmetic may be called the science of exact limitation of matter and things in space, force, and time.

Nothing useful can be constructed without the use of that mode of limitation called numbering. Not the simplest article of furniture, not an instrument, tool, machine, nor building, can be made without exact measurements. Commerce would be impossible without the measurement of weight and bulk of articles. There could be no relation of values without number. All progress in science is absolutely dependent upon number. Any knowledge of geography, geology, chemistry, and above all else physics, is impossible without accurate measurements of volume, weight, force, and time. That mode of judgment which we call numbering enters into every activity of life, and into every relation of science or business—into the kitchen, the parlor, the workshop, manufactories, commerce—and marks all human progress. Numbers enter into all acts of practical life, into all intellectual attainment; they are essential factors in all human development.

What is number? What are the nature and function of those

acts of the mind which number? By what mental process do they become known? Number is a mode of judgment.[1] There are no numbers or acts of numbering outside of consciousness. Number is the product of mind, and does not exist outside of the mind. All that lies outside of, and acts upon, consciousness may be considered as causes of effects in consciousness, but is entirely separated from the causes.

An act of judgment in numbering is an act of limitation.[2] The little child spontaneously begins his preliminary studies of number just as soon as he tries to measure with his arm the distance between himself and any object, or the distance between himself and a chair, when he begins to creep or walk. All his early experiences are mixed up with vague strivings after definite limitations of weight, distance, and single things. When these vague inferences rise to positive and accurate judgments they may be called acts of numbering.

The limiting adjectives, some, several, many, much, few, small, little, great, high, tall, long, short, are the expressions of inexact or vague inferences. These inferences are not acts of numbering; they are but the beginnings, the initial steps, which create the necessity for accuracy, and therefore lead up to numbering. Indeed, all efforts to measure distance, areas, weight, force, and time may be referred to that spontaneous action out of which exactness and accuracy may be developed by necessity and education.[3]

The tendencies of the child's spontaneous or instinctive activities are the perfect indications of what he should study, and the natural method of study as well. The best clew to the nature and function of number, as with all other subjects of thought, is to be found in the innate tendencies of the child manifested in his spontaneous activities—in what nature demands that he shall do in order to know.[4]

Many, if not most, of our pedagogical errors have their origin in the ignorance of the nature and functions of the subjects taught. We were in the dark concerning the practical educational value of color and the method of teaching it until scientists like Helmholtz discovered what color really is. Those subjects which have been taught for the longest time, such as reading and arithmetic, are, as a rule, the least known. They are buried "full five fathoms deep" in tradition and pedantry.

From this standpoint of a child's natural activity then, let us again ask: What is number and what is function? First, the child enters a visible, tangible world. His environment acts upon him and arouses and develops mental life. His knowledge depends utterly upon the mental energies which respond to the action of external forces. He is surrounded by objects that stimulate judgment—forms of differing size, weight, and dimensions. He is utterly dependent for his knowledge of an object, and his inferences in regard to an object, upon its correspondence in consciousness. That correspondence is non-spacial. Form and size are the exact limitations of an object in space. The knowledge of the form and size of an object is not only indispensable to the knowledge of that object, but also of its relations to other objects, in comparison, classification, and consequent generalization.

Size has three dimensions—length, breadth, and thickness. The spontaneous tendency of the intellect is to know length, breadth and thickness. Whatever may be the innate or *a priori* tendencies of the mind, this much is sure—*a knowledge of form and size must be acquired entirely by self-activity*. Every act of the child, every movement of the body, involves measurement of size. That the child at first has no knowledge of distance is shown by his reaching for the moon as confidently as he does for a lighted candle close to him. All his knowledge of size must come through experience. Definite experience in any direction is acquired by habitual self-activity in that direction. Knowing or inferring distance is a positive and inborn aptitude of the child.

He strives to measure distance, area, and volume by the attention of all his senses, and by the expressive acts of his whole body.

It cannot be too often repeated that the first attempts at measuring are exceedingly vague and obscure. They are the invariable signs of exceedingly crude individual concepts. Nevertheless, the child is incessant in measuring and judging distance, area, and volume. For this purpose all his muscular activity, his muscular sense, is brought into continual action. In creeping and walking the child is always measuring with his eye, with his hands, with his feet, and, indeed, with his whole body. The first act of a child in walking is an act of measuring. He attempts to take his first steps by calculating with his eye the distance between him and the outstretched arms of his mother. He creeps toward an observed object by first measuring the distance between himself and the object. Just as he makes for himself instinctive gestures and language, so he makes for himself measures of distance, measures of area, and measures of volume. As his individual concepts rise from obscurity to clearness, there is a necessity for exact measurement. Then come the conditions for higher education, and an arbitrary scheme of mensuration takes the place of the child's instinctive plan. He knows intuitively one step and more than one step. He learns from one step, two steps, if the proper conditions are presented. He infers the distance of one foot, one yard, and with that mental limitation he measures two feet, two yards. He gains these measures by his own experience, assisted by the language and directions of adults about him.

The so-called abstract numbers mean nothing whatever to the child. To him they are worthless unless applied. When the proper opportunities arise, he learns one inch, one foot, one yard, one square foot, one inch cube, etc. Thus, from mere spontaneous activities is developed the necessity for exactness and accuracy. When the child feels the need of knowing distance, area, and volume, the proper conditions being presented, he will measure and learn length, breadth, and thickness. Thus, numbering activity is organically related to form activity. The mere form of an object finds its highest importance in size. The knowledge of form is the initial step, the knowledge of size, an absolute consequential necessity.

Form and size are really one in mental act, for there can be no individual concept corresponding to external form without some judgment of the size of that form. The educational question is: Is that judgment an exact one? This brings fully to our minds the necessity of numbering. An object may be infinitely small or infinitely great, as to its dimensions, but identical as to its form. A sphere one inch in diameter has exactly the same form as a sphere twenty-five thousand miles in diameter. The difference is in size, and that difference can be known only by the exercise of that mode of judgment which we call numbering. Apply these facts to the study of the central subjects and we shall see what a vast field these present for the constant and continual exercise of the faculty of numbering.

Turn to geography: the form of a continent one mile in length may be the same as the form of a continent—Eurasia, for instance—which is more than ten thousand miles long. A little brook-basin may have the same form as the basin of a mighty river. The differences are in size. Knowledge of area of the earth's surface and the area of any given characteristic unit of surface is fundamental in all study of geography. As the forms gained by observation determine precisely the imagined forms that lie beyond the sense grasp, so the measure of lines, areas, and volumes, that are gained by direct and immediate experience in observation, are the indispensable criteria by which we measure all space outside our sense horizon. Whatever the accuracy of these measures is, so will be the accuracy of our measures estimated by the imagination. There can be no exact individual concept of the area of a continent. Most, if not all, the measures of space by the imagination are approximate. These measures are adequate just in proportion to our experience. We travel a thousand miles upon the cars at the rate of thirty miles an hour. We measure vaguely the time by hours, and by that measure we form some approximate estimate of the distance, and that becomes, in turn, the measure of another thousand miles, and another, and so on. The habit of accurate measuring is acquired solely by the exercise of the numbering faculty, which grows out of present and immediate necessities ever presenting themselves. Geography is a study of form and size; form is the fundamental step, and size the immediate sequence. If the child had no other study than that of geography, and the exercise of the numbering faculty met the necessities of the child's increasing knowledge both of observation and imagination, these opportunities would give him a sound basis for the acquisition of the knowledge of arithmetic, as it is now understood. The teacher must always know when there is a necessity for measuring, must always know when the numbering faculty should be exercised. In all outdoor work and excursions, the length of the slope, the breadth of the river or brook, or the area of the lake, should be approximated. It goes without saying that unless the conditions for these necessities of knowing are presented to the child, the child's measuring power will remain in vagueness and obscurity, but the moment the necessity of knowing is presented, then the child acquires the habit of estimating the distance which he passes over, which he views with his eyes and which he measures with his feet. Thus effective knowledge of the natural areas of the earth's surface, or the areas of political divisions, is developed by this exercise of the numbering faculty. After a study of the structure of the United States, for instance, how many practical questions, appealing to the pupil's sense of right, can be made by comparing the sizes of the different states, one with another! How many Delawares in Texas? How many Englands in the United States? How many Hollands in Russia?

I have spoken of the study of form and geometry in the study of mathematical geography, and what is said of form is also true of arithmetic. To gain anything like a clear knowledge of the distribution of sunshine over the earth's surface, and the natural means of that distribution, arithmetical problems must come in at every step; and there is no textbook of arithmetic extant that contains the number of problems, to leave out entirely the practical side of the question, which such a study would bring to the pupils. The study of number is inherent in the study of all the central subjects. First-hand observations necessary to gain a knowledge of distances, areas, volumes, are numberless and indispensable. They are intrinsic to the subjects themselves, and inherent in the child's tendencies.

Although form and size constitute the foundation of all search for truth, we must add here the importance of the knowledge of another great property of matter, and that is weight, the measure of gravitation, and the examination into its laws. Just as a child begins his inquiries with size he begins his experience with weights. The weight of his own body, the weight of a cart he draws, the weight of the doll, the weight of the knife and fork, all his lifting and carrying, are the beginnings of the after-knowledge of exact weights. The child begins instinctively to weigh and to compare weights; to compare the weight of one doll with another, or the kitten with the cat, and he also makes his own standards of weight. He feels the weight of a pound, and he compares that weight with a lighter and a heavier. This strong, instinctive tendency to weigh portions of matter is a preparation for later accurate numbering by weighing.

One of the fundamental properties of matter is density. Density, the compactness of atoms or particles, is ascertained by weighing, and by comparing weights with volume or size. Thus size and weight are closely related. A pound of feathers weighs as much as a pound of lead. The difference is in the volume or the space occupied by the two portions of matter. The knowledge, then, of weight and density is an indispensable factor in all study of matter. For instance, in the study of minerals, density, which is measured by weight and comparative size, is as important as a knowledge of form. The weights of different metals, comparative weights of soils and of woods, are all prominent factors in investigation.

The principal means of knowing energy or force is to measure it. The child when he lifts a ball to throw it instinctively measures the distance between himself and the target, and as instinctively measures the force necessary to throw it. He automatically measures the distance of his steps in walking and running, and in the same way determines the force necessary for the proper movement. He builds a little mill-wheel in the brook, and this measures indefinitely the force of water. These are a few illustrations of the vague beginnings of the measurement of force, which are to grow into higher educational value when the means used for measuring are exact. All true study is the study of invisible energy, and of the direction of that energy which we call natural law. Number is a mode of judgment by which energy is measured; form is a result of peculiar differences in the kind of energy acting; size is the extent of that energy; weight is but another term for the measurement of energy—the energy of gravitation. Thus, all these subjects of form, size, weight, and force are sequences of the same subject.

Time is known only by accurate judgments of the duration of moving objects. All matter is in space and moves in time. There can be no measuring of force without a corresponding measuring of the time taken for its action. I need hardly refer to the child's measurement of time: the morning and the night, the darkness and the daylight, breakfast-time and dinner-time,

time of going to school, time of waiting for some promised pleasure, time to Christmas, time to the Fourth of July. Later come in more approximately accurate inferences. The sun, the darkness, and finally the clock, are used as measures, each and all exercising either the preparation of the mind for numbering, or actually numbering in itself.

The relation of time to the study of the central subjects is inherent in all effective attempts to study, but it may best be shown in history. History moves on in space through time in great parallel lines. Comparative chronology measures the evolution of civilization; thus the memory of dates and their relation to each other is an indispensable factor in understanding history. A date, which marks some event or period interesting to the pupil, is a symbol which recalls a long series of events. The populations of cities and countries; the number of people who live upon a square mile, the relation of the number of inhabitants who occupy one country to that of another—all these are questions in arithmetic which clarify the study of history.

The natural unit of number is an individual concept, a concept which the ego discriminates from all other concepts. If it corresponds to some external object, it is inferred that that object is one object, and therefore it is discriminated from all other objects. The power to limit numbers of objects by this natural unit is the foundation of the number faculty.[5] The numerical relation of single objects and things, which is usually placed first in the discussion of number, I take the liberty of placing last, on account of the great law of all human growth and human progress—necessity. Distance, area, volume, and weight are earlier necessities of knowledge than the numerical relations of single things; however much these relations have in themselves of value. The presentation of single objects in teaching a child number, objects which in themselves are in no way necessary for the child to know, do not stimulate and arouse mental action by that strongest motive, a feeling of necessity. You place three sticks and three sticks before a child, and he may be led to see six sticks; but he does not feel any great urge for the information.

One necessity, however, does appeal to the child, and that is a knowledge of equivalent values; knowledge of the relation of money as an agent of purchase. Most of our arithmetics are filled with this one subject of money-equivalents. They form the bulk of all the problems in arithmetic, overstimulating, too often, the sordid nature of the child. Arithmetics are filled with percentage, interest, banking, etc. This is the so-called practical value of arithmetic, that the child may be able sometime to make change in a grocery-store. Now it is not to be denied that a knowledge of the immense ethical value of money, and its purchasing power, should be acquired as a great means of education; but in spite of all the arithmetic studied in the schools, and the vast amount of time consumed, knowledge of money-values is really acquired only by the handling of money, by the actual necessity presented in commerce, whether it be the buying of a stick of candy for a cent, a pound of raisins for twenty cents, or a gold mine for a million dollars. When money and its relations are taught merely from its so-called practical standpoint, with commercial use as the sole end in view, it has very little educational value. It should be taught from a much higher standpoint of civics, in the light of its ethical relation to human progress, and it is to be hoped that the future arithmetic will contain some problems that bear directly upon the higher and more valuable knowledge, and fewer upon that which aims to make merely a competent clerk or accountant.

Heretofore, as above stated, the learning of arithmetic has been made an isolated subject, learned by itself, and practically applied as sparingly as possible. Yet, illustrations need not be multiplied to show that no study can be pursued adequately in itself without the continual application of arithmetical facts.

Teaching children numerical figures without their application is merely cultivating the recollection of meaningless forms, without any exercise of the judgment. There is not the slightest exercise of the judgment in simply repeating the fact that four and five are nine. A judgment is the essential element of reason, and when a child is actually measuring objects he is reasoning. When he is learning the figures in the multiplication table he is cultivating his verbal memory, to be sure, but working even in this at a disadvantage because ignoring the laws of necessity, of use, and of association, reasoning having nothing whatever to do with the process. The wastefulness of this meaningless method we realize when we consider the almost universal evidence of merchants and bankers, to the effect that a boy enters the counting-room after having studied money-values eight or ten years continuously with very little practical knowledge of bookkeeping and accounts.

The subjects of number, trying to comprehend both the real subjects of number and the general relations of these subjects to all study, are: lines, areas, volume, bulk, and the measurement of energy, time and single things, including money-values.

Economy and effectiveness of teaching are in proportion to a child's recognition of the purposefulness of the matter taught. To illustrate, the child is called upon to learn the fact that four and five are nine. Now which is the better way—for the child to feel a necessity for learning that the cleat for the box-cover which he is making is four inches plus five inches requiring a board nine inches long, or to simply repeat the fact that four and five are nine? Grant even that he uses a better device, with objetcs before him, and learns that four objects and five objects are nine objects; he still feels no necessity for this fact, but he does feel a necessity for knowing how to measure lengths of the article he makes in the wood-shop. He must measure in order to do exact work. It has been proved by actual experience that a child can learn all the facts of numbers under twelve through the necessity of daily use of the ruler.

The reason why children do not exercise their reasoning powers in studying arithmetic is because there have been very few objects taught in school which admit reasoning. The mere formal learning of words does not admit any exercise of inference or judgment; to learn empty forms and dry facts for future application is always a forced external demand. In its infancy, number had little practical use until it occurred to some thoughtful mind that there was more than astrology in the knowledge of the heavens, and myth was raised to the dignity of a science by the practical application of mathematics.

We are to-day face to face with the proposition of putting subjects of thought, the sciences, into our schools; and therefore this discussion is of profit to those who see the relation between the knowledge of number and the knowledge of matter—or better, to those who seek to apply the knowledge of natural laws.

[1] Frobel, *Education of Man* (Appleton), pp. 206-208.
[2] MacLelland and Dewey, *The Psychology of Number* (Appleton), Chap. II.
[3] MacLelland and Dewey, *The Psychology of Number* (Appleton), p. 79.
[4] Caroline Pratt, *Experimental Practice in the City and Country School* (Dutton), p. 22-23.
[5] MacLelland and Dewey, *Psychology of Number* (Appleton), pp. 80-83.

V

WHAT CAN BE DONE WITH NUMBERS?

LET us bear in mind at every step that numbering is a mental act. There are no numbers in reality outside of consciousness and conscious activities; the relation of external forces or objects to number is the relation of their action upon consciousness, and the mind alone numbers.

All numbers are abstract; they are the products of judgment. Numbers may be either applied, or pure, numbers. When a number is used as a numeral adjective limiting things by ones or units, it is applied; when a number is not applied or used as a numeral adjective, it is a pure number.

The attention is now called to one number. All that can be done with that number is to divide it, and the same can be said of any number. We can divide the number twelve into a number of equal numbers, as: twelve divided by four equals three fours ($12 \div 4 = 3$); twelve divided by three equals four threes ($12 \div 3 = 4$); twelve divided by six equals two sixes ($12 \div 6 = 2$); twelve divided by two equals six twos ($12 \div 2 = 6$). By these statements we ask how many fours are there in twelve; how many threes are there in twelve; how many sixes are there in twelve, etc. For instance, twelve inches divided by four inches equals three, which means that there are three four-inches in twelve inches. This process is the division of a number into equal numbers.

A number can be divided into equal parts. It is necessary very often to find the value of one equal part of a number, or the number in one part. This is an entirely different operation from finding the equal numbers in a number. In finding the equal numbers in a number, we must know the number to be divided into equal numbers, and we must know one of the equal numbers into which the number is to be divided, then we find the number of equal numbers in the number to be divided. We divide twelve into equal parts in order to find the number in one part. We divide twelve into four equal parts, and we find the number in one part is three or three ones. We write: one-fourth of twelve equals three (¼ of 12 = 3).

The child should be helped to realize that dividing a number into equal numbers and dividing a number into equal parts are two materially different processes, with different operations and different answers. For instance, twelve apples divided by four apples equals three groups of four apples (12 apples ÷ 4 apples = 3). One-fourth of twelve apples equals three apples (¼ of twelve apples = 3 apples). In dividing a number into equal numbers, the quotient is equal in value to the dividend; in dividing a number into equal parts, the quotient is an equal part of the dividend. It is of exceeding importance, as will hereafter be seen, that these two mental operations are kept distinct.

We can divide a number into two numbers, equal or unequal, when we know one of the numbers. We can divide twelve into seven and another number. The arithmetical sentence is, 12 − 7 = 5. We can divide twelve inches into three inches and another number of inches. We write, 12 in. − 3 in. = 9 in. The mental operation is the division of twelve inches into three inches and nine inches.

All that can be done with a number is to divide it, and we can say that there are three different kinds of division stated:

Dividing a number into equal numbers in order to find the number of equal numbers.

Dividing a number into equal parts in order to find the number in one of the parts.

Dividing a number into two numbers in order to find the value of one of the numbers.

We cannot fix too firmly in the mind that all that can be done with any one number is to divide it, and that there are three cases of division.

All that can be done with a number of numbers can be stated in one simple sentence. Numbers may be united, or in other words, a number of numbers can be taught as a unit; "united into one sum or amount," is tautology. A number of equal numbers may be united, as three fours are twelve, four threes are twelve, two sixes are twelve, and six twos are twelve. A number of numbers, equal or unequal, may be united, as $5 + 4 + 3 = 12$. We make the general statement again, that all that can be done with a number is to divide it into equal numbers, into equal parts, or into numbers equal or unequal. All that can be done with a number of numbers is to unite them. Equal numbers may be united, and numbers equal or unequal may be united.

The student is earnestly invited to criticize with great care and closeness the following definitions of the five operations in number:

Division is dividing a number into a number of equal numbers.

Partition is dividing a number into a number of equal parts in order to find the number in one part.

Subtraction is dividing a number into two numbers, one of which is known.

Multiplying is uniting a number of equal numbers.

Addition is uniting a number of numbers, either equal or unequal.

Considerable repetition may be necessary in order to make these very simple definitions plain and explicit.

Division is dividing a number into a number of equal numbers:

III, III, III, III.

A dividend in division is the number to be divided into a number of equal numbers.

A divisor in division is any one of the equal numbers into which the dividend is to be divided.

The quotient in division is the number of equal numbers into which the dividend is divided. (The quotient, or number of equal numbers into which the dividend is divided, is equal to the dividend.)

The arithmetical statement is as follows: $12 \div 4 = 3$; three is a numeral adjective limiting four, and means three fours. Thus, in division, the quotient must be equal to the dividend, as the quotient is the number of equal numbers into which the dividend is divided. Ask the question: How many three-cents are there in twelve cents? And the answer is: Four three-cents. The arithmetical sentence is, $12\not c \div 3\not c = 4$, and the four means four three-cents. 12 in. $\div$ 3 in. $= 4$, or, in other words, there are four three-inches in twelve inches. Again, we ask the question: How many two-pints are there in twelve pints? Arithmetical sentence, 12 pts. $\div$ 2 pts. $= 6$. The answer is, six two-pints, or six quarts. How many one-fourths are there in one half? Arithmetical sentence, $\frac{1}{2} \div \frac{1}{4} = 2$. The answer means there are two one-fourths in one-half. How many two-thousandths are there in twelve-thousandths? Arithmetical statement is, $.012 \div .002 = 6$. The answer is, six two-thousandths. The value of the quotient is known by making it the numeral adjective limiting the divisor.

Six limits two-thousandths. (Otherwise the quotient has no value.)

There is a second case or kind of division which may be called partition, or, as the Germans call it, *Teilen,* and, as has already been said, must be kept entirely distinct in thought from the process of dividing a number into equal numbers. Using the word partition, then, for this kind of division, the definitions may be made as follows:

Partition is the division of a number into a number of equal parts in order to find the number in one equal part.

The dividend in partition is the number to be divided into equal parts.

The divisor in partition is the number of equal parts into which the dividend is to be divided.

The quotient in partition is one of the equal parts of the dividend.

Subtraction is dividing a number into two numbers.

The minuend is a number to be divided into two numbers.

The subtrahend is one of the numbers into which the minuend is to be divided.

The remainder in relation to the subtrahend is the other number into which the minuend is to be divided.

Multiplying is uniting equal numbers.

The multiplicand is one of the equal numbers which are to be united.

The multiplier is the number of equal numbers to be united.

The product is the equal numbers united.

Addition is uniting numbers, equal or unequal, as 3 apples $+$ 4 apples $+$ 5 apples $=$ 12 apples; $\frac{3}{4} + \frac{1}{2} + \frac{3}{6} = \frac{9}{12} + \frac{6}{12} + \frac{6}{12} = 2\frac{1}{12}$; $.4 + .3 + .2 = .9$.

The questions for the teacher are: Are these definitions perfectly simple, exact, and true? Can language be used to express the facts in a plainer way? Are the definitions comprehensive?

That is, does each definition include everything that can be thought of in the process defined?

Since mathematics is the one exact science—should it not have an exact language to express it? Most arithmetics declare that the quotient in division is abstract. To illustrate: twelve dollars divided by six dollars equals two. Twelve dollars is a so-called concrete number, but the quotient two is not concrete, not two six-dollars, it is abstract! Why is the quotient, the two six-dollars, any more abstract than the undivided twelve dollars? Reasoning of this sort is at least too abstruse for the common understanding, as well as unnecessary, when the whole matter is perfectly adjusted and can be made perfectly plain to all minds by using the two sentences, $12 \div 4 = 3$, and $\frac{1}{4}$ of $12 = 3$. There is absolutely no need, as has already been said, of using one sentence to express two distinct meanings. There is no difficulty in the way of a common use of these two sentences, and by such use the arithmetic of division and partition can be made utterly simple. There are abstruse things enough in this world which are natural and essential, without the necessity of creating artificial mystification.

How does the mind acquire that mode of judgment called numbering? The answer to this question is very near at hand. We learn to judge by judging. Number is an exact mode of limiting single things, lines, areas, volume, bulk, force, time, and commercial values, by units or exact standards. Therefore the mind learns to number by numbering, that is, by measuring, weighing, learning to estimate lines, areas, volume, etc. There is no other way by which the judgment in numbering can possibly be exercised, and, indeed, no other way is necessary. All that can be presented to the mind, externally, for its action, consists of objects or forms of matter.

Attention is holding the mind and body in the attitude of reception, or for efficient action of external objects. In the efficient exercise of that mode of judgment which is called numbering, attention plays a very prominent part. The standards of number are developed by observation; the mind can attend to acts of numbering just so far as these standards are developed and become forces of the mind; just so far and no farther the mind can act in exact measurement of numbers of things, lines, weights, etc. The direct contact of the mind with numbers of things, and the direct action of the mind upon objects in acts of numbering, are absolutely essential to acquiring the power of numbering. The acts of the mind in recalling numerical facts, for instance, in recalling three fours are twelve, four threes are twelve, one-half of twelve is six, four and three and five are twelve, are not acts of numbering, they are merely acts of recollection. There is no reasoning in these acts; there is no mental power exercised except the mere power of recollection.

Now these facts, it is well known, may be memorized by the mere repetition of the sentences; but it is of the greatest importance that teachers should understand that all exercises in the processes of adding, multiplying, dividing, and subtracting are not in any way acts of numbering, *per se,* or in any case a direct exercise of judgment in numbering. It is granted that certain facts, a certain power of recollection of numbers, and the relations of numbers are an absolute requirement in the economy of thought; but at the same time it is also just as necessary to know that the mere acquisition of knowledge of numerical facts in recollection in no way exercises the reasoning faculties.

In what direction is the exercise of judgment in numbering developed? The first answer to this question is one usually urged in regard to the development of the race in civilization. The lower the grade of development in the human race, the less there is known of number. It is said that certain savages of low order do not know more than three. As the necessity of knowledge increases, just in that measure numbering power is acquired.

It may not be a valid hypothesis to say that in the mind of each child numbers are developed precisely in the order that they have been in the development of the race; still it is something of a guide in attempting to answer the question in what direction should number be developed in the child. The line of development is apparent. The answer to the question, where should we begin with every child in numbering, is also plain. *Begin with the child just where his numbering power is found to be.* If he understands two, teach him three; if three, teach him four. Ascertain at first exactly what the child knows of number, and let this form the germ of all his after-growth. *One* forms the center of the natural horizon of number, and this center is enhanced by one or two, and that by one or more, and that also by one. It is not presumed that this line should be rigidly followed. The line of progress is governed by the necessities of growth, and whenever and wherever a child needs numerically to limit an object or objects, he should then and there learn to know the number necessary for needed exercise of his judgment, and to hold that knowledge ready for immediate application.

It is, however, a very important question to ascertain what it is to know a number:

I I I I

The knowledge of number may be summed up in the following general statements of facts to be acquired:

First, all the equal numbers in a number.

Second, all the equal numbers that united make a number.

(These two facts are correlative, and one cannot be known without the other. One cannot know that there are two twos in four without knowing that two twos make four.)

Third, the numerical value of any one of the equal parts of a number.

Fourth, the division of a number into any two numbers.

Fifth, the union of any two numbers.

A practical knowledge of number is comprehended in these five general statements. There is, however, one question still to be answered, and that is: What facts should be known automatically? Automatic knowledge is that knowledge which requires the least effort of the will in recollection. It is that knowledge which approximates the spontaneous action of the mind. In other words, automatic knowledge is a habit of knowing, so fixed that the least possible effort is required in order to recall it. Now, it is not to be supposed that the five operations above mentioned should be automatically known to an unlimited extent. One should be able to ascertain any fact by numerical processes in the five operations. It can lead to an overburdening of the mind to endeavor to make much of this knowledge above stated automatic; *but certain numerical facts should be absolutely automatic.* Automatic knowledge in the principal directions means the freedom to act; means the least possible time, the least possible effort; it means also no obstructions in the way of quick and exact action of the mind. Therefore, the question of what numerical facts should be made automatic is one of the first importance. Custom has fixed, to a great extent, the demand for these facts. There should be a less comprehensive limitation made. For instance, the knowledge of the equal numbers that make the number one hundred, inclusive, is absolutely sufficient for the most rapid calculation in that direction. The union of the numbers expressed by the nine digits is sufficient for addition; the division of a number into two numbers not exceeding twenty is sufficient for subtraction. Custom has made one hundred and forty-four the limit in division, multiplication, and partition.

The prevailing method of teaching number is the acquisition of certain conventional facts, without any relation to number itself; but, notwithstanding this criticism, the acquisition of automatic knowledge is of immense importance. *At the same time, it must be repeated that the acquisition of the power of number is absolutely dependent upon the exercise of the judgment in numbering;* that is, the application of number to objects, or, speaking more psychologically, to the development of individual concepts. There are two ways of gaining these facts: one is by verbal acts of memorizing, and the other is by acts of numbering. In the one case, as has already been said, the direction of the mind, so far as the exercise of judgment is concerned, is too often omitted; in the other case, the conditions presented are such that the mind is continually judging. In the mere exercise of the verbal memory there is no demand for reasoning power and no feeling of any necessity for numbering, except the mere will of the teacher.

It is at this point that the question of economy comes in as a very important factor. It was found that children of Italian parents, in Boston, whose business it was to sell fruit upon the streets, knew numbers up to eighteen, twenty, and twenty-five readily, when they entered school at six years of age. The reason is apparent: they had simply, by the necessity of the exercise of judging money-values, acquired this knowledge rapidly and completely. This fact, one among the many which could be cited, points to the true method of teaching number. *Present the necessity for acts of numbering, and the facts will be acquired.* How much drill is necessary in number? The old question, like Banquo's ghost, will "not down," reason, common sense, and experience to the contrary. Let it be said then, that *just so much drill is necessary as will render the facts above given automatic.* The less the mind is exercised in actual acts of numbering, the more drill necessary. On the other hand, the more the mind is exercised in numbering, the less drill is necessary—the equation is apparent: the more reasoning, the less conscious memorizing of figures.

Two reforms in number that have been instituted in English-speaking schools in this country consist, first, in the use of objects in teaching number, and, second, in the immediate organic relation of the five operations to each other. When the facts are merely memorized, the more distinct from each other, and the more isolated, the better. Numbers have intrinsically perfect relations to each other, one fact cannot be known without its correlative; but in the mere memorizing of words and sentences operations have absolutely no relation to each other, and to teach them together would lead to confusion and weakness. To a child who does not feel the necessity of knowing the fact that three fours are twelve, and at the same time, that there are three fours in twelve, the facts in his mind have no relation really, and should not be learned together. When his attention is put upon objects themselves, when he is numbering, measuring, or weighing objects, he cannot learn one without knowing the other, and a failure of the teacher to relate the facts is simply to fail in knowing either. To know that seven and five are twelve, and not to know that twelve less five are seven, and twelve less seven are five, is impossible to a mind that is actually number-conscious, but to the mind that is simply trying to recall words in themselves, these facts are not related. When numbers are learned—numbers, not figures—all the five operations are essentially related to each other, and each kind of fact should be associated with the knowledge of the other correlated facts. This can be readily seen by the analysis of the number twelve:

I I I I I I I I I I I I

Now, what can you see in twelve marks? The conclusion you must make is that you know every one of the five operations in knowing twelve, and that these five operations are intrinsically related. You say there are three fours in twelve, also that two sixes are twelve, that one-half of twelve is six, that twelve less six is six, and that six and six are twelve, or two sixes are twelve. You grant without question that the five operations are intrinsically related. When we look at numbers *per se,* the light is full and distinct, and the conclusion is inevitable.

The five operations in learning numbers must be acquired together; in fact, it can almost be said that they can be learned in no other way, and that the artificial distinction used in the Arithmetic pertains entirely to mere memorizing of stated facts, without the least exercise of reasoning. The five operations should be taught together, not only from one to twenty, but from twenty to one hundred, and all through the development of arithmetic. In the common teaching of arithmetic very much is made of notation and numeration, and the economical processes of finding results in numbers too great for automatic knowledge. For instance, the process of writing numbers, reading numbers, of adding, multiplying, dividing, large numbers are all economical processes. The Arabic system of notation and numeration is the basis of the great economy in numbers; *it is therefore of great importance to study the history of the evolution of notation and numbering.* It is also very well to note the uneconomical processes that were used for ages, notably the Roman system of numbers. [1]

The question for us to answer here is: When should notation and numeration and all these operations be taught? What is the pedagogical line of development of these processes? Out of the foregoing these questions can be easily answered. When should a child write numbers? When there is a necessity for him to use the number in expressing his thought. When should he write the different forms of the different figures and signs? For instance, when should he write fractions? When he has occasion to use fractions. From the first, when he learns to read one-half and one-fourth in words, he should learn them at the same time in figures, and they should mean the same thing to him. When should he use decimals? When he is taught ten. He should always write one-tenth in decimals, and the same can be said of all the decimal notation. When should he add large numbers, and go through the process of borrowing in subtraction? He should learn these operations when he uses numbers demanding such processes. The wonders of the Arabic decimal system should be open to him when the necessity requires. One answer is valid for all these questions. When should he multiply a number greater than twelve, or divide by the process of long division? When such economy of mind is necessary. The habit of knowing the processes should come with the doing. *Bring the child face to face with absolute necessity in his thought and action, and difficulties are easily overcome.* If great stress is laid upon the exactness and skill in these processes, they may be easily cultivated when the necessities arise.

It will be granted by all that a course of study should be an adaptation of conditions to the development of the mind, and that the enhancement of conditions should keep pace with the stages of the development of the mind. The so-called logical arrangement of subjects has been a fixed matter of tradition and is deeply rooted in custom. It remains for us to examine anew this arrangement, and to question if it is necessary to divide up the subjects of arithmetic in this way, to have one subject succeed the other, and in each subject to have new terms and new definitions, new rules and new mysteries?

The intrinsic relation of the five operations has already been discussed; also the necessity of acquiring skill in economical numerical processes has been explained. Of all confusion, worst confounded, we can take the subject of *fractions* as the climax. The difficulty of fractions does not consist in the exercise of the numbering faculty, but in the use of complex forms, rules, and definitions. It can be said, in a word, that fractions should be learned precisely like whole numbers. The only difficulty in fractions, a difficulty which is more artificial than real, is the identity of the fractional unit. Thus 12/12 ÷ 3/12 presents no greater difficulty than 12 ÷ 3. In studying lines—for instance, in studying the foot—we have, twelve inches are three four-inches, or four three-inches, one-half of twelve inches, one-fourth of twelve inches, one-sixth of twelve inches, etc. A child can readily see that one-half of twelve inches is six, one-fourth of twelve inches is three, and three-fourths of twelve inches are nine—and the foundation of the fractional unit is laid. In other words, it is perfectly easy to teach all there is in fractions in the development of numbers, step by step, from two upward.

The putting off of the teaching of fractions to the fifth and sixth grades is simply putting in abeyance an essential means of developing the mind. The child, when he reaches the fifth grade, may know all there is to be known of fractions with the greatest ease, if fractions have been really taught—not mere notation and phraseology about fractions. Therefore we must conclude that fractions, as in the usual arrangement of arithmetic, coming after the four operations, is illogical, unpedagogical, and wrong. *Fractions should be taught from first to last, and the same can be said in regard to decimal fractions.* Decimal fractions in notation have a great advantage over common fractions. Decimal fractions are perfectly easy and should be taught when ten is taught, and the notation of decimal fractions should always be learned and used when required in the development of number. Many pupils, after they have passed through a high school, and are asked to divide eight-tenths, two-tenths, put down four and do not know what it means. That is, they do not know that there are four two-tenths in eight-tenths. This ignorance is due to the fact that the proper work has not been done at the proper time.

All there is to be known of United States money can be taught to a child of the number one hundred. I know the claim will be made that the difficulties of multiplication and division of fractions are so great that they should be taught as one subject. This is certainly true if the pupil is plunged headlong into the mysteries of decimal notations without any previous steps, but to develop the notation along with the development of the number there are really no difficulties—no more difficulty in knowing two-tenths than in knowing two, the whole number.

Then we come to the matter of *compound numbers:* addition, subtraction, multiplication and division of denominate numbers. It seems almost sufficient to ask the question of any intelligent person: Why should not all tables and processes of denominate numbers be taught when the number is developed? Why should not two pints be taught, or three feet, or twelve inches, or sixteen ounces, right along in the development of number? Why should not all the operations of compound numbers come in with the five operations? There is every reason why a child should use lines, weights, values, etc., from the first. Is there any reason in putting off this essential knowledge until the seventh grade in the school? If a child is adding, why may he not add pounds? If he is dividing, why not miles or yards? If he is multiplying, why not dollars, pounds or inches? It would be very difficult to answer these questions in the negative. The logical place of compound numbers is in the normal development of number, and nowhere else; and each of the necessary tables should be learned as the practical use for these table necessitates. We have great complaint that children go out of school, after four or five years of study, without any knowledge of arithmetic, and the cause for this is that these subjects are introduced with disregard to their pedagogical relation. They have an artificial illogical place in the course. Tradition has taught us to put off these things until a certain time comes—a time when one-half of the children of the United States are out of school. The genuine demands for a child's growth always include the best for practical life at each stage of his growth.

We now come to the subject of *percentage,* or the decimal fractions of hundreds. With little thought here, we can refer all the per cents, or the division of hundreds into equal parts, to the teaching of one hundred. As has already been shown, the child can learn a decimal just as soon as he learns ten, and that growth in the knowledge of decimals can be continued in all the five operations to one hundred, and when the child learns one hundred he can learn all that there is to percentage. Percentage is merely the practical application of decimal fractions.

Of all subjects, the subject of *interest* has been made the most mysterious, complex, and most confusing; still, the subject of interest in itself is perfectly simple and easy. Bookmakers have crowded their terms of rate per cent, base, etc., upon us; and when the pupils come to it they suppose that they are coming to a brand-new subject, when the fact is, if the subject of number has been developed, there is nothing essentially new to learn in interest. The subject can be taught whenever a child is mature enough to realize that men pay for the use of money. It is based upon a knowledge of percentage and therefore offers no new arithmetical idea or manipulation.

The matter of *proportion,* or comparison of numbers, is a matter that should enter into the warp and woof of all arithmetic teaching. The relations, as well as the values of numbers, consist in comparison—comparison of lengths, areas, volumes, weights, force, time. The form of a ratio and the form of the relation of rates may be used when the child understands that $\frac{1}{2}$ of $4 = \frac{1}{4}$ of 8.

Then we come to those great subjects that were so difficult in our youth. When should a child know *square root?* When should he know the square of a number? When he knows a number can be squared, or of which the square root can be found, he should know them. When he knows four, he should know the square root of four. When he studies a square area, he should know its square root. He should know the square of three, and the square root of nine. The knowledge of the one is the knowledge of the other. Precisely the same thing can be said of *cube root.* When he knows eight, he should know that two is the cube root of eight. He can discover for himself the cube roots and the cubes with the necessary objects in studying volume. But it may be said that the processes of finding roots are difficult; they are difficult because they have been taught as an isolated new idea. If the child through the manipulation of squares and cubes knows how to find area and volume, and if he knows how to find one dimension if the area of a square, or volume of a cube, is given, then when he comes to these processes of finding the power or root of a number the difficulties will vanish.

The present arrangement of subjects in arithmetic is decidedly unpedagogical; and when we consider, again, that the subject of arithmetic takes at least, to put it within bounds, one-third of all the time spent in school, and that one-third of the millions spent for the education of children is put into arithmetic, it is for us, as teachers, to reconsider the whole subject.

I have endeavored to show how illogical these subjects are arranged, and that the beautiful subject of mathematics, the subject that is essential to all human growth and all human thought, is an inheritance of mystery. This piling of mystery upon mystery had made a dark and dead wall in the way of education. It is an imperative duty of every teacher to reconsider this whole subject, to study the essentials of arithmetic anew and to apply them as the necessity for these essentials arises in the child's experience.

---

[1] Herman T. Lukens, "Preparation of an Exercise on Historical Methods in Arithmetic," *Studies in Education,* Vol. II, pp. 30-33. (These volumes are published by the faculty of the Francis W. Parker School, 330 Webster Avenue, Chicago. Price 50 cents.)

VI

ATTENTION

ATTENTION may be partially defined as a mental process immediately caused by the action of the attributes of external objects. This definition needs for its explanation a brief résumé of the psychology of the relation of external objects to subjects of thought or activities of consciousness. The first question to be considered is: What are external attributes?

Light is a mode of motion, differentiated into external colors. An external color, shade, or tint consists of waves of ether of a definite shape and a definite rate of motion. A wave of color touches the end-organ of sight, the retina of the eye, and arouses in the brain its corresponding elementary activity. Similarly, external sound is a mode of motion, modified by the matter through which it acts. It consists of vibrations of air of different forms, particular shapes, and degrees or rates of motion. The special external energy which produces an elementary idea of sound touches the end-organs of sound, and arouses a certain definite conscious activity, which, we infer, corresponds to the external activity or attribute which created it.

All external attributes which definitely affect consciousness are simple energies acting through differentiated qualities of matter. That which is known of the nature of external colors and sounds may be inferred of touch, taste, and smell. Whatever

matter may be in itself as a whole or in its differentiated qualities, all that we know of it depends utterly upon the effects of
energy acting through it upon consciousness. Thus we infer that
a certain attribute is an energy acting through a certain definite
quality of matter. We say that that wall is yellow. The basis of
the judgment is an act of consciousness, induced by the repeated
action of that partciular external attribute or energy we call
yellow. We know little of the nature of that which differentiates
light into this special external color. So far as the human judgment is concerned, all externality consists of simple energies or
attributes, acting through matter, and by the action of these
attributes upon the mind we are able to infer the nature of
the external attributes themselves, and the qualities of matter
through which they act.

An attribute is a simple energy acting through a quality of
matter. Attributes by repeated action develop their correspondences in the mind. That which an attribute creates in the mind
may properly be called an elementary idea. This is the simplest
form of mental energy. An object, then, in its relation to the
mind is a unity of attributes acting through differentiated qualities of matter.

The brain is an organism created and developed for the differentiation, reception, and action of external energies. All activities
of consciousness depend fundamentally upon the action of these
external attributes. To illustrate: Given a complete nervous tract
for the transmission of the vibration of waves of light, and a
complete brain organism upon which external colors may act,
still, without the action of these external colors there can be no
consciousness corresponding to them. Whatever the ego may be,
this much is true, that the elements of all conscious activities
are set in motion by external energies, and the unities of these
psychic elements are known to, and acted upon, by the ego.

The organism of the brain, with its convolutions, its sub-organisms, its fibers and filaments, and all the differentiated parts of the sensorium, comprehending all the nervous tracts and the great central ganglion, determines exactly the number, kind, and nature of the external energies which may act upon, and through, it. The action of the brain, then, is the immediate medium by which conscious energy is known to the ego. The number and kind of external energies which can act upon, or in, the brain are determined by the sensitiveness of the nerve tracts and the quality of the brain itself. There are countless attributes of color, sound, taste, smell, and touch of whose effects the most highly developed brain can never be conscious, because the physical organism is not adequate to their reception.

We are informed by good authority that the child is born deaf, dumb, and blind; in other words, it has little, if any, conscious activity. Its brain consists of physical potentialities for such activities, but until there is due action of external attributes in arousing these latent possibilities there can be no conscious activities. The presence in consciousness of an elementary idea corresponding to an external attribute determines absolutely the possibility of the possessor's knowledge of that attribute and the quality of matter though which the attributes acts.

No elementary idea appears alone in consciousness. A state of consciousness contains units of elementary ideas which may correspond to external objects or units of attributes. The knowledge of external attributes as a whole depends utterly upon the corresponding unit of elementary ideas in the mind. The analysis of an external object depends entirely upon the analysis of its correspondence in consciousness. We have, then, on the one hand, the physical organism with capabilities of receiving and retaining elementary ideas created by external attributes; and on the other, the power of the mind to unite these elementary ideas into wholes, or individual concepts.[1] That which is of especial moment to us in discussing attention is the fact that all the ego has to do in the processes of the creation of elementary ideas and their unification into individual concepts, is to present proper physical and mental conditions for external and internal action. The ego cannot originally create an elementary idea, nor can it directly combine elementary ideas into wholes. This creation and unification is automatic and unconscious. It is the product of external energy. Most of the mistakes in the science and art of teaching have arisen from the false notion that the ego itself can directly create fundamental ideas or individual concepts.

Verify this fact by some simple investigations or experiments near at hand. Look at the objects about you, and name them as rapidly as you can. You say, "I see a house," "I see a flower," "I see a chimney." Listen and you have the same effect in kind— "I hear a locomotive," "I hear a bird singing."

These successive acts of the mind are the results of objects or certain attributes of objects acting upon the mind and raising elementary ideas above the plane of consciousness. They appear to the ego as wholes or units of ideas. The synthesis, association, unification, or recollection of the ideas is perfectly unconscious and automatic, so far as the ego is concerned. The ego is conscious of the results only, on the units of elementary ideas. You can analyze, compare, classify the results, but you cannot directly unite or arrange the ideas. Of individual concepts, elementary ideas alone lie below the plane of consciousness. There is no difference in the kind of action of an object, whether it be the first or any subsequent act; the effect of an object is always the union of elementary ideas, which repetition has a tendency to accelerate.

In each and every act of the senses, that is the act of attributes in creating and energizing elementary ideas, the function of the ego consists wholly in the attitude of body and mind. The rule is: the more receptive the organism, the more effectively external and internal energies act. Receptivity is in proportion to the capacity of the individual to adjust body and mind so as to limit mental action to particular stimuli. This ability to limit conscious stimulation is sometimes called inhibition.

The psychological fact that the unification of elementary ideas is automatic, not a conscious effort of the ego, is highly significant pedagogically, and many pedagogic errors have resulted from ignorance of this fact. The "A, B, C"-methods, the countless phonic and word-building methods, the systematic, prescribed, and predestined object-lessons, are all the bad results of ignorance in regard to this powerful, persistent, and spontaneous action of the mind.

Experience proves that every human being is conscious of mental activities during his waking hours, from the dawn of consciousness to the close of mortal life. Waves or states of consciousness succeed each other in general with great rapidity, and this succession of conscious states cannot be prevented by acts of the will. These conscious activities consist of units of elementary ideas, and the inferences which the ego derives from them. Every human being has these states of consciousness; nevertheless, comparatively few of the human beings born upon earth are becoming educated. Waves of consciousness, or a prolonged succession of conscious states, are not in themselves educative. An educative act always conditions an educative subject and an educative self-effort; the act is effective to just the degree that self-effort is intense.

Self-activity is the fundamental principle of education—a principle universally believed and generally neglected.[2] It is, however, of vast importance that we discriminate with exceeding care the exact functions of self-activity and the conditions which make self-activity possible; that we in some measure comprehend the physical and mental conditions which are the basis of conscious energy, and the spontaneous, instinctive movements and creative power of that energy by means of those conditions. In comparison with creative power and created results, independent of self, self-activity sinks into insignificance. Heredity, birth, physical organization, the instinctive sympathetic acts of body and mind, digestion, breathing, and sensation, it goes without saying, are not the direct products of volition. It is a correct interpretation of an old theological doctrine when we affirm that everything is done for man; that external power creates and sustains him, gives him marvelous powers of body and mind, and is ever ready to render divine assistance at every step of his development. I say divine assistance, because origin and source cannot be discriminated among all the mighty energies that create, nourish, and sustain an organism of life. One differentiated energy cannot be called divine and another material with scientific accuracy.

> To make such a soul,
> Such a body, and such an earth for inspiring the whole.

Notwithstanding all that is done for man, the eternal power that creates and is ever creating him—his individual development is a result of self-activity. *Education depends upon the use the being makes of the conditions in which he finds himself the center.* As he uses that which is given him and done for him will he be educated. The highest economy of self-effort may be attained only by a right discrimination between that which is done for the being and that which the being can do for itself. Overstepping the boundaries of self-effort results in weakness rather than strength; the overstraining in effort, the fearful consciousness of self, the mental entanglement in forms of thought-expression are all the outcome of mis-directed self-effort. Poise, equilibrium, passive and receptive attention, mature reflection, ease in expression, and consciousness of power spring from wisely adjusted self-effort. "Be still, and know that I am God."

The power of the will in attention consists in holding the body and the mind in the most economical attitude for the most effective and complete action of external attributes through nerve tracts upon consciousness.

The special interest of the ego dominates and controls the body and the mind in an act of attention. The principal act of the will consists in the stopping, hemming in, or obstructing the onward movements of consciousness, thereby *intensifying* conscious activities.[3] Let me illustrate this by acts of reflection, which are the same as acts of attention, minus direct external stimuli. You will please think of the house in which you were born. Instantly, when I say "house in which you were born," there comes a mental image, an individual concept, into your mind, brought there by my words. Hold that image, that individual concept, by an act of your will, and what is the result? The first synthetic result is a mental image with dim outlines. It immediately begins to build in elementary ideas of color; forms rise above the plane of consciousness and complete the first vague outlines. You enter the house, you go from room to room; the floors, the ceilings, the paper, the furniture, all enhance the individual concepts. Associations then come in; old experiences, former judgments, emotions without number crowd this picture. What have you done? By an act of your will you have held this state of consciousness, and thereby the picture has been enhanced, filled up, intensified. The longer you hold the central concept corresponding to the house the more ideas will rise, fill, and intensify it; the act of recollection is continually enhanced by your mental attitude. You do not bring in certain elements, certain subjects of thought in relation to the central subject—they come in themselves. You cannot by an act of the will create an elementary idea—*you cannot directly recollect, unite, synthesize, or associate ideas, but you can control the conditions necessary to the effectiveness of these acts.*

Attention means stopping the otherwise continuous flow of conscious states; it means the inhibition of all extraneous activities; it means the concentration upon certain definite conscious activities aroused by the objects which the ego is to know, to analyze, to compare, to classify, and to make the basis of all inferences. The danger comes when the ego ignorantly attempts to do that which does itself, or is done by immutable laws, not controlled but conditioned by the ego. Attention is a process of mental or conscious action stimulated, excited, aroused, induced, or caused by the attributes of external objects upon consciousness.

At every step and every stage of education, the action of the will in controlling the organs of the body in such a way that the most complete action of consciousness can take place must be recognized. In other words, the whole environment of consciousness, which consists of the brain, the body, and external energies, makes self-activity possible, and determines its nature, its kind, and the probabilities of its continuity.

There are three modes of attention or study: first, observation; second, hearing-language; and third, reading.

The educative value of an act of observation consists in the individual concept which corresponds to the object acting upon consciousness. Observation is the continuous action of an object upon consciousness for the purpose of developing and intensifying its corresponding individual concept. In the mere casual action of objects, through the senses, crude, incomplete, and inadequate concepts are produced; but by the continuous action of one object upon consciousness it will be readily seen that the concept corresponding to the object acting is intensified—it is filled up, enhanced, made to approximate adequacy. This individual concept is a direct factor in itself in the development of the mind in which it acts; and becomes, through the action of observation, more and more a complete basis for inferences of analysis, comparison, classification, and generalization.

Attention is educative thinking. Thinking, or continuance of conscious action, is not in itself educative, it becomes educative only when the conscious action is intense and the conscious activities are immediately needed for development. The fundamental action of consciousness is synthesis or association.[4] The same action takes place and the same laws control synthesis, association, recollection, remembrance, and imagination. These acts may have direct external causes, or may be the products of the action of the ego without direct external stimuli.

The second act of consciousness in which the ego is the immediate cause is inference or judgment. Acts of inference may be classified as acts of recognition, analysis, comparison, classification, and generalization. Allow me to repeat, then, what I consider to be the most important fact in all psychology—*that each and every act of consciousness contains in itself every kind and variety of acts of which the human being is capable.* Development consists, then, not in the introduction of new kinds of conscious acts, but in the continued intensity of all these acts. The intensity of an act of consciousness means that the contents of the acts are to be continually enhanced by new psychic units, or individual concepts, and more vivid elementary ideas, consequently, making possible those inferences which approximate the truth. Thus, acts of observation, hearing-language, and reading are identical in kind of mental action, the differences consisting in the differences in external causes and intensity of effects.

Two great classes of objects act upon the mind. One we may call, for the sake of classification, non-symbolic objects. A non-symbolic object is one whose correspondence may have a direct educative value. The other great class of objects consists of symbols. A symbol is an external object which arouses in consciousness certain definite activities. The conscious activites which a symbol arouses or stimulates we will call in this discussion appropriate activities, in contradistinction to corresponding activities, and it is well to make a careful distinction between the two. Corresponding activities are the activities directly aroused by the object itself. The first action of any object, whether a symbol or non-symbolic, is to arouse its correspondence in consciousness. A symbol has but one function, it was made for but one purpose, and that purely a mental one. A pure symbol is used to arouse in consciousness certain definite activities, which do not correspond to any part of the object itself. The immediate relation of a pure symbol to development of educative action consists entirely in the effect of the correspondence in recalling appropriate activities.

Each and every object has one immediate effect upon the mind, let me repeat, and that is the production of its correspondence, which is in itself an individual concept. This immediate effect, correspondence, or individual concept, arouses other definite activities which I have called appropriate activities. You can test this very easily. I write upon the board certain words, for instance: "horse," "cow," "goose," "fence." While I am writing you shut your eyes. I say, "Open your eyes and tell me the immediate effect of these objects, that is, these written words, upon consciousness." You are able to say immediately, "The horse that I thought of was chestnut, or white; it was running or standing still." Thus, these words, that I have written on the blackboard, are immediately functioned. They arouse their appropriate activities. But suppose you were not acquainted with the language used, and that I should write the words *"Pferd," "Kuh," "Gans," "Cavallo," "Hest."* These objects have the same functions as the others, and produce their immediate effects, but those effects in consciousness do not produce effects for which they were made; they are consequently not functioned in your mind.

Oral and written words are objects; they have length, breadth, and thickness, and they act upon consciousness precisely like any other object; but if these effects do not immediately become causes and arouse other definite conscious activities, they are of no immediate use.

Symbols may be divided into two classes. One class I will call partial symbols. Partial symbols consist of pictures, drawings, models, and all objects not purely symbolic, which are made to awaken in consciousness certain definite activities. The conscious activities awakened by a partial symbol, it will be seen, do not fully correspond to the object awakening them. In other words, the direct effect of a partial symbol is precisely like any other object; but this direct effect arouses definite activities, and the effect itself becomes a part of those definite activities, a part of the individual concept aroused—thus I call them partial. For instance, a picture arouses its correspondences, and this in turn arouses its appropriate activities, and the correspondence to the picture sinks, to use a figure of speech, into the individual concept itself.

In order to make my meaning clearer, I will attempt to describe the second great class of symbols, which we will term pure symbols. A pure symbol, like a partial symbol, is an object made to arouse certain appropriate activities; but it is also an arbitrary invention made to produce a certain definite effect in consciousness, which in no point corresponds to the cause. A partial symbol, for instance a picture, functions itself by the same kind of action as a pure symbol. You will understand me when I say that a little child sees a picture and knows what it is, or a statue and knows what it is; that is, the partial symbol has an immediate effect, and needs no other conditions than its presentation or its action upon consciousness; but a pure symbol [5] requires the presentation of certain definite conditions for its use in consciousness. Interpretation through a standardized meaning is essential to its functioning. The process of making written or printed words function is the technique of reading. Indeed, the teaching of reading, at every step, from beginning to end, consists in presenting conditions for functioning words. The law under which all words are functioned will be carefully discussed in Chapter IX.

Hearing-language is thinking by means of the action of oral words, arranged in sentences. The process of hearing-language is a mental process caused by the action of external objects called oral words arranged in sentences. An oral word is just as much an object, as I have already said, as a written word, a tree, or a mountain. The mind does not act upon the word, but the word upon the mind; and therefore upon the attitude of the being depends the power of hearing-language after the words have been functioned.

Reading is thinking, or mental activity aroused by the action of written or printed words arranged in sentences.[6] Precisely the same reflections may be made upon reading as upon the action of oral language; the conscious activities aroused are the same in kind. It is often justly urged that an act of hearing-language, or reading, is not in itself an act of attention, does not arise to the dignity of an act of attention; but I beg you to bear in mind that I am discussing education, and also the fact that educative acts consist wholly of intensity of mental acts in hearing, and intensity of mental acts in reading. Observation is an intense act of consciousness. Educative hearing-language is also intensity of conscious acts. Study of text is intense reading. The three modes of attention are means of intensifying conscious activities.

The function of the object itself in an act of observation is to intensify its corresponding individual concept; the function of a pure symbol is to arouse appropriate activities. The correspondence to a pure symbol has no direct educative value. In an act of observation the mind is absorbed in the direct products of the object in consciousness. In the acts of hearing-language or reading, the mind should be absorbed in the appropriate activities, with the least possible consciousness of the effects of the words.

The body, with all its physical organs, its nervous tracts, and great central ganglion, the brain, is an instrument for utilization of the action of external attributes. I have already presented the fact that the organism itself determines the nature, the number, and kinds of external attributes which may act through it. These sense products form the basis of all self-activity, and that self-activity has a very prominent part to play in attention.[7] Every self-act has a motive.[8]

By motive I mean that which primarily impells the ego to attend continuously. It may not be easy to define or analyze motive. The content of motive is usually interest heightened by the anticipated pleasure which the being believes will result from the act. This motive may have for its content immediate pleasure or the pleasure of fancying subsequent pleasure.

An act of attention may be analyzed as follows:

(1) The external stimuli which act upon consciousness
(2) The physical response to that stimuli
(3) Intellectual action aroused
(4) Motive of an act of attention.

In the economical act of attention these factors immediately succeed each other, are simultaneous. In other words, there should be perfect unity of action. This fact is illustrated in all spontaneous acts of attention. The motive is aroused by the object presented, and under that motive the act is sustained, the thought stimulates emotion, and the body becomes an unobstructed medium through which the attributes act. *This unity of action or effort of the whole being is the central educative moment; it is in education a supreme act, bringing about the*

*conditions necessary to a most economical use of the body as an
instrument for the action of external energies.*

In order to explain this more fully, allow me to speak of
the physical attitude of attention. The attributes or external
energies act through certain nerve tracts. The nature of the nerve
tracts over which the attributes act determines the attributes
which act through them. In a complete act of attention, the ego,
through the will, controls the whole body; all extraneous muscular activities are inhibited, that is, physical action is limited
to the reception of certain definite external energies. Special nerve
tracts are cleared for action. That which is true of muscles and
nerve tracts, is just as true of the brain. We know, from long
observation of the body, when it acts most effectively, it acts as
a whole; that although one organ or one sense tract may be the
center of that action, still the whole body, every organ, every
muscle, and every nerve, contribute to the one central action;
every organ, every muscle, every nerve, concentrate and enhance
the one central act of attention. Or, to put it in another way,
just so far as the action of the whole body is inhibited, and therefore concentrated upon the one act of attention, just so far will
the intellectual action be enhanced. On the other hand, any
part of the body, any portion of the muscular system, that does
not enter into this act of attention, weakens the act.

We are all instinctively students of acts of attention in others,
and I think if we will but reflect a little upon our own somewhat spontaneous and intuitive generalizations, we will come to
a common conclusion. A speaker watches his audience—it may
be an individual, it may be thousands of people; he judges
whether his words have their desired effect by the physical
attitude of those before him. The slightest mark of inattention
discourages him, and, on the other hand, signs of attention
prompt him to better thought and expression. The story-teller's
first thought is: Are my auditors listening? He judges by their

attitude; a movement of the arm, the head, the facial expression, in fact the whole body tells him whether his words are having their effect or not. Artists portray animals in acts of attention; a fawn or rabbit in the act of listening. A critic who detects in the attitude of the body any lack of coördination or unity in so far argues the failure of the artist. In a word, *there is a complete physical unit of action in a perfect act of attention.* The organs of the body, the muscles, the nerves, the whole sensorium, contribute to the one central act. Or, to put in upon the negative side, if the body is not in a perfect physical attitude of attention, if the arms or legs are not disposed for the best action of external stimuli, then the conscious act is obstructed. The maximum physical action in attention is the concentration of all muscular and nervous action to one act. If, then, there is a complete normal physical attitude of attention, if the blood in its rapid flow through all parts of the body enhances the complete act, then educative acts of attention have a great influence in developing the body, not only developing it in health and strength, but enhancing its function as an instrument of attention.

The motive of all physical development should be the training of the body as a perfect instrument of attention and expression, for action and reaction upon external objects. The perfect physical attitude of attention is a healthy attitude. What has been said of the whole body may be said of the brain. The will has the power to bar out extraneous conscious activities by hemming in intrinsic conscious activities, or by excluding that which is not pertinent to immediate moments of attention. *One central point in the theory of concentration is that in all acts of attention there shall be perfect unity of action.* An economical act, an intense act, is that perfect unity of action in which every part of the body, every fiber of the brain, enhances the mental act; and conversely, any failure to inhibit the action of the body or the brain, any disconnection or lack of response on the part of any agent or sets of agents, renders the central act of attention incomplete.

The importance of the unity of the whole being in all educative acts cannot be overrated, for the reason that unscientific teaching and training may permanently break or disconnect this unity, and thereby weaken both the body and mind.

An act of reading is brought about by the action of printed words arranged in sentences upon consciousness. In such acts there must be an impelling motive, the physical attitude of attention, the mental results, and consequently the instantaneous action of the forms of the words. *The right motive should precede every act; the most economical mental acts should take place superinduced by a complete physical attitude of attention.*

Suppose the motive is attention to the forms of the words, then there can be no educative effect. If the motive is brought to bear entirely upon the forms of the words, the real motive must be in abeyance; in this case, the mental action consists entirely of the correspondences to the words themselves, and there can be no genuine thought action. The unity of the action is broken, and if this systematic teaching, in which the forms of the words are the end and the aim of the teacher, continues, the breaking up of the unity of action will be effectual, and mental weakness in reading and study will be a permanent result. The word should perform its function instantly; there should be the least possible attention to the forms of the words. It is possible, under the scientific teaching of reading, to absorb the mind to such an extent that the action of the words becomes unconscious or automatic. Its opposite is also possible: the habit may be easily cultivated with little children of complete absorption in the forms of words, and anything like clear, lucid, enlivening thought prevented. The reason why the acquisition of the forms of words is made the end and aim of much teaching is that the teacher anticipates great difficulties in the objects themselves, the words, and the whole power of the child is put on the acquisition of dead forms, with the supposition that at some future time thought may be aroused by them or expressed through them.

That which has been left almost entirely out of the discussion of how to teach the first steps in reading has been the means needed to arouse strong, continuous, and cumulative interest in the thought expressed by the words themselves, and how to develop that motive with its content of interest which will most effectually overcome difficulties.

The educative habit of attention is purely a cultivatable one. In simple spontaneity, without direction, there is very little development of the habit of attention. There may be many acts of attention, but they cease before they reach the educative point, or they have no organic relation each to the others. *The cultivation of the habit of attention is the main factor in education—the habit of observing closely, listening intently to language, and of reading intensely are the fundamental means by which self-activity is induced and developed.*

The cultivation of the habit of attention depends fundamentally upon the condition of the body, the brain, the nerve tracts, in fact, the whole physical system. Teachers should study and thoroughly understand how long an act of attention can be sustained. The effect of exercise of brain and nerve power is similiar to the effect of continued muscular activity and can be illustrated by physical exertion. When a muscle is exercised the waste matter is eliminated, and there is an immediate flow of blood to the muscle to repair the loss. If the exercise is continued too long, the waste matter cannot be carried off fast enough, the flow of blood is insufficient, and exhaustion sets in. Continue the action of the muscle longer, and the result is disastrous. Physical exercise carried beyond the point of exhaustion, it will be granted by all students of physical training, weakens instead of strengthens the body. Moreover—and this is the main educational point—there is always a dislike of exercise, and an unpleasant emotion aroused through over-action.

The human brain is the most delicate, the most complex, physical organ in existence. Whatever is true of the over-exercise of a muscle is still more strikingly true of the over-exercise of the brain. An act of attention is conditioned entirely upon the physical strength of the brain—upon the elementary ideas held or retained by the physical qualities of the brain below the plane of consciousness. In an act of attention the blood flows through millions of delicate arteries to reinforce and sustain the action of the brain. If a muscle becomes exhausted after repeated acts of the same kind, how much more quickly the delicate fibers of the brain will become exhausted: The teacher who really strives to develop pure acts of attention on the part of the child should remember that no matter what the object of attention may be, how strong the motive which prompts the interest, or how delightful at first the mental act, exhaustion sets in with children very quickly.

In fact, while I use the little child for illustration, it is equally true of all persons who have not trained themselves in the habit of attention. You might perhaps try to experiment on yourself by listening to some sermon or lecture upon philosophy or pedagogics. A person who can listen for forty minutes, for instance, with the closest attention to any elucidation of an unfamiliar theory has an immense power of attention; in fact, has attained the one preëminent habit of education.

Habits of attention are acquired with exceeding slowness. The moment the brain of the child becomes exhausted, no matter how beautiful the object studied may be in itself, the immediate result is a sort of mental nausea or disgust with the subject. A weakness is caused which afterwards prevents free action, because the moment the object, or subject, is again presented the associated emotion takes possession of the mind. You know a subject and love it, and take delight in studying it; in fact, no one can ever study any subject really and truly without loving it, for truth is beautiful always. Try to teach these same truths so appealing to you, to the child, and you are surprised at his attitude of disgust. In nine cases out of ten this undesirable result is the product of brain exhaustion. Under the control of traditional education, the false meaning of the word "thorough" has done serious damage. You feel, as a teacher, that the child must see as you see, have the same action that you have, and you try to bring it about by the proper conditions. He cannot have the same action, and when he becomes exhausted through futile efforts to attend, the product is disgust. He dislikes the topic because it is beyond his thought grasp, and his dislike is a barrier to future action in that direction.

In reality there is no need whatever, in careful teaching, of this brain exhaustion and its unfortunate results. The child without guidance observes briefly many objects in succession. He does this spontaneously, without exhaustion. Change rests the brain. A great variety of related objects should be used in teaching, extending gradually the time of each act of observation, so that the healthy interest may be sustained. The direction that I would give to all teachers is: *Watch the child, watch his attitude of attention.* Is it spontaneous? Is the light of pleasure in his eyes? *Is interest the motive which controls him?* So long as that exists there is no danger; but before the pleasure fades, the action should be stopped.

Another great pedagogical error is the attempt to sustain attention day after day upon one series of subjects. The old pedagogical belief was that the child must take one subject, and observe, investigate, classify, and follow that subject logically to its higher generalizations. Let us fall back upon the premise, which is absolutely true, that the organism determines that which shall enter. The growth of the organism is exceedingly slow, the individual concepts are at first obscure and vague. The conditions are there for spontaneous, not scientific, classification. *Endeavor, in a course of lessons which require attention, to force the child's mental acts in any one direction so that he may arise to generalizations though series of inferences based upon careful observations, and you will produce the same effect that I suggested in regard to brain exhaustion in prolonged and futile acts of attention.* You disgust the child with the subject, and render all after-study difficult in the extreme.

In the plan suggested in the discussion of the central subjects, I beg leave to recall to your mind that the child begins all subjects spontaneously; at least he is interested in everything, and begins instinctively the investigation of all subjects before he is six years old. He goes from bird to bush, from grass to flower; in fact his whole environment acts in succession upon him, and there is no exhaustion. The teacher is there to present conditions so that these external objects will act just a little more, sufficient to sustain interest, not enough to induce exhaustion and consequent dislike.

The method that we have now adopted continues that which every child has already begun; keeps interest keenly alive by using a great variety of subjects; makes the ever-changing phenomena of the "rolling year" the basis of observation, experience, and investigation; presents the same subjects successive years to be met by continually enhanced interest, power to observe and reason.[9] Beyond the limits of the pupil's capacity lie only sterile regions of empty word-learning.

One other error as potent for evil as brain exhaustion and logical sequence, is study with a conscious effort to prove an hypothesis presented by the teacher, or previously formed by the pupil. If there is any prejudgment or fixed supposition of what will be found or proved, there can be no free act of attention.[10] Under such a motive there can be no real investigation in regard to the truth. The attitude of the mind is merely: "There is something I wish to prove, and this act of attention will prove it." The attitude of prejudice is a cramped attitude of the mind into which nothing can enter, where there can be no enhancement of facts, no fresh, vivid, original inferences. I can illustrate this by conventional drawing. The pupil learns to draw the typical fish from a flat copy. He gains, therefore, merely a conventional image of a fish. Afterwards in the study of zoölogy, when required to draw a real fish, the pupil naturally recalls and reproduces the conventional form, and the benefit of self-effort in continuous observation has been lost.

Teaching is but the presentation of external conditions for educative self-effort. The work of the teacher in educating is confined to the presentation of these conditions. All these conditions consist of objects and their movements in space. It is of tremendous importance that the teacher appreciate the philosophy of external energies, and the psychology of their creative and stimulating action upon the mind. All education is by self-activity, but when this self-activity oversteps the bounds and tries to do that which nature does perfectly herself, it defeats its own end. Self-activity has certain boundaries; for instance, in attention the boundary is the holding of the body and mind in an attitude for the action of external energies. I repeat this over and over again, that a certain overstraining of the mind in self-activity destroys its purpose.

> The eye—it cannot choose but see;
> We cannot bid the ear be still;
> Our bodies feel, where'er they be,
> Against, or with our will.

Nor less I deem that there are Powers
Which of themselves our minds impress;
That we can feed this mind of ours
In a wise passiveness.

Think you, 'mid all this mighty sum
Of things, forever speaking,
That nothing of itself will come,
But we must still be seeking.

Education may be defined as the development of the attitude
of the being toward truth. Over-action, over-straining, and prejudgment are obstructions in the path toward freedom; although
self-activity is of the utmost importance, still undue interference
on the part of the ego may be such as to obstruct rather than
further the highest development of the being.

Every subject of thought, every object of attention, truly studied and freely observed, must arouse in the mind emotions of
pleasure. In a word, the test of whether you know a subject,
whether you are really studying a subject, is your love for that
subject. I think I can say positively that no one knows a subject
unless he loves it. Certainly the test that proves that one has
never studied a subject, is a feeling of satisfaction when he has
"finished it," when he has "been through it," passed examination, and the stint-work is done.

All true study develops an apprehension of unity—unity of
design, unity of purpose, unity of love. By these tests, and with
this goal, educative acts of attention may be cultivated. The
opportunities for attention in the central subjects of study are
infinite—infinite in direct observation and boundless in reading
and hearing-language. The highest duty of the teacher is to
adapt the right conditions for mental action to the individual
mind.

Every step in the right direction brings new light and new

love, arouses curiosity, enhances desire, and stimulates prolonged, ·
persistent study. Every fresh discovery opens new vistas, deepens
perspective, and cultivates humility, that humility of spirit which
leads upward to the Kingdom of Heaven.

And thus looking within and around me, I ever renew
(With that stoop of the soul which in bending upraises it too)
The submission of man's nothing-perfect to God's · all-complete,
As by each new obeisance in spirit I climb to his feet.
                                        —Robert Browning, *Saul.*

[1] "The acquisition of definiteness and of coherency (or constancy) of meanings is derived primarily from practical activities. By rolling an object the child
makes its roundness appreciable; by bouncing it, he singles out its elasticity;
by throwing it, he makes weight its conspicuous distinctive factor. Not through
the senses but by means of their reaction, the responsive adjustment, is the
impression made distinctive, and given a character marked off from all other
qualities that call out unlike reactions." John Dewey, *How We Think* (D. C.
Heath), p. 122.

[2] Froebel, *Education of Man* (Appleton), p. 30—§23-26.

[3] Wm. H. Kilpatrick, *Foundations of Method* (Macmillan), pp. 110-119,
concerning focus and margin of attention.

[4] John Dewey, *How We Think,* Chaps. VI-XI which constitute Part II of
the volume and deal with "The Nature and Normal Growth of Thinking."

[5] E. B. Huey, *Psychology and Pedagogy of Reading* (Macmillan), pp. 164-165.

[6] John Dewey, *How We Think,* p. 176—§2, p. 178.

[7] "Concentration does not mean fixity, nor a cramped arrest or paralysis of
the flow of suggestion. It means variety and change of ideas combined into a
single steady trend moving toward a unified conclusion." John Dewey, *How
We Think* (D. C. Heath), p. 40.

[8] Wm. H. Kilpatrick, *Foundations of Method* (Macmillan), Chaps. VI-VII,
"Coercion and Learning"; Chap. X, "Interest."

[9] Wilbur S. Jackman, *Nature Study.* Suggestive outline for seasonal study
of "rolling year" for third through eighth grade.

[10] Colin Scott, *Social Education* (Ginn & Co.), pp. 176-183.

VII

OBSERVATION

OBSERVATION as a mode of attention, its relations to the central subjects of study, and its place in teaching, has significant educational value.

Observation may be defined as a mental process induced by the continued action of objects upon consciousness.[1] To the conscious products synthesized by external objects we give the name *individual concepts*. This is a term used to limit a unit of elementary ideas which the ego discriminates from all other conscious entities. The relation of the ego to external objects in observation consists in holding the body and mind in the best possible attitude for the most economical action of external energies.

The relation of elementary ideas and individual concepts to knowledge of the universe may be stated as follows: first, an elementary idea is the absolute basis of all knowledge of its corresponding attribute, all externality so far as mind is concerned consisting of attributes; second, the individual concept corresponding to an object is the absolute basis of all knowledge of that object. Upon the individual concepts as here defined depend all elementary inferences: first, the simple inferences of recognition; second, the inferences of analyses of the individual concept; third, the inferences of comparison; fourth, the inferences of classification; and fifth, the related inferences of generali-

zation. An equation may be formulated thus: as is the degree
of intensity or vividness of the individual concepts, so be the
inferences, analyses, comparisons, classifications, and consequent
generalizations.

The individual concepts of children, and the individual concepts of most persons who live and die in this world, are exceedingly vague, crude, and obscure. That is, they are crude, vague,
and obscure in comparison with any approximation to adequacy.
This can be tested in many ways. Try to form a mental image
of that which you have seen thousands of times, and you will
immediately be seized with a desire to see the object again; that
is, you have a feeling of its obscurity or incompleteness. If there
is a demand made upon you to paint, draw, or model an object
which you have seen over and over again, the desire to see the
object becomes still more intense. You feel a necessity for a more
continued action of the object upon your consciousness, because
you are aware that the concept corresponding to it is imperfect.
*Upon the growth, development, and approximation to adequacy
of individual concepts depends almost wholly the development
of intellectual power.*[2] An adequate concept, a concept which
perfectly corresponds to the attributes of an object, must correspond to the arrangement and relation of those attributes to the
whole object. First, an individual concept must have for its content just the number of elementary ideas that its corresponding
object has of attributes. Second, the individual concept must have
its elementary ideas correspondingly arranged and related to
each other exactly as the attributes of the corresponding object
are arranged and related to each other. Third, each elementary
idea corresponding to an external attribute must have the same
degree of intensity or vividness that the attribute has in itself.
If this hypothesis be accepted, it will be evident at once that
an adequate individual concept is the basis of perfect judgments
of form, size, etc., of the corresponding object. All analysis of

an object depends upon the analysis of the individual concept. All comparisons, of two or more objects, depend for their results on the approximation to adequacy of the compared individual concepts. No comparisons take place outside of consciousness, and the result of the comparisons depends entirely upon that which is in consciousness at the time of comparison. The scientific value of all classifications which are the result of comparison depends upon the distinctness of the individual concepts. Upon individual concepts and approximation to adequacy depends all our knowledge of the external world.

Taking for granted this attempted definition of an adequate individual concept, the following inferences may be made: that simple mind energy, which I call an elementary idea, never can equal in power or intensity the external attribute, for the reason that no brain has the physical basis of such adequacy; no individual concept can have for its content all the elementary ideas which correspond to the attributes of an object, for the simple reason that all the attributes of an object cannot, from the nature of the brain itself, act in and through it. It follows, therefore, that the arrangement of the individual concept must be vastly inferior to the arrangement of attributes in the object. In a word, an adequate individual concept is purely ideal; no such result was ever yet produced in the human brain or synthesized by the mind.[8] I refer you to what I have already said in the talk on attention, that the attributes which act upon consciousness, upon the highest developed brain, are exceedingly vague compared with the attributes which compose the great All-Energy of the universe. The development of the brain is along the line of its power to receive more and more of external attributes, to increase its power of correspondence, that each attribute may act with greater definiteness, and produce higher results in the way of clearer elementary ideas, and more nearly complete individual concepts.

I do not wish to exaggerate in any way the importance of the growth and development of individual concepts, but I believe that a little reflection will confirm what I have said in regard to the value of distinct correspondences in consciousness to external objects.

The psychology of to-day depends upon the closest observation of the physical basis of consciousness and the relation of brain and the whole sensorium to mind action. Individual concept corresponding to objects and bodies of matter of which the universe consists are the products of searching investigations and the most indefatigable study: from such concepts have sprung the marvelous discoveries in modern progress. All study of the universe has for its sole aim the knowledge of those energies which act through qualities of matter. When we thoughtfully appreciate the all-importnat truth that the universe is the manifestation to man of Eternal Love and Power, we get some apprehension of the priceless value of observation and investigation.

There are thinkers and educators in this world of ours from whose writings we seem to gather the inference that the creation of the senses is not altogether a success; that although the senses are of some use, still the sooner the mind gets into the region of abstraction, and away from the domination of the senses, the better, and that a few sense-products are amply sufficient for the evolution of the highest philosophy. When the educative value of observation is urged, these profound abstractionists ᐧcite, with a presumption of finality, the case of the savage who is surrounded by all the beauties and glories of nature. "Why," they say, "is this child of nature not educated, when he has complete educational means at his command?"

Motive determines all intellectual action and growth. It is stated that the savage has wonderful sight, wonderful hearing, wonderful acuteness and sharpness in listening for the steps of the approaching foe or watching the trace of the flying game, and it is true; but the motive is entirely limited to self-preservation, either in self-defense or as a means of satisfying his hunger and limited personal wants. His acuteness and sharpness are narrowed down by his motive. It has the very lowest educative value. When his motive rises to the preservation of his family, his observation takes a wider sweep, and still broader when he is incited to work for his community or tribe. Compare these low motives in evolution with the high motive of the love of truth for truth's sake, or a deep, strong curiosity to know, or, with the still higher motive, the belief that much can be found for the good of humanity. Finally, environment in every stage of evolution, from the lowest grade of savagery, has had its particular effect in the evolution of man. That which is called education is the conscious presentation of conditions for the evolution of the whole being. The savage has had no scientific conditioning for evolution of thought. So it seems to me that this argument, so often brought up, regarding the savage, that observation is not the foundation of all human development, falls utterly to the ground, and the fundamental necessity for observation is indisputable.

The other great means for education we find in symbols, the greatest number of which are in oral and written languages. These symbols are used for the expression of man's thought, as the universe is the expression of God's thought. In spite of this, throughout the ages, educators and authorities have clung tenaciously to the delusion that the greatest and most effective means of education consists in the study of books. Words have been their fetish, everlastingly adhered to; clung to as a pagan clings to his idols. The greatest problem of the past, in which the paramount idea was "control of the many by the few," was how to make man believe he was educated, and at the same time deprive him of the power of original thinking. The whole machinery of authority and the immense power of tradition

were brought to bear upon the solution of this question, how
to keep the masses from anything like true education. One
solution of the problem was to separate the soul from the truth
by means of the written page. "Study, learn, believe, and follow
me!" is the echo of oppression in all the past; the same command
is still written in ignorant souls, in human beings struggling in
darkness all over the known world, and even, alas! in our own
republic, in which we have lately decided that society can rule
itself.

A careful comparison of the relative educational values of
reading and observation is of the first importance to teachers.
Many who will readily grant that the written page is an
absolute necessity to human development, will at the same
time positively deny that the printers' ink has ever or can
ever reveal to man eternal truths so efficiently as by the direct
manifestation of God through the universe.

We can reasonably hold to the hypothesis that that All-Love
and All-Power, that Unit of divine energy, God, manifests Itself
to human minds through matter; that the energy becomes elementary, is differentiated in and through matter for the direct
purpose of revealing itself to man's soul; that the leaf and
flower, the mists and the clouds that tell their stories of the far-
off ocean, the pebble on the beach, and the coal that burns in
the grate, are, in themselves and considered with their causes,
revelations that human souls are capable of understanding. There
is no beam of light that strikes the eye and colors the mind
but says to man: "Follow me, and find me." "Behold, I stand
at the door and knock." The divine energy surrounds man, forms
his environment, and acts upon his soul with unspeakable
power. "He that hath ears to hear, let him hear."

Myth-creating, common to all mankind from the time that
light first kindled the fire of curiosity in human souls, has
been and is the strong mark of the universal tendency of man

to find God through His manifestations in nature. Shall we say that this tendency is wrong because imperfect observations, by struggling minds, have led to tentative and imperfect conclusions? Is it not better to believe that this all-controlling desire is divine in its nature, pointing man to that higher knowledge, the Creator's revelation of Himself, which will finally lead to the truth?

These two hypotheses have been the central cause of the conflict between man and man: man's duty is to know and obey the behests of human authority; man's soul was created for and endowed with the power to seek and find eternal truth for itself. I would not overrate the value of observation, or underrate books as means of education; I only state to you, my fellow teachers, that which comes to me with overpowering force. "We have climbed up some other way"; we have said: "This is nature, this is science, and that is God."

History in spirit is the mirror of man's prejudices, the expression of his self-conceit, his subserviency, his serfdom, his worship of kings, forms of government, and creeds. Goethe has put this in a few expressive words:

> Was ihr den Geist der Zeiten heisst,
> Das ist im Grund der Herren eigner Geist,
> In dem die Zeiten sich bespiegeln.
> Da ist's denn wahrlich oft ein Jammer!
> Man lauft euch bei dem ersten Blick davon.
> Ein Kerichtfass und eine Rumpelkammer,
> Und höchstens eine Haupt und Staataction,
> Mit trefflichen pragmatischen Maximen,
> Wiemsie den Puppen wohl in Munde zieman!

> What you the Spirit of the Ages call
> Is nothing but the spirit of you all
> Where in the ages are reflected.
> So, oftentimes, you miserably mar it!

At the first glance who sees it runs away.
An offal-barrel and a lumber garret,
Or, at the best, a Punch and Judy play,
With maxims most pragmatical and hitting,
As in the mouths of puppets are befitting!
                    Translated By Bayard Taylor.

It is true, following the lead of Niebuhr, that the study of
history is fast becoming scientific; one of our great American
writers of history, John Fiske, has helped us essentially in this
direction. The best we can say of past history preceding the
scientific period, is that the human environment (the *Zeitgeist*)
controlled in a marked degree written history. History is in
spirit and truth a written account of the evolution of man. The
great question which modern scientists are seeking to solve is:
how, by the study of human records, can we find the truth
in the mass of chaff and fiction? First of all, we must be able
to estimate the spirit of the times, the controlling motive of
the writer, and his surroundings and limitations. We can illustrate this by recent history. Take histories of our late Civil War—
one written from the Confederate standpoint, and one written
from the Union standpoint; the study of either history alone
would inevitably lead to errors that must develop bigotry and
extreme prejudice. How can we find the truth in history? How
can the wheat be sifted from the chaff?

Personal experience is the fundamental means or basis of
judgment of the experiences of the race in all ages. A child's
observations and experiences in family, community, social, religious, and school life lay the foundations of his after judgments
of human life, both present and past. If a strong, tyrannical
government controls him in the family or in the school, he will
either reverence or hate that form of government as he compares his own life with the lives he finds in history. "He who

possesses the youth, possesses the future," may mean that a child's early life should be "cabined, cribbed, confined" by tradition, bigotry, and prejudice. If his experiences and observations open his soul to the love of truth and the love of mankind, if his school life breaks the awful barrier of hate, then he can read and interpret history in the divine light of love to all mankind. If history is dogmatically taught, the history of a church, or the history of one form of government, the students are led to believe implicitly the printed statements, and the result is the perpetuation of narrow mental and moral limitations. Such study bars the path of liberty to freedom. The student must have the means, the mental power, to judge for himself, and the bases of that judgment are the products of his own personal observation. Dogmatic teaching is the perpetuation of dogma and creed in government and church. The teaching of history which presents the proper conditions and leaves to the student his own inferences and his own generalizations leads to the education of the true citizen and the development of the highest type of manhood.[4]

What textbooks shall be used in teaching science? The distinguished head of a Scottish University is quoted as having said that a textbook upon science more than ten years old cannot be profitably used by university students. This statement but echoes the opinion of all scientists. All textbooks upon science, then, which do not present the latest inductions and generalizations are to be relegated to the history of the evolution of science. To a student of such history the works of the scientists of the past are of great value, because they present the protracted study and struggles of great thinkers who arrived at tentative and incorrect conclusions from insufficient data or inaccurate observations and experiments. The whole history of science is strewn with the wrecks of theories. It is true that no scientists ever worked in vain, that even "our failures are a prophecy," but the prin-

cipal truth acquired in the study of the science of the past goes
to prove the weakness and incompleteness of inadequate observations. The most important lesson taught by this continual sur-
render of generalizations is that the theories of to-day are simply
tentative; that although progress in science has been marvelous
in its outcome, still the human race is but upon the threshold of
the discovery of new truths, which will no doubt put in abeyance
many important modern conclusions. In a word, the great danger
in teaching science, as in everything else, is to teach a perfect
reliance upon human authority.[5]

Some one has said that the greatest discovery of the nineteenth century is [winter in 1894] the "suspended judgment";
in other words, the true scientific attitude toward discovery and
investigation. Whatever a working hypothesis may be, the genuine scientist is just as anxious to prove its falsity as its truth, and
he bends all his energies to collect the data for either result.
A very good working definition of education is: the development of the attitude of the soul toward truth. That attitude can
be cultivated only by the self-activity of the mind with unprejudiced judgment intent on the direct discovery of truth. A
too early study of textbooks has a strong tendency to prejudice
judgment and restrict the attitude of the mind in its original
ingenuousness: "Except ye become as a little child.[6] "

The human mind has, in general, two opposite poles. One is a
tendency to inertia, from which arises a longing desire for a
fixed and final belief in dogmas.[7] The other pole is curiosity to
discover truth, stimulated by an honest doubt of presented generalizations; "doubt is the beginning of wisdom." There is no
better way to develop and cultivate this heaven-born attitude of
the soul toward truth than by bringing it directly in contact
with truth along the shortest line of resistance—God's manifestation before man's representation. Observation is a fundamental
means of cultivating a love for truth and an earnest desire to

know it. On these grounds the two great antagonistic motives meet and have their conflict; one of which is that a human being should believe implicitly in human authority, and the other, that a soul shall doubt human authority and try to find truth for itself. In the former, books alone are the first and efficient means; in the latter, unprejudiced observation. One is the study of textbooks made by man; the other, the study of the book of nature, the direct revelation of God to man. The cultivation of the love for science is the cultivation of the love for truth, for beauty, and for goodness.

That laboratories for direct investigation, observation, and experiment are indispensable is now recognized by all universities, most high schools and a few elementary schools. The true leaven has begun to work in secondary education, aroused, it is true, by the great practical value of discoveries. But I wish to enter here a special plea for the children, having already shown that they begin all these subjects of science spontaneously. I wish to earnestly protest against making school-children wander through a long desert and wilderness of words before a few of them, who intellectually survive, can have the inestimable privileges of direct observation found in the laboratories of universities. When pupils in the lower schools study science throughout the course there will be a hundred students in our universities where now there is one.

I can here safely give the reason why children are not taught science, and I think you will all agree with me: teachers do not really know science themselves, on account of textbook methods. So we should hail with great joy the fact that laboratory methods everywhere mark the study of science. Speed the day when the little ones, on entering school, shall be brought face to face with the truth manifested by the Creator through His works.

Here I present an argument often used and venerable—used

not so much to-day as yesterday—an argument put in the form
of a question, which seems to settle the matter in the minds of
those who ask it: "Shall the child in his search for knowledge
go through all the experiences of his race in finding it? Must the
child discover for himself all the generalizations which he is to
make his own?" This question would seem to imply that there
is in the minds of some reformers in education an idea that past
experiences are of little use to the child. While this is untenable,
on the other hand, it is not sufficient for the child to learn only
what great discoverers have found, to memorize their facts and
generalizations, and thereby gain the required knowledge.

What has the past brought to the child of the present? Certainly the child should not go through all the mistakes in observation of those scientists who offer him their incomplete products.
"There is no royal road to learning" means, if it means anything, that self-activity is the fundamental law of human growth,
that each human being must "work out his own salvation," that
he must discover truth for himself. It means that there are immutable laws of human growth and development; that the conscious activities and the laws of consciousness, synthesis, analysis,
comparison, classification, and generalization, are precisely the
same as they were in the beginning; that the powers of a human
being may be enhanced by heredity, but the laws of the mind
remain the same; that there is no human education possible except by self-educative effort, and that all the products of the past
do not diminish in the least the necessity for the succession of
self-efforts in the direction of higher development. Past achievements merely form a new foundation upon which to base self-
activity.

The vast treasures which the past has brought may be divided
into two principal factors of education: first, a better knowledge
of the human being, of anthropology, ethnology, psychology, and
all those sciences which embrace the knowledge of the origin,

growth, and development of man; second, the discovery of the external conditions of human growth, the knowledge of nature and its laws. The science of pedagogics is the science of the application of external conditions for human growth, physical, mental, and moral. The delusion that books in themselves necessarily induce human growth, that there is less self-effort, less struggle, less persistency, less will-power necessary, is one which does much harm. All the past has brought us, with its wealth of inventions and discoveries, may be sumed up briefly: more effective means for better development and for a more effective character-building.

All inventions and all progress consist in one thing—economy of energy in the direction of human development. The forces of the universe have been ever-acting, never decreased or diminished; from the beginning unchangeable laws have been discovered and applied for the use of man. If the economy of energy, then, is the summation of all discovery and all progress, the highest product is found in the economy of human energy, or education. Education is the economizing of the energies of the human being. How shall the child judge of the past, of the history of man and his discoveries? By his own discoveries, by his own insight, by his own self-effort; without this, it matters little what has been brought down the long ages, the child is helpless.

One of the saddest things in this world is that a student may earnestly and honestly study for long years, only to find himself lacking in power to know and to apply the truth. The conditions of education must conform to immutable laws, else there can be no true education. Knowledge of laws and conformity to them concenters all the knowledge of the past. "Be ye not conformed to the world, but be ye transformed in the newness of light."

The unconscious synthetic and associative acts induced by observation are in themselves precisely the same kind as those acts of synthesis caused by a direct act of the ego through the will. We name the former acts observation, from their cause, external objects; we name the latter acts imagination, from their cause, the ego; but the acts themselves, so far as I can see, are precisely the same. In observation the ego controls the body and mind and holds it in an attitude for the most economical action of the object. The result is a synthesis or unification of elementary ideas into wholes; the ego is conscious of the result of this, not of the process; in acts of imagination the ego, without the immediate action of external energies, puts itself in a mental condition for the unification of ideas, consisting of parts or wholes of former individual concepts, of elementary ideas lying below the plane of consciousness, and of individual concepts which have formerly been in consciousness.

The part that imagination plays in education cannot be overestimated.[8] By imagination the human being can go outside of the sense grasp, can picture that which lies beyond his own immediate environment. That world beyond, of everlasting change in nature and man is a world that the imagination must reveal, else study is vain and profitless.[9]

The relation of the products of observation to the products of imagination is exceedingly close. The mental acts in observation or unification of ideas, and the mental acts of imagination, are, as I have already said, the same in kind, and they will also be in the one individual the same in quality and the same in intensity. The products of observation are used in imagination. Whatever the products of observation are, so will be the products of imagination, if the imagination is properly exercised. If the products of the senses are vague, obscure, and incomplete, it is reasonable to suppose that the products of the imagination will have the same incompleteness. If the knowledge of the environment is weak and insufficient, the knowledge of that which is beyond the environment will have the same imperfections. All great scientists have been persistent, close observers, and their generalizations, universally applied, are the products of that observation. Their imperfect or wrong conclusions have been derived from insufficient observation.

There are eminent educators who seem to believe that reading is the key to all knowledge; that if the child is taught to read, the portals of truth are opened to him. Granting at the outset the vast, the indispensable value of the action of the printed page upon the mind, still it can truthfully be said that the far greater instrument of education is observation. Most reading done by children, and for that matter by most persons not truly educated, falls short of anything like educative effect. The inefficiency of much reading is found in the failure of the reader's power to imagine. Nearly all of the educative reading of children in the eight grades of the elementary schools consists fundamentally in the exercise of the imagination, that is, consists of descriptions of facts in history and science, which in order to be known must be truly imaged in the mind. *Reading arouses conscious activities, and the whole question of the value of reading lies in whether the activities aroused are educative.* More reading, like all desultory and promiscuous conscious action, may be anything and everything but educative. An educative act has for its fundamental condition intensity of conscious action upon worthy content.

I have already shown that mere conscious activities in themselves are not educative, nor do they in themselves lead to strength of mind. They are indeed the bases of mental power, but unless they become intensified, unless they rise from obscurity to clearness and distinctness, there is practically no educative movement. Now the question very plainly is: What should be the effects of the printed page upon the child's mind? First of all, it should stimulate intense acts of imagination. There should be a richness and vividness of elementary ideas ready to rise above the plane of consciousness when excited by words. There should be a great store of related concepts already formed in consciousness.[10]

The common saying that reading is getting the thought of an author is not scientifically correct. Strictly, no one can ever have any thought but his own. The mental value of intense reading, or the study of text, depends entirely upon the ideas which lie below the plane of consciousness; upon the individual concepts that have formerly been in consciousness, and upon personal experiences, inferences, comparisons, and generalizations. Upon the richness, fullness, and quality of one's own mind depends the action of printed words. Sentences recall former concepts, unite new ones, and arouse the power to understand or to draw original inferences. The quality of all imaginative acts is determined by the quality of previous acts of observation. Thus we see that reading is not the key to knowledge; it is rather the corridor beyond the broad door swung open by observation.

Let us look for a moment upon that common scene, which would be a laughable caricature were it not so sad: Here are the children in the schoolroom with their heads bent over a so-called "Primary Geography," learning definitions of mountains, capes and bays, of islands and plains. They learn the definitions, they recite the definitions, and then become satisfied with the delusion that they know something about geography. Let them lift up their weary heads and look out of the window, and there are the mountains themselves! There is the bay, its waters sparkling in the bright sunlight; there are the plains! Long experience shows that the child who learns the text of a primary geography rarely ever dreams that the objects about which he reads are ever before his eyes when in the open air. The German teachers learned long ago that the only way to teach geography is by observation in field excursions. Yet with us the fetish of word-learning holds thousands of teachers soul-bound by its superstitions. They still believe that the words are of more educational value than the things themselves.[11]

Thousands and tens of thousands of pupils go through the high-school textbooks on physics, botany, and zoölogy with little or no observations; if they are sometimes fortunate enough to observe objects used for illustration, the specimens are too often paraded as something out of the ordinary, held in the hands of the teacher, or placed upon the table, merely to prove facts stated in the textbook.

I am making an argument here for observation that is as old as human thought. Every great thinker and every educator, from Socrates down to Froebel, have urged the study of the great textbook of nature. The Master illustrated all His teachings by scenes from the hills of Judea. The fact that confronts us in this discussion is that, although these truths have been urged for ages persistently, although they are generally believed by thoughtful men, still the real educative life-giving work of observation has reached in our republic very few children, and the reason for this sad state of things is that very few teachers themselves have had an opportunity actually to study science in this vital way.[12]

Outside of the school windows, in many a beautiful country-place, the birds sing in the trees, the clouds float overhead, the trees, hills, plains, valleys, all cry out to the child; all nature yearns to speak through his senses to his soul; waits with awakening power to open the sealed fountatin of his being, to stir in him the germs of feeling that link his soul to the great over-brooding Soul of the Universe.

> Wisdom and Spirit of the universe!
> Thou Soul that art the Eternity of thought,
> That giv'st to forms and images a breath
> And everlasting motion, not in vain

By day or starlight thus, from my first dawn
Of childhood, didst thou intertwine for me
The passions that build up our human soul;
Not with the mean and vulgar works of man,
But with high objects, with enduring things—
With life and nature—purifying thus
The elements of feeling and of thought,
And sanctifying, by such discipline,
Both pain and fear, until we recognize
A grandeur in the beatings of the heart.
                —William Wordsworth, *The Prelude,* Book I.

But the children, the poor children, are confined to dead words, as if there were some mysterious power in them to awaken intellectual and moral life. "Behold, the fields are white, and ready for the harvest." "Come and learn of me," "Know me," "Love me"; but he who is buried in the dead formalism of the past has not ears to hear nor heart to understand the longing cry. All-sided observation of nature has for its grandest result a profound love and reverence for God's glorious manifestation of Himself in the universe. No one can study nature without loving her; no one is ever alone, is ever where there is nothing to love and to be loved by, who listens to the voice of the Eternal sounding and singing through all that He has created and is creating.

One of the most encouraging movements of modern times, in education, is the bringing of literature into the life of the child, replacing dry textbooks with great expressions of essential truth. But upon what mental conditions does the power to understand, appreciate, and love good literature depend? The first quality of literature is genuineness; genuineness is an unalloyed revelation of the soul. The fact of genuineness is the fundamental fact of literature, and next to and higher than this is the manifestation of the soul in its evident struggle to know and to express the truth. Good prose and the masterpieces of poetry are full of truths of the invisible world based on observation of the visible world; indeed, take the descriptions, the teachings of nature, out of poetry, and a bare skeleton only would be left.

Whence have come the grandest inspirations of thinkers and writers in all ages? The greatest preacher of our age was a devoted student of nature; the poets whose works live are filled with the closest observations of nature, and generalizations therefrom. Nature speaks with no uncertain voice to him who penetrates her deeper mysteries.

> Flower in the crannied wall,
> I pluck you out of the crannies;—
> Hold you here, root and all, in my hand,
> Little flower;—but if I could understand
> What you are, root and all, and all in all,
> I should know what God and man is.

Is it true that a study of nature leads to a knowledge of God? Consider Job who, in spite of all his wretchedness and woe, was established in his faith by the contemplation of God in nature. Anyone who can read with understanding these words of Lowell has a wellspring of moral power within him.

> Whether we look, or whether we listen,
> We hear life murmur, or see it glisten;
> Every clod feels a stir of might,
> An instinct within it that reaches and towers,
> And groping blindly above it for light,
> Climbs to a soul in grass and flowers.

Or these sublime words of Thomson:

> . . . The rolling year
> Is full of Thee. Forth in the pleasing spring
> Thy beauty walks, Thy tenderness and love.
> Wide flush the fields; the softening air is balm;

Echo the mountains round; the forest smiles;
And every sense and every heart is joy.
Then comes Thy glory in the summer months,
With light and heat refulgent. Then Thy sun
Shoots full perfection through the swelling year;
And oft Thy voice in dreadful thunder speaks,
And oft at dawn, deep noon, or falling eve,
By brooks and groves in hollow-whispering gales.
Thy bounty shines in autumn unconfined,
And spreads a common feast for all that lives.
In winter awful Thou! with clouds and storms
Around Thee thrown, tempest o'er tempest rolled,
Majestic darkness! on the whirlwind's wing,
Riding sublime, Thou bid'st the world adore,
And humblest nature with Thy northern blast.

Mysterious round! what skill, what force divine,
Deep felt, in these appear! a simple train,
Yet so delightful mixed, with such kind art,
Such beauty and beneficence combined;
Shade, unperceived, so softening into shade;
And all so forming an harmonious whole,
That, as they still succeed, they ravish still.
But wandering oft, with brute unconscious gaze,
Man marks not Thee, marks not the mighty hand,
That, ever busy, wheels the silent spheres;
Works in the secret deep; shoots, steaming, thence
The fair profusion that o'erspreads the spring;
Flings from the sun direct the flaming day;
Feeds every creature; hurls the tempest forth;
And, as on earth this grateful change revolves,
With transport touches all the springs of life.

Just in proportion as man is a true student of nature can he
interpret the study of literature, and enjoy and understand what
the poets have expressed. I grant that there may be a cold, hard,

materialistic study of science, but the true study of science results in the power to understand the best that there is in literature.

The ethical use of science should not be overlooked. Summed up as a whole, most of the discoveries in science have for their highest use the improvement of conditions for human comfort, happiness, and consequent development. No one can study science without acquiring the means of enhancing the value of home and the happiness of the community in which he lives. The things we almost wholly neglect in our teaching are the earth we live on, the air we breathe, the water we drink, and the life and powers that impinge upon us from every side, the things of health and wealth, of true success and real education. History tells us what man has been; science, what he should be. My earnest plea, then, to you, my fellow teachers, is, that our children, the future citizens of our country, shall have the privilege and the means of studying science throughout their whole school course.

And here it may be well to refer to the countless opportunities there are for the study of elementary science. In a country school, surrounded with the bounties of nature in the way of lands, woods, vegetation, and animal life, let the teacher take the children out into the fields during school sessions, and study upon the farm that which is of the most importance for the farmer to know, undertake to study something about the soils, fertilization, something of the insects injurious to fruits and trees, something of meteorology. To deal with those things which are nearest and most evident in the child's environment is a happy choice of material. "Familiarity breeds contempt" only to the ignorant and narrow soul.

Education can be made so much better, so much richer in means and influence and breadth, by making observation the foundation. I have tried to present some arguments in favor of the study of elementary science, and, in conclusion, allow me to turn to an authority which few will deny—to the argument of all arguments:

> The law of the Lord is perfect, converting the soul:
> The testimony of the Lord is sure, making wise the simple.
> The statutes of the Lord are right, rejoicing the heart:
> The commandment of the Lord is pure, enlightening the eyes.
> The fear of the Lord is clean, enduring forever:
> The judgments of the Lord are true and righteous altogether.
> More to be desired are they than gold, yea, than much fine gold:
> Sweeter also than honey and the honeycomb.
> Moreover, by them is thy servant warned:
> And in keeping of them there is great reward.
> Who can understand his errors?
> Cleanse Thou me from secret faults,
> Keep back Thy servant also from presumptuous sins;
> Let them not have dominion over me:
> Then shall I be upright,
> And I shall be innocent from the great transgression.

There is only one study, and that study is the law; the conversion of the soul is through the knowledge of the law gained by the personal experience and insight which comes from self activity. The ideal is that there is a perfect law, that the study of that law "rejoiceth the heart," that the law, when found by the soul's search, is "sweeter than honey and the honeycomb." The Psalmist is alive and aware of the dangers that beset a soul that is not in touch with truth: "Who can understand his errors? Keep back Thy servant from presumptuous sins." The isolated study of textbooks has for its main product the presumption of knowledge—a self-satisfaction which is a bar to all future development. True humility, which has for its gain the "Kingdom of Heaven," can only come to the one who gains some apprehension of the boundlessness of knowledge and of the depths of truth by actual personal experience. The highest product of observation, and that which no other study and no other work will bring, is some idea of the infinity of knowledge and the finiteness of man; out of these conclusions alone comes the knowledge of the true attitude and righteous progress of man toward the truth and toward God. "For He made us in His own image."

[1] John Dewey, *How We Think,* Chap. XIV.

[2] John Dewey, *How We Think* (D. C. Heath), pp. 129—§5,-134; *also see* John Dewey, *My Pedagogic Creed* (Progressive Education Assn.), Article IV, paragraph 2.

[3] E. B. Huey, *Psychology and Pedagogy of Reading,* pp. 160-161.

[4] Edward Yeomans, *Shackled Youth* (Atlantic Monthly Press), pp. 37-42.

[5] W. H. Kilpatrick, *Education for a Changing Civilization* (Macmillan), pp. 8-50.

[6] John Dewey, *How We Think* (D. C. Heath), pp. 64 (a)-67; 150-156.

[7] John Dewey, *How We Think* (D. C. Heath), pp. 145-149.

[8] Porter Lander MacClintock, *Literature in the Elementary School* (U. of C. Press), pp. 18-26.

[9] John Dewey, *How We Think* (D. C. Heath), p. 223.

[10] " . . . our power to think effectively depends upon the possession of a capital fund of meanings which may be applied when desired." John Dewey, *How We Think,* p. 118.

[11] Edward Yoemans, *Shackled Youth* (Atlantic Monthly Press), pp. 13-25; pp. 106-109.

[12] Chap. XIV of *How We Think,* by John Dewey (D. C. Heath), on "Observation and Information" parallels this discussion and illuminates it.

VIII

LANGUAGE

IN THE history of education the discussions of the principles and methods of teaching language, especially methods, occupy by far the largest place: this is true of language from the days when the Humanists held universal sway up to the present time. The relations of language to the evolution of the human race are of the closest nature: so close, that some psychologists, notably Max Muller, strive to prove that there can be no thought without language.[1] Whether this be true or not, there can be no question that language is by far the most prominent factor in education.

The relation of language to the people who speak it and whose ancestors created it is similar to the relation of the mind to the body, and inversely, the body to the mind. It is a well-recognized fact that the attitude and bearing of the body and its gestures are marked indications of the mind's character and influence. Thought controls, modifies, and develops for better or worse physical organs and physical power.

Emotion of different kinds set in action involuntarily the whole body: joy is easily recognized by the attitude, bearing, and inflections of the body, the particular state of the mind out of which it arises, modifying the action of the whole organism. Fear has its strong influence, checking nerve currents and contracting muscles. Each emotion, either of pain or pleasure, influences in a marked degree nerve and muscular action. A person in a state of constant merriment has a characteristic bearing; one controlled by continual despair has a characteristic bearing; one animated by hate of mankind carries the indications of this hatred in every muscle. It is past all question that every emotion has its corresponding effect upon the body, influencing the growth and development of physical power.

The sensorium, muscular system, and sympathetic nerves all contribute to the most effective act of attention, enhancing the thought. Acts of educative attention are in essence a means of physical training which insures the higher development of the body as an instrument of attention.

In expression the use of the body is more pronounced than in attention. The agents of expression are continually modified by the various muscular adjustments necessary to expressive acts.

In pure reflection, although the body is not immediately used as an instrument of reception, it still indicates mental states. Its attitudes are best adapted to the mental effort necessary to reflection, in which state all receptive and executive action of the organism is suspended until the particular line of action has been determined. In other words, there is no absolute inertia of the body in any mental act.

The mind to a marked extent creates the body; every fiber of the brain, every nerve tract, every bundle of muscles, indeed, all the organs of the body, strongly indicate the influence of the mind upon the body. This is true of each individual; but each individual is only one of a series of individuals coming into the world with a body that is to a great extent the product of ancestral development. The mind is continually creating the body.

The relation of a language to a people who created it has much the same relation as has body to the mind. A language is a body created not by one individual, but contributed to by all of the individual units of a people and their progenitors from the beginning.[2] The development of language is an absolute necessity to thought development, following the law of all forms of expression. The general thought of a people, whatever the degree of civilization to which it has arrived, is indicated by the language of that people. A dialect is generally recognized as a case of arrested development. It is not an idiosyncrasy or eccentricity: it is simply an indication that a people who use the dialect has not kept pace in its development with the higher civilization of the race who use a common language.

It is impossible to trace any language back to its origin; but the beginnings of language, it is not impossible to suppose, sprang from the crude necessities of a race just emerging into something like intelligence. Every word, no doubt, sprang from the immediate necessity of thought. Every idiom marked a peculiar phase of thought. Every modification of subject or predicate indicated a step in human progress. As in the past, so in the present, new inventions, discoveries, explorations, not to consider newly awakened perceptions of being and feeling, make demands for new words or old words with new meanings. In languages like the German, the original language of the people serves them in using old words with changed and higher meanings; while in English the source of new words is found in the Greek, Latin, and other languages.

It is not my purpose to give a general indication of how language is developed, but to show the close relation of the growth of a language to the growth of a people. A language in itself indicates better than any other means the exact stage of the growth and civilization of the people who speak it. A geologist reads in a characteristic area of the earth's surface the geographical history of that surface. This fact has a far deeper significance when applied to language. Although *philology* is a comparatively new science, yet as a means of studying the spiritual life and growth of a people it is incomparable. Ruins and implements give fleeting, disconnected insight into a people's history; but the language of a people, the tracing of even one word back to something like a supposed origin, is a vista in the life of that people.

The language also indicates the environment of a people. When it was found that in Sanscrit there were no names for animals of Asia that live in the Oxus basin, it was taken as a proof that the Aryan race did not have its origin there. A language is the ethnographic body of a people, reflecting the life and thought of that people, from the beginning. Just as the nerve tracts and muscular coördinations of the body indicate the growth of the mind of an individual, so do the words, idioms, and syntax of a language indicate the development and growth of the accumulated experience of a race.

The one insuperable argument in favor of the educative value of dead languages is that in no other way can the spirit, the genius, and the inner history of a people be so thoroughly understood as in a language. The Greek language, for instance, is the body that remains to us of a departed soul, showing what that soul was on this earth—how it struggled and grew, what its imaginations, its religions, its aspirations, and its victories were. Greek history can be best understood through its language. The study of a language, dead or living, is a study of the human spirit. This fact gives us the method and motive for the study. The study of dead forms, whether in our own vernacular or in a language of the past, is of the lowest educative value; but the study of a dead language that has for its sole aim the revival of pictures long gone by, an understanding of the inner life of the people once using it, what they thought, how they struggled, how they conquered or failed, gives the student an impulse in the right direction, and determines the method by which all languages should be learned—the method which arouses the deepest interest and attains the most valuable results.

The literature of any language contains in itself the history of the highest life of the people. The loftiest aspirations of the Italians we get from Dante, of the Romans from Virgil and Horace, of the Greeks from Homer and Xenophon. Because the methods of the Humanists consist, in general, of empty formalism, because much of the study of modern language, and even our own, is of the same nature, a direct inheritance of our pedagogical ancestors, because language has been taught with the least educative effect—presents no valid reasons why the study of dead or living languages should be discarded. A knowledge of each and every language which has poured its flood of words into English speech reveals to the learner the otherwise hidden might of his own vernacular and enhances greatly his power of thought and expression. "A modern language is the mirror in which one sees his own language." The unscientific methods of teaching languages are the reason why so many students, after years of drill in dead forms, know little of what they have tried to study.

It may be well for us to glance for a moment at the method by which a child learns the spoken language. The subject should be of deep interest to the teachers, especially under the teachings of Preyer, Perez, Darwin, Taine, Romanes, and other scientists who have assisted so materially in this direction. In the first place, a child makes his own language—a language of gesture, a language of babblings, which has its vague but significant meaning to the child. Then comes the language that he hears spoken around him. What are the difficulties that a child has to overcome in learning this language? Because every child learns the language with such ease, we are apt to think that the difficulties are slight.

I am now discussing how a child learns to hear, or to understand, oral language. It is true that hearing and speaking have exceedingly close relations to each other, but they are two things entirely different in themselves and in acquisition; hearing is learned by a series of acts of attention; speaking, by practice in uttering thought.[3] In anything like scientific investigation the two must be kept separate.[4]

Let us consider the tremendous obstacles a child must overcome in learning to hear language. These difficulties may best be described by a partial analysis of speech. Pronunciation is the main factor in oral language. It may be generally defined as making oral words by means of the vocal organs. The pronunciation of a word consists of, first, the enunciation of each sound element; second, the articulation or uniting of the sounds enunciated. In articulation there is an imperceptible pause between two successively uttered sounds, and a perceptible pause between syllables; third, in words of more than one syllable in most languages inflection of voice or accent upon one of the syllables; fourth, a slight inflection less than accent, which is called rhythm, in the utterance of every syllable. In the analysis of pronunciation we have enunciation, articulation, pauses—perceptible and imperceptible—accent, and rhythm.

The second great obstacle to be overcome in hearing-language is the mastery of idioms. The idioms, i.e., the general arrangement of the words in sentences, differ greatly in form in different languages; indeed, the principal obstacle to be overcome in learning a foreign language is the idiom, and it is reasonable to suppose that this same difficulty confronts the child. A sentence consists of words related in conventional order. The function of each word is to arouse certain definite activities; the sentence arouses these activities in a certain definite relation. The idiom, being an arbitrary and conventional relation of words to each other, must be acquired by the association of the thought with the conscious effect of the idiom.

The foundation of the spoken language is voice, or vocalized

breath, modified by the organs of speech. The shape of the vocal cavity or the exact position of the organs is an indispensable
condition for the making of definite voice elements. These definite qualities or voice elements depend upon the shape of the
organs anterior to the vocal chords. In the utterance, then, of a
sentence we have articulation; the pronunciation; the relation of
words to each other, or the syntax of the sentence; the rhythm
of each syllable, which we call melody; and the combined
rhythm of all the syllables, or harmony; back of this, emphasis,
the spontaneous impulse of the voice in inflection, is the direct
reflex of the highest impulse of the thought itself; force of voice
which denotes the intensity of the being; and quality, which
shows the kind of emotion or degree of earnestness which moves
the speaker. Vocalized breath or voice, rhythm, melody, harmony, and emphasis are not obstructions in learning to hear
language; they are helps spontaneously generated and understood.

The difficulties to overcome in learning to hear language consist principally of pronunciation and idiom. Learning to hear
language consists of functioning words and idioms. A word is
functioned when it acts upon consciousness and arouses instantly
certain definite activities—activities which the word was made
to arouse. The activities which a word when functioned arouses
in consciousness we shall call appropriate activities. The general
law of association may be stated as follows: When two activities,
either simple or complex, immediately succeed each other in
consciousness, the after appearance of one of these activities has
a tendency to recall the other. The particular law relating to
functioning of words is: When the mental correspondence of
the word is immediately succeeded by its appropriate activities, or
vice versa, the reappearance of the correspondence to the word
has a tendency to recall its appropriate activities, or *vice versa.*

An oral word, through the ear, arouses its correspondence in consciousness, and this correspondence in turn arouses certain activities, which I call appropriate activities, in contradistinction to corresponding activities. A word that merely arouses its correspondence without any further effect in consciousness is not functioned. The law for the functioning of every word may be stated under the general law of association. Two activities must immediately succeed each other: the first activity is the effect of the word, or its correspondence; the second activity is the appropriate activity. When these two activities immediately succeed each other in consciousness, the appearance of one has a tendency thereafter to recall the other. There is no other law by which a word can be learned. Words are learned by acts of association—the association of the effect of the word itself with the appropriate activities, or the activities which it was made to recall. A word is learned by repetition of these acts of association. *The more intense the acts of association, the fewer the number of repetitions necessary.*

The intensity of these acts of association with children depends entirely upon interest. That interest is aroused by a desire to understand what other people are saying. There is no interest in the effect of the word itself; the interest is entirely dependent upon the emotions aroused by the appropriate activities which the correspondence to the word recalls. We have briefly stated the difficulties which children must surmount in learning to hear language, and also the action of the law by which the difficulties must be overcome. Each word is made by itself, each sound in an oral word is made by itself, and must really be heard by itself; still the process of mentally synthesizing these sounds is perfectly automatic. The child is vaguely conscious of the effect of the word as a whole, and although the sounds are continually uttered in his presence, he never makes an attempt unprompted to analyze an oral word into its component parts.

A word acts instantaneously like any other object, and acts as a whole.

To illustrate this point: an object is presented to the child— a doll, or a dog. An immediate interest, or emotion of pleasure, is aroused in consciousness by the presence of the object; the child has activities appropriate to the word at the same time the word "doll" or "dog," is spoken. The conditions of the act of association are perfect, and the associative act takes place in consciousness. The greater the interest of the child, the more intense, and therefore, the more effective, the act. The child must first have the appropriate activities in his mind to be brought into consciousness, and the effect of the word must follow in immediate succession. Thereafter, if the act of association is an effective one, when the word "doll" or "dog" is spoken the appropriate activities come into consciousness.

Idioms are learned in much the same way. The difference is that the effect of the idiom is to unite conscious activities in immediate succession, as, "A dog runs"—which idiom unites the idea of dog with the motion of the dog.

The child begins to hear language long before he begins to speak. He begins instinctively and spontaneously to follow the law. Parents have intuitively a method of teaching children to hear language. They make no attempt whatever to divide the oral word into its component sounds. They understand perfectly that if the child is attentive and deeply interested in an object it will have no difficulty in learning its name.

Under this law and under these general relations the great work of acquiring vocabulary and idioms begins with the child. First a few words are learned—the names of objects in which he is immediately interested: "mamma," "papa," "cat," "dog," and so on. Then follow the words united into idioms, the learning of each word and each idiom springing directly from the necessities of thought, a child rarely ever remembering a word which has failed to arouse certain definite conscious activities. The attention of the child is controlled by the words which recall thought, or by the desire to know the name of an object.[5]

We look upon the common fact of a child's learning language in two or three years as something very natural, always to be expected, and having in itself nothing of the marvelous; yet when we study the matter closely and compare it with some of the methods used later in school, it is indeed a wonderful process of mental action. A child acquires in three years the foundation of his own vernacular; the pronunciation and fundamental idioms of the language are in this comparatively short time within his power. There do not seem to be any great obstructions in the way; every step is met and overcome with great ease.

Parents never attempt to teach words which are not needed for immediate use; that is, words that are not directly associated with appropriate activities. The language which a child acquires is adapted to the immediate necessities of thought; thus a certain body of language becomes his own, to be used in hearing and expression. The language conforms to the thought; thought and speech become a unit in hearing and speaking.

The simplicity or complexity of the sentences a child learns to use depends upon the simplicity or complexity of his thought. When this wonderful process is explained to teachers, and it is presented to them as an example of what spontaneity will do for the child, the answer often comes, "This is natural," "The child learns that naturally."

This word "natural," like charity, covers a multitude of sins —a multitude of sins of ignorance.[6] It may be well for us to look at the word in its true significance, or in its scientific application. There is a vast difference between that which becomes natural through habit, and that which is according to nature. The word natural can have no scientific meaning other than conformity to the laws of the being. Teaching is the presentation of conditions for the normal or lawful action of the mind. That teaching is most natural which is best adapted to the laws of mental action. If, then, the child learns to hear the oral language naturally, by conforming to the laws of his own being, why should the child not continue the process by the same method? Why should he not learn the written language and all other languages by conforming to an immutable law of the human mind?

The forms, correct and incorrect, of language are acquired almost entirely by imitation.[7] Whatever speech a child hears at home, in the street, and in society he imitates; he forms strong habits of language, good or bad, which it is well nigh impossible later in life, even under the best teaching, wholly to eradicate. All this imitation of language, it must be remembered, is acquired and controlled by a desire to understand and express thought; there is little or no imitation of meaningless words; the child has a motive in his acts, and adheres tenaciously to that motive.

The child when he enters school has learned more of language than he ever afterward can learn. We shall best enhance his knowledge of and power over language by the same natural method which he has pursued so assiduously in his first years. It is an educational error fraught with serious results to believe that the school should introduce a new method which has for its basis the hypothesis that form of speech must be learned for form's sake, unrelated and unimpelled by the immediate necessities of thought. His language, his sentences and their modifications must grow with the growth of thought, conform to thought, be adapted to thought, arouse thought. Words must not be learned by themselves and for themselves, with a vague belief on the part of the teacher that at some future time the child may have the thought necessary for their use. It is possible to enhance this magnificent spontaneous product by continuing the same method in teaching, that is, adapting language to the conditions of mental growth. It is possible to make thought development the center and adapt the teaching of language to every step in thought.

The child has been unconsciously learning the forms of language, including etymology and syntax, from the beginning; that he should continue the study of grammar is beyond doubt. A very serious question is: How should he continue this most important branch of knowledge? Is grammar to be taught as a special subject, isolated from all other subjects? Must the knowledge of language outgrow the necessities of thought with the supposition that it will some day be needed when perchance thought is evolved? On the contrary, grammar can be made the warp and woof of language which springs directly from thought, under the strong impulses to hear and to express thought. It must not be spun and woven by itself without regard to inner necessities or without direct adaption to the activities of consciousness.

There are two fundamental uses of language and the grammar of language. The first is to enhance, to deepen and to broaden the understanding of speech and printed language; the second is to make language, both spoken and written, an adequate means for the expression of thought; both motives are a unit in the action and reaction of language, in the intensification of conscious activities. Hearing, reading, speaking, and writing are the formal modes of learning language; a most significant educational fact is that the power to use language, and the correct habits of language, are acquired by a continuous effort to express thought adequately.

The purely formal studies of the past have been in a great degree a stern and awful necessity; there was little else to teach besides spelling, copy-writing, parsing, analysis, and construction. It is only within a few years, comparatively, that abundant means of thought evolution have been brought to the doors of the schoolroom; new-born sciences, a real geography, and a reformed history—to-day all these are ours to use as the highest conditions of human development. The necessity for the old extravagant waste of time and energy is gone forever. These magnificent subjects have come to the doors of the school and will make the learning of language meaningful and vital. Language should become then the habitual and proper channel for the expression and intensification of thought.

[1] John Dewey, *How We Think* (D. C. Heath), pp. 170-172; also *My Pedagogic Creed,* Article III, p. 15, "I believe that at present we lose much of the value of literature and language . . ."
[2] E. B. Huey, *Psychology and Pedagogy of Reading* (Macmillan), pp. 125-133.
[3] E. B. Huey, *Psychology and Pedagogy of Reading* (Macmillan), pp. 133-141.
[4] That this is equally true educationally in teaching reading and writing, *see* this volume, p. 192.
[5] John Dewey, *How We Think* (D. C. Heath), pp. 180-186 (i, ii, iii).
[6] E. B. Huey, *Psychology and Pedagogy of Reading,* pp. 329-334.
[7] E. B. Huey, *Psychology and Pedagogy of Reading,* pp. 123-125.

IX

READING AND ITS RELATIONS
TO THE CENTRAL SUBJECTS

READING is a mental process. It consists of a sequence of mental activities immediately induced by the action of written or printed words arranged in sentences. I propose to discuss the psychology and pedagogics of reading as a mode of attention.[1] Oral reading is a mode of expression and comes under the head of speech. Many of the grossest errors in teaching reading spring from confounding the two processes of attention and expression. Reading in itself is not expression any more than observation or hearing-language is expression. The custom of making oral reading the principal and almost the only means of teaching reading has led to the many errors prevalent to-day.

Observation is thinking; hearing-language is thinking; reading is thinking; and, in anything like a reasonable discussion of the psychological nature of reading, the subject of oral reading must be referred to its proper place as a mode of expression.

Reading in itself has no educative value; it does not give rise to a succession of educative acts any more than does seeing, hearing, or touching. The value of reading in education depends entirely upon the educative subject presented and upon the intensity of the conscious acts. Ordinary reading, then, is not educative. It may consist of a succession of conscious states without any appreciable degree of intensity; it may consist of intense immoral states degrading to the mind: in a word, reading in itself is not moral, neither does it necessarily induce educative action. Reading may lead to the pollution of the soul; or, under the right conditions, it may be made the means of its highest development and elevation. The educative value of reading, then, depends (1) upon what is read; (2) upon how it is read.

With these very important modifications in view it is readily seen that reading in itself may be made, next to observation, the greatest factor in education. Reading opens all the historical records of the past, all the discussions and discoveries that have been made throughout the ages. By reading, poetry and literature may become essential means of human growth. Here I wish to repeat what I have already said in discussing attention: A reader does not think the thought of an author, he simply thinks his own thought.[2] By the action of words upon the mind ideas arise above the plane of consciousness; individual concepts and judgments that have formerly been in consciousness reappear and are recombined and associated; new units are formed and fresh judgments suggested; but the mental results of written or printed words upon the mind are predetermined by the mind itself. If it were true that reading is "getting the thought of an author," then we should have to suppose that the reader has the power to think as the author thinks, the same power of imagination, the same power of inference, of generalization; in fact, the power to follow the same processes of reasoning.

Reading is thinking, and thinking depends utterly upon the individual power of the mind. The difference between reading and studying books consists entirely in the fact that the latter action is more intense than the former. In ordinary reading, waves or states of consciousness succeed each other with more or less rapidity; but in the study of text, states of consciousness are held under the action of the will. In reading, a sentence arouses a thought which is immediately succeeded by another, and another, and so on; in study, the thought aroused by the sentence is delayed or hemmed in, more distinctly presented to the ego, and therefore intensified by the action of the will. The result of this hemming in and intensification is a more vivid imagination, and consequently more valuable inferences. Ordinary reading is the essential preparation for study, as the exercise of the senses is for observation.

The psychology of reading, and at the same time of study, plays such an immense part in education, that its comprehension is a prime necessity.

A written or printed word has one function and one only, and that function is to arouse or recall into consciousness certain definite and related activities—activities which the word was made to recall; in other words, those activities which, by convention, are assigned to the action of the word itself. A word is an object: it has length, breadth, thickness, and weight; it is made up of parts; it acts upon consciousness by the same law and in precisely the same general manner that any other object acts; it acts instantaneously through the nerve tracts of sight; it is the cause of an effect in consciousness, which effect, as with other objects, corresponds to the object that caused it. Any and all printed words act in the same way, producing an effect or mental correspondence.

This mental correspondence of a word has no value in itself; it is merely and solely a means to an end. When the word is functioned, its effect in consciousness recalls certain definite activities. The appropriate activities are recalled by the correspondence of the word to itself.

Certain words, nouns for instance, either common or proper, arouse definite activities which are not of necessity immediately related to other activities. Other classes of words, such as conjunctions, prepositions, adjectives, adverbs, and verbs, have for their function the arousing of certain definite activities in immediate relation to other activities; that is, their effects have only a suggestive relation to other activities. Thus we have the sentence consisting of subject and predicate and modifiers of both subject and predicate. The sentence arouses certain definite activities in relation each to the other. The arrangement of words in sentences, or syntax of language, is an arbitrary relation. The idiomatic relations, we all know, differ in a marked degree among different languages. The idioms are generally learned in hearing-language, and the habit of mind which induces the proper action of an idiom is easily formed in the child's effort to understand oral language. In printing or writing the English language the arrangement of sentences is from left to right; in other languages it may be from right to left, up or down; thus the order of arrangement is arbitrary.

In the reading of a sentence the related words arouse a certain state of consciousness, or a sequence of associations. The arrangement of the words in a sentence recalls in consciousness ideas or conscious activities in a certain, definite, related order. The first action of words, whether isolated or in sentences, is precisely the same as the action of objects upon consciousness; but the function of words, more strictly speaking, is to recall certain appropriate activities—activities appropriate to the words, themselves. The action, too, like the action of all objects, upon consciousness, is instantaneous. In observation the action is continuous, but in reading, when the word has performed its function it is of no more immediate use: it is therefore of the utmost importance that words act instantaneously, that they in no way obstruct the action of the mind, that they simply and easily perform their function, and that there be no absorption of the mental power in the forms of the words themselves.

Teaching reading consists entirely in the presentation on the part of the teacher of the conditions for the functioning of words. This is true not only with the little child, but it is just as true in all stages of human development, and pertains quite as much to foreign languages, ancient or modern, as it does to one's own vernacular.

It is the question of questions for those who teach reading, and in fact for all teachers of language: What is the law by which each and every word is functioned? The general law, the law upon which fundamentally all recollection and remembrance depends, may be stated as follows: When two activities, either simple or complex, follow each other immediately in consciousness, the reappearance of one of these activities in an after state of consciousness has a tendency to recall or arouse the other.[3,4]

Associated activities are those which follow each other in an immediate succession. Now from this general law we deduce the particular law by which printed words are functioned. The activities which are immediately to succeed each other are first, the effect of the correspondence to the word itself; and second, the appropriate activities. The law, then, for functioning words may be stated as follows: The effect of the word or its correspondence must be succeeded immediately in consciousness by the appropriate activities which the word was made to arouse; or, conversely, the appropriate activities must be immediately succeeded by the effect of the printed word upon consciousness. It follows that when these two activities immediately succeed each other, the appearance of one of these activities has a tendency to arouse the other—that it, the effect of the word when it appears in consciousness has a tendency to arouse the appropriate activities; and when the appropriate activities appear in consciousness they have a tendency to recall the effect of the word.

I have here used the phrase, "has a tendency." If one act of association were always sufficient to function a word, the teaching of the first steps in reading would be a very easy matter indeed. This, we all know by experience, is not true, but that, as a rule, repeated acts of association are necessary. In fact, the whole difficulty is to bring about these acts of association. There is much desultory and promiscuous discussion in regard to methods of teaching reading, but no matter what conditions may be presented, no matter what so-called method may be used in teaching reading, the effect of the word and the appropriate activities must be associated, they must be associated under this stated law, and can be by no other. So we can lay down the principle here and follow it: *Whatever assists in the immediate succession of the effect of the word and the appropriate activities may be used in teaching reading;* whatever interrupts this associative act should be omitted. This principle gives us a sure guide in the application of the law.

Children suffer from violation of this principle. Too often conditions are presented which obstruct the action of the law by which every word must be learned.

Following out this fundamental principle, we can make the following statements of other and subsidiary principles:

(1) Every printed word must be learned by one or more acts of association.

(2) The less the number of acts required to function a word, the greater the economy.

(3) The greatest economy in learning a word would be, therefore, one act of association.

We can say, then, that that teaching is best which presents conditions by which a word is learned by one act, or in one state of consciousness. We seek, therefore, for conditions that will bring about those acts of consciousness by which a word may be most economically learned.

First, in this discussion, we turn to the word and its effect upon consciousness; and we can confidently affirm that the effect of a word upon consciousness in itself arouses no pleasant or agreeable emotions in the child's mind, except, perhaps, by anticipation. A word is an object to which a child is totally indifferent. On the other hand, it may be as confidently stated that if the effect of the word were pleasant to the child, if it aroused his interest, or, in other words, induced pleasing emotions, reading, as Dogberry says, would come "by natur." Were there not the resistance of indifference which often amounts almost to aversion on the part of the words, the child would learn the pure symbols, the printed words, with the same ease that he learns the partial symbols of pictures and models.

When we turn to the history of methods of teaching reading we find numberless illustrations of the truth of this statement. In the first attempts to teach reading, the alphabet-method, pure and simple, no doubt was used; the drudgery consisted in learning the names of letters and afterwards combining them by oral spelling. A suspicion was aroused that this seemingly necessary toil might be lightened by interest. The Romans carved the letters in ivory; Basedow, the Philanthropin, made the alphabet in gingerbread, and rewarded successful attempts at naming the letters with delicious bites—a sugar-coating to a bitter pill. We have had countless primers full of gorgeously colored initial letters as baits —"A is for apple, so round and so sweet; B is for the baby, so clean and so neat"; and so on, *ad infinitum, ad nauseam.*

Another prolonged attempt to lessen the difficulties of overcoming words is found in the so-called phonic- and phonetic-methods. The phonic-method was at the time of its introduction, over 350 years ago, a very profitable departure from the pure alphabetic method, and had its origin in some of the earnest minds that worked contemporaneously with Martin Luther. The phonetic and word-building methods have all been earnest attempts to make the words easy and pleasant—like the old device, of late revived, of comparing elementary sounds to the noises made by animals and in nature; as "ch" is the sound made by a locomotive, for instance. The struggle has been a long one, an earnest and an honest one, but has failed because of no reasonable appreciation of the action of the mind in learning words. We are, on this side of the question, about where we began three centuries ago. Baked letters and sweetened sounds still "hold the fort" for artisan teachers.

The history of another phase of the pedagogy of reading is that brought about by the great reformer Comenius—indeed we may give him for lack of further knowledge the credit of originating it. This movement consisted in arousing the appropriate activities in order to make the associations more effective. Comenius' work began in the time when the Humanists had complete control, and dead languages were nearly the sum and substance of all that was taught. His famous "Orbis Pictus," now reproduced, is open to all teachers for study.

On page 1 of this book we find:

ORBIS SENSUALIUM PICTUS,

A World of Things Obvious to the Senses Drawn in Pictures

I.

Invitation   Invitatio

(Here a picture of a teacher with his finger beckoning, inviting the boy who stands before him, hat in hand.)

The Master and the Boy.	Magister et Puer.
M. Come, Boy, learn to be wise.	M. Veni, Puer, disce sapere.
B. What doth this mean, to be wise?	P. Quid hoc est, sapere?
M. To understand rightly.	M. Intelligere recte, etc.

On page 3, opposite a picture of a crow:

Cornix cornicatur,—
The crow crieth.

Opposite the picture of a lamb:

> Agnus balat,—
> The lamb blaiteth.

This, as I have said, was an attempt made by Comenius to associate the appropriate activities and the word by means of pictures.

This device, which is the supposed beginning of the so-called thought-method of teaching, has continued down to our time, principally by the use of pictures; nearly all readers for primary grades have followed this plan.

It was found, however, by inquiring teachers, that the object itself aroused the appropriate activities more vigorously than the pictures; and in the *Normal Worter-Methode* we find objects freely used, and some special methods named after the object which is first used—as for instance, the *Ei-Methode,* so called because an egg is used in the first step. It is safe to say that all along the line on both sides, overcoming the obstacle of the word and the arousing of appropriate activities, there have been countless methods, and that these methods have been converging and combining at every step.

The so-called word-method was the first recognition of the plain and simple psychological fact that a word acts as a whole just like any other object, instantaneously, and that there is no instinctive attempt on the part of the child to analyze the word into its parts, or to associate it consciously with its corresponding oral word. Any attempt at analysis, at first, weakens the action of the word, is entirely unnecessary and unnatural. Another great step was the sentence-method and this idea is a representation of the thought-method, and is pregnant with possibilities for the economical teaching of the first steps in reading.

I have very briefly indicated some of the struggles to find the way to the best method of teaching reading, many of which have been steps in progress, while others have simply gone back to the starting-point. The work of Comenius, followed by that of Gallaudet and Webb with the word-method, and Farnham with the sentence-method, have been tendencies in the right direction.[5] *The ideal method has not yet been attained; it can be reached only by a complete application of the law under which all associations are made.*

It must be established in all thinking minds beyond peradventure that pleasurable emotion must come from the arousing of appropriate activities;[6] that the difficulties may be overcome by the association of the word with the appropriate activities under the white heat of thought; and that the question left for us to decide is: How can the mental result of the appropriate activities be made most effective? Intensity of mental action consists in the holding of mental states in suspension—the hemming in, so to speak, of a mental state for the educative action of the ego.[7]

One cause of educative action is the will. The will may be controlled by present interest in the act itself or by anticipated pleasure. With the child, immediate pleasure must be the all-powerful motive of intense action; the motive must have for him an immediate content—interest. The greater the interest of the child, the more intense the action. The immediate emotional effect of the word in itself can be, at best, anticipated pleasure; under immediate pleasure, however, of which the appropriate activities are the cause, there is always an intensity of action. *The more intense the act of association, the less the number of repetitions necessary for the functioning of a word.*

I have already discussed at some length the spontaneous activities of the child. I have shown that the child is a born naturalist; that he loves both nature and human nature; that he revels in fancy, in the myth. I have shown that the child learns to overcome the difficulties of the oral language by that persistent energy which springs continually from desire and interest. I hold that the difficulties in the oral language to be overcome by the effort of the child are far greater than the difficulties to be overcome in reading. An oral word is far more complex than a written word. More than that, in learning the oral language a child overcomes a difficulty far greater than that of hearing words—the idiom, or peculiar relation of words to each other in sentences.

When the child comes to the learning of reading, he comes with the most important part of the oral language spontaneously acquired; he comes with his mind full of activities, full of experiences; he comes with the habit of learning language; and his everlasting question is: What is that? He is never satisfied until he knows the name of the object which excites his interest. Face to face with a new problem of reading, it seems evident that he should go on in the way that he has already begun the learning of language.

What is the greatest source of interest to the child? What does the child love best? I may seem heterodox in my statement when I say that the child loves best that which is best for him; he loves nature and he loves human nature. This statement may shock some persons who are continually looking upon the negative side of human nature, who see only the bad in humanity, whose commandments always begin with "Don't." The child is attracted only spasmodically and ephemerally to that which is bad for him; things which excite his sensuous nature, satisfy his hunger, or his desire for pleasure. A beautiful doll is but for the hour, and then packed away; but a doll which requires a long stretch of fancy to imagine it a human being is dear to the little girl's heart. The child loves permanently the best means for development.

The use of pictures and objects, as I have already said, is a tendency in the right direction; but we find in the study of the central subjects, in the study of geography, physics, mineralogy, and botany, an inexhaustible source of pleasure and of interest.

We see also that in the study of these subjects there is an organic growth and development of thought. Indeed, mental life is developing continually if the right conditions are used.

Language should grow with the thought itself; the language should be made a means of arousing thought in the child's mind and making new units or combinations by apperception of that which is already below the plane of consciousness. The studies of science, myth, and history are of inexhaustible interest and pleasure to him, and they develop his thought in the best possible way; when the thought is being developed, when the interest is most intense, the printed words may be associated with the greatest ease, that is, unconsciously associated.

Here I meet a strong traditional objection: the child learning to read only the printed words that spring from the immediate necessities of his thought would not fancy that he was learning to read; his parents would not think that he was learning, and the result would be dissatisfaction in regard to the school-work. I cannot resist here the temptation to lay down a rule fundamental in all education: *That which is best in education, that which is best for the body and mind and soul, is unconsciously acquired.*

No traditional opinion has a stronger hold upon many teachers and most parents than the supposition that the pupil must be painfully aware that he is learning;[8] that he must feel deeply the pressure of the amount of knowledge (*sic*) he is acquiring; that he should rejoice in the pages learned, the quantity memorized, the examinations passed, the promotions attained. A child skips home from the kindergarten, or from the primary school, and the fond parents ask, "What have you learned to-day?" "Nothing," is the reply; "I've had a good time." The despairing mother takes this answer in its most literal meaning, and seeks a school in which the weight of learning is measured, and progress definitely marked. No suspicion ever enters her head that the real indication of progress in character-evolution is not the record of pages learned, but in the acquisition of moral power, demonstrated in habits of action.[9]

I come back to my point of the intense mental action aroused by appropriate activities. From the time the child first enters school, the purpose of the teacher should be to continue in the best possible way the spontaneous activities of the child in the directions which nature has so effectively begun. We will suppose that he has lessons, experiments, observations, and investigations in all the central subjects; that they form the core of the work done by the teacher; that the child's mind, his whole being, is brought face to face with truth, and consequently with intrinsic thought; and that at the moment when the word is required it is given orally, and at once written rapidly in a plain, beautiful hand upon the blackboard. I am now speaking from considerable experience. The child is interested in the appropriate activities; they have been aroused in his mind, they have become intense, and just at the right moment the word from the blackboard acts upon consciousness, is associated with the appropriate activities, and one act of association is often sufficient for the functioning of the word. Not only are the words presented, but sentences showing what the child has discovered in experiment and investigation are also there.

It will be readily granted that a theory of teaching reading which adapts in the most economical way the conditions for the action of mental laws is of the utmost importance. Taking into consideration the vast amount of time spent in learning to read and the unquestioned pedagogical value of reading, an approximately true theory of teaching reading must be of first importance. In the history of education there are more theories and methods of teaching reading than of teaching any other subject; therefore, at the risk of some repetition, I shall present the theory of the method of concentration, for the purpose of giving a working hypothesis for your investigation:

First, under this theory, the entire time of the learners can be spent in the study of the central subjects. These subjects, if adapted to mental action, will excite and continually enhance interest. Second, the intrinsic thought developed will create the necessity for both spoken and written words and sentences, the latter to be presented to the child from the blackboard. Third, the teaching of reading is to be, on the part of the pupils, an unconscious auxiliary to the development of thought; the difficulties of the written and printed word will be overcome by the energy aroused by intrinsic thought. Fourth, the presentation of the words and sentences at the proper moment will serve to enhance the thought itself, because the printed words are made a necessity, and, as such, will react upon the mind and assist in mental action. When a sentence which has grown out of a child's investigation, and which has been made by the child, appears upon the blackboard and is read by the child, this action cannot fail to continue and enhance the original thought. Fifth, the teaching of the mere words and sentences in reading will take comparatively little time either of the child or the teacher; thus reading will continually serve as a means of enhancing thought.

This latter proposition, I grant, is indeed a very strong one, and it should not be accepted without the most careful study and investigation on the part of teachers; but I firmly believe that the proof of the theory is at hand.[10] It may be here asked why this theory has not been applied to any great extent. The greatest factor, hitherto, in all teaching has been the study of forms under the hypothesis that forms must be first learned by themselves for use thereafter in the development of thought-power. The history and present status of work under this hypothesis is well known to us as teachers.[11] The hypothesis under the doctrine of concentration is that *each and every step in the*

*development of reading-power must be taken under the immedi-
ate impulse of intrinsic thought.* Under the doctrines of concentration, reading is subsidiary and auxiliary to the study of the
central subjects.

Science in the elementary school is still an innovation, and, as
a rule, has been taught as a subject by itself. Many teachers still
consider it an intruder infringing upon the time of both pupils
and teachers. Yet countless opportunities for the study of science
and history, which require at every step the adaptation of language, exist; and there is no doubt that this learning of subjects
in relation to each other establishes a development of mind which
is organic.

This exposition would be incomplete without some reference
to the strong influence of expression upon the acts of association
required in the learning of words. The paramount act of expression which should follow and enhance acts of association is that
of reproducing immediately the word or sentence written upon
the blackboard by the teachers. The pupil sees the teacher write
the word rapidly and beautifully. His fixed habit of speaking
that which he thinks, and of imitating that which he sees, is carried over and made permanent in the habit of expressing thought
by writing the words he sees written.

I have discussed the marvelous facility with which the child
learns and overcomes the difficulties of the spoken language,
which are without question greater than those of the written or
printed language. We know that children will do wonderful
things spontaneously, unless a feeling of difficulty restrains them.
It is easy for a skillful teacher to arouse an intense interest in an
educative subject. Just at the moment when the interest is at its
height, she introduces a word orally, immediately writes it upon
the blackboard, after one glance by her pupils, erases it, saying,
"Say that with the chalk!" The little ones rush to the board and,
under a strong desire to express the thought, quickly reproduce

the word. The first attempts may be crude, but they are genuine efforts and with repetition will improve. Many children write words for the first time with ease, decision, and distinctness, when the unity of the action is unbroken by fear because the influence of the thought arouses the appropriate activities with which the word is associated.

Too often teaching of reading—in fact, teaching of every subject—consists in presenting difficulties and impressing children with the obstacles to be overcome, thus stultifying their otherwise free action. When a child attempts to write a word under the impulse of thought, the act of association is continued, made more intense and therefore more effective. He makes the word that is being functioned; this word afterwards will act upon the consciousness and recall its appropriate activities.

We all agree to the statement that the child's attempts to speak assist him in learning in the most effective way the oral word: this is as true of the written word. Carry the idea further: the child makes discoveries by his experiments in physics or by his investigations in botany; he wishes to tell something. He tells it orally, and is easily induced to express the same thing in writing. He goes to the board and tells what he has seen. He does this with great earnestness; there is a unity of action of mind and body, his desire to express thought overcoming many technical difficulties. In this way pupils may be taught to write original sentences, spelling, punctuating and capitalizing with complete accuracy.

Naturally the question follows from the teacher: What have you written? He looks at the sentence so fresh in his mind and tells his teacher just what he has written, in a perfectly natural tone, because alive and interested in the thought. This is the proper beginning of oral reading. The child, as he glances along, the sentences, may express his thought in the words he has already written, or he may express the same thought in other words. The effect of expressing his thought in either way, in the new words or the words he has himself written, is the same; that is to say, *the oral expression of thought enhances the thought itself, for it is genuine, and is the immediate reflex of his conscious activities.*

The oral word plays a very important part in teaching the written word. The child, when he enters the school, has mastered oral language adequate to his own thought; he can hear every sound in the language; he does not distinguish these sounds as separate and distinct, but hears the oral words as wholes—for all practical purposes, he is master of them: they act instantly upon the consciousness, and the appropriate activities are aroused—so that he knows each oral word. Further, he can use the various elements in the pronunciation of words with ease. Teaching is the presentation of conditions for the most economical educative effort. The effort of the child is directed to investigate, to experiment, to think under the highest effort of the mind, and the printed words or their correspondences in consciousness are thus melted, fused, and blended with the appropriate activities.

These acts of association are continued by the attempts of the child to express thought in written words and original, written sentences. To repeat a fundamental statement, everything that economically assists in acts of association should be used; everything that does not assist in such acts should be eliminated.

One cannot fully discuss the subject of teaching reading without discussing some of the arguments for the formal methods which have little and sometimes no relation to the thought itself; which propose to overcome the seeming but unnecessary difficulties of words themselves. To the "A, B, C"-method very little attention need here be given, except to expose this very important fact: When the child learns painfully one letter after the other, the names of which have no relation whatever to the pronunciation of the words, the whole attention of the child, so far as it can be gained by the energy, tact, and devices of the teacher, is

concentrated upon the forms of the words. By an artificial and
arbitrary method the child's power is sunk in the form. His whole
attention, whole conscious action, is absorbed in the form of the
word, and consequently the appropriate activities are left entirely
in abeyance; there can be no act of association when the child's
whole mental power is bent upon the forms of the words and the
parts of the words. In this intricate formal study there is little or
no educative mental action. No method illustrates this so strongly
as the A, B, C-method.[12]

The phonic-method, which succeeded the alphabet-method, as
before stated, was the first attempt to improve the latter method,
and its value consists in lessening the apparent but not real difficulties. In the word "method," the written word as a whole is
associated with the oral word as a whole; the child learns written
words precisely as he has learned oral ones. By the phonic-method
the pupil is trained directly and consciously to associate the separated and isolated elementary sounds of which the oral language
consists, with the separated and isolated characters of which the
printed language is composed, for the purpose of developing the
power of associating, independently, the sounds of words with
the letters, and by this means gaining independent recognition of
words. There are two ways to associate sounds with letters: The
first is independent of the written word, the pupil acquiring the
relation of sounds to letters without regard to the written words
themselves, so that the characters of which a printed word is composed may recall the corresponding sounds and thus enable him
to combine the sounds into oral words; the second is by teaching
sounds in direct relation to the printed words, pronouncing the
words slowly or spelling by sound. This is, I believe, a fair statement of the general processes of the phonic-method.

The written English language, however, is fearfully and
wonderfully made. Its spelling, or combinations of printed characters, is one of the awful and unnecessary obstructions in the

way of English-speaking children. A single sound must be associated with a number of characters, different letters, or combinations of letters. This great difficulty educators have sought to overcome by the introduction of phonetic methods of teaching reading.

It must be granted that phonetic methods can be used with great facility and great apparent results. A child who has nothing better to interest him will make out new words, however difficult, with marvelous ease by the skillful use of phonetic methods; but the same objection to the alphabet-method may be applied here— the child's attention is mainly directed to making the association between the forms of the printed words and the united sounds. The intense formal action of the mind hinders or prevents the appearance of the appropriate activities. By the use of each and all of the formal methods of teaching reading, a fixed habit of attention to the forms, and the forms alone, is the inevitable result. The spontaneous unity of action is broken and can be regained only with the greatest effort on the part of the victim. The miserable oral reading which is so common, and which teachers too often in the older grades hopelessly strive to overcome, is a direct product of this broken unity of action. The unnatural and monotonous tones of readers show that their attention is absorbed in form, and there is little or no free thought-action.

An argument very commonly and effectively used in defense of these obstructive methods is that if the child learns the words as wholes he will never acquire the power to make out new words. It has even been claimed that the word-method is a "Chinese method." Nothing can be farther from the truth than this ever-recurring stock argument. The printed word acts upon consciousness precisely like any other object. The power on the part of any or all persons to recognize new forms or new objects, units of attributes, whose elements lie below the plane of consciousness, is beyond all doubt. The child sees a new tree or a new face or a new house, which he recognizes instantly and discriminates from all other objects. The same can be said of words the child has never seen before. The power of association or synthesis is a fundamental power of the mind, ever acting spontaneously, ever recognizing and classifying by means of analogies. This may be illustrated by learning to hear language. Our spoken language consists of forty-two (more or less) distinct elements; the same sounds are ever recurring in new words acting upon the ear. When a sound is known, the recurrence of that sound in any word acts in the same way. The child is perfectly unconscious of any analysis, but the law of analogy, of synthesis, or apperception, powerfully and persistently acts, and thus the power to hear words is enhanced, and the process becomes easier and easier.

That which is true of the acquisition of speech is just as true of the acquisition of the printed language; whatever is spontaneously acquired in one form of language may be similarly acquired in the other. The word-forms of printed language consist of twenty-six characters. These characters are identical in an immense number of words, the same recurring in many words; the influence upon the mind of a familiar character in a new word is the same as in all the previously acquired words, precisely as the color red is instantly recognized in countless objects. Thus the "Chinese" argument has no foundation in psychology.

The many methods and devices—alphabet, phonic, and other schemes of teaching the first steps in reading—which entangle pupils' attention in word-forms and word-analysis are really so many obstructions to the development of thought power, and do not economically assist in thinking by means of printed words. Many inventions sought out and applied by teachers, with arguments which seem to be right, are really devices which defy the plainest and simplest laws of mental action. "There is a way that seemeth right unto a man, but the end thereof is death." If a child, acting under the energy aroused by the appropriate activities, through the study and investigation of subjects which arouse pleasant emotions, can learn the word immediately on its presentation, and can reproduce that word rapidly upon the blackboard, then the question of method is settled. He writes words without knowing the names of the letters, or without being able to analyze them. He does it spontaneously, in precisely the same way that he has learned to hear and to speak. Every word he writes, acting under the energy of appropriate activities, strengthens the association and prepares him for the learning of a new word. The beautiful, and the true, fact in regard to the method suggested, is that the child's mind is absorbed in intrinsic, educative thought, and the acquisition of words is incidental.

Still the question may be properly raised: *Cannot the power of the child to make independently the associations of new words with the appropriate ideas be enhanced? Is there a strictly pedagogical use of phonics?*

An oral word consists of one sound or a unit of sounds articulated in immediate succession. In words of more than one syllable there is a slight perceptible pause at the end of each syllable, and in uttering sentences there are also perceptible pauses between the words. A syllable is a unit of sounds uttered in immediate succession. Each sound requires for its utterance a definite position of the vocal organs. In order to utter each succeeding sound, there must be a change in the position of the organs; this change is made in time, and therefore, though the pause is imperceptible to the ear, there must necessarily be a pause between the utterance of two sounds in a syllable. If this imperceptible pause did not exist, there would be a great complexity of intermediate sounds which would modify the word radically. That these intermediate sounds do not exist is proved by the fact that if the words are pronounced with a perceptible pause between consecutive sounds children will understand them readily and will, indeed, perceive no difference between the common utterance of syllables and the slow pronunciation.* The child has power to hear oral words and to utter oral words. He has been in full practice for five or more years in this direction, and it is certainly not unpedagogical to pronounce words slowly before children—that is, with perceptible pauses between the sounds—and have them immediately recognize what is said. By repeating these processes in the first grade without any association with the printed words, the child takes a step in ear-training which will enable him to relate the sounds in words slowly pronounced.

By writing words the pupil gradually and consciously discriminates the characters that make up the word; and by holding in his mind the oral form of the word and intensely associating it with the written characters—a necessity in writing—the elements of both forms of the word reach a stage in consciousness when, by a little judicious, careful teaching, the power of analogy may greatly assist in associating the word with the appropriate activities. Little children will readily understand any word when pronounced slowly, if it is done naturally; and after a short practice in hearing-words they may be led to pronounce slowly themselves. Thus phonics may be effectively used without breaking the unity of thought and expression. Here, as in every method under consideration, the test is always as to whether it assists or obstructs the child in getting thought directly from the symbol.

It should be ever borne in mind that the real use of words is to arouse educative thought. There should be the least possible entanglement in the form of the word; the action of the printed word upon the mind should be instantaneous and effective. There should be the minimum attention to the word, the minimum consciousness of it. No one can observe the work of pupils from the primary grades to the university without being amazed at

---

* The term "slow pronunciation" is here used instead of "spelling by sound" of "word-analysis." It is a term used by the Germans, who have had most to do with the teaching of phonics—*langsamer Aussprache*.

the impotency of many to think by means of the printed word; the ability really to study text is rare, the ability merely to memorize words is common.

The study of text differs from common reading in the intensity of those acts of the will that hem the flow of consciousness. Now if the child early forms the habit of believing that he reads when he pronounces words—and by the tricks of the phonetic-method he can acquire great facility in mere pronunciation—there is great danger that he will never acquire the fixed habit of thinking by means of words. He will suppose that the pronunciation of words is reading, and that getting the reading content means committing words *verbatim*. This is one of the most terrible evils in all teaching—this habit of pronouncing and learning words disassociated from the thought.

The great benefit of the method of concentration in teaching reading here presented, is that the child will never fancy that he is reading unless he has the thought aroused by the words; if the words do not arouse the thought, he will struggle to that end, will read aloud with the closest thinking, and will study with the most intense thinking.

One awful product of isolated word-learning is the pedant, who fancies that he knows a great deal because he can recall a great number of pages. *The only valuable thing is the thought itself and the development of the reasoning powers.* Reading is accessory to these, and is a necessity at every step. Under the concentration-method of teaching, reading, written words, and sentences are made the immediate means of intensifying thought. The sentence which the child writes upon the blackboard, and the sentence which he reads from the blackboard, or from the printed page, immediately enhance the thought evolved by investigation.

The concentration-method of teaching reading proposes still more: It proposes that reading shall be used from beginning to

end, in the enhancement of intrinsic thought; that there shall be
no desultory or promiscuous reading in relation to education. A
child who learns to read properly will practice a great deal at
home; he will read books, magazines, and newspapers—and this
is good if the material chosen is appropriate.[18]

The great economy of these suggestions is apparent. The interest in reading will be continually strengthened, for no subject
can be really studied without a continual growth in interest. The
interest is excited, stimulated, and enhanced by the concentration
of all reading upon the cumulative processes of thought.

Most school reading is desultory, promiscuous, and unrelated
to the subjects taught; some of it is in a good sense educative;
much of it void of sense, and of no literary value whatever. The
proposition of the theory of unification is to concentrate directly
all reading—first, last, and at every step—upon the central subjects of study in hand: It proposes that geography shall be enhanced by descriptions of counties, travels, and stories; that
interest in science shall be kept aglow by delightful accounts of
research and discoveries; that history shall be illuminated by the
most precious literature, and explained by the mythical treasures
of the ages. When, for instance, the story of the first battle of
the Revolution is studied, the pupils shall hear "A hurry of hoofs
in a village street," shall see "a shape in the moonlight, a bulk in
the dark, and beneath, from the pebbles, in passing, a spark"
which "kindled the land into flame with its heat." Or when the
story of the Greeks is told, it shall be accompanied by the glorious
lyrics of Homer.

Nothing but good literature should be read by children. It
may be difficult to define literature, but briefly, literature is the
adequate expression of truth. The truth itself is beautiful, and its
expression should, therefore, conform to that which it expresses.
Literature is the genuine expression of truth, the pulsation of the
soul. Every sentence in literature says something. There are no

extraneous forms, no forms of speech without a direct purpose. Children should read only the best.

It is a common mistake to fancy that because children cannot pronounce every word, or because they do not understand the meaning of every word, they are not ready for that reading. Experience proves, beyond a doubt, that a child will learn words like "temperature," "aquarium," "hydrogen," "dissolved," just as easily as he does "cat," "rat," and "mat," if there is behind the long words an intensity of interest. It is the mental energy that impells the acquisition of the word. The mechanical learning excites the lowest grade of interest and energy. The question to consider is not regarding the size of the word, but the value and adaptation of the contents. *Reading is thinking, and not the pronunciation of words.*

The demand here made is, then, that from beginning to end the child shall *think;* that the action of his mind shall be upon that thought which he most needs for his own growth and development; that symbols shall act upon his mind immediately, attracting to themselves the least possible attention; that he shall early form fixed habits of thinking when he reads and of never fancying that he is reading unless he is thinking. Thus reading may be made, next to observation, the greatest means of mental and moral development.

[1] E. B. Huey, *Psychology and Pedagogy of Reading,* Chap. II.

[2] Wm. H. Kilpatrick, *Foundations of Method* (Macmillan), pp. 226-331.

[3] Already given in the discussion of Hearing-Language, pp. 180-181.

[4] Wm. H. Kilpatrick, *Foundations of Method* (Macmillan), pp. 45-53 (The physiological basis of learning).

[5] German teachers, Graser, Bohme, and others, have worked very effectively in this direction.

[6] Wm. H. Kilpatrick, *Foundations of Method* (Macmillan), p. 30, *law of satisfaction and annoyance* and all of Chapter II bears immediately upon this discussion.

7 "Direct immediate discharge or expression of an impulsive tendency is fatal to thinking. Only when the impulse is to some extent checked and thrown back upon itself does reflection ensue." John Dewey, *How We Think*, p. 64.

8 Dr. Dewey has dealt repeatedly with the false "analytic" methods of instruction in *How We Think*, see pp. 111-115; 214-217. "The ways of teaching criticized in the foregoing pages as false analytic methods of instruction all reduce themselves to the mistake of directing explicit attention and formulation to what would work better if left an unconscious attitude and working assumption." "To be forced to dwell consciously upon the accustomed is the essence of ennui . . ." *How We Think*, p. 215.

9 Wm. H. Kilpatrick, *Foundations of Method* (Macmillan), pp. 8-11.

10 This statement made many years ago by Colonel Parker has ceased to be hypothetical and the wonder increases that anywhere this theory is not being applied.

11 John Dewey, *How We Think* (D. C. Heath), pp. 51; 52, paragraph (b) "overdoing the mechanical and automatic"; *also see* E. B. Huey, *Psychology and Pedagogy of Reading*, pp. 348-349.

12 Colonel Parker recognized one practical use for learning the letters of the alphabet in order. Every child in the primary grades of the Chicago Normal School kept a *self-made dictionary* to which he added the new words which he would constantly use as they were functioned in his work. The dictionary was used for self-help, and all drills in spelling were based upon the childrens' dictionary lists.— F. J. C.

13 The need for home and school coöperation in the choice of reading material offered the children is obvious. This was a point much emphasized by Colonel Parker with both teachers and parents. "Children should read only the best literature adapted to their ages and interests."—F. J. C.

X

MODES OF EXPRESSION

ATTENTION and expression are the two processes of human action which have had most to do in the intellectual evolution of the human race. If we admit the working hypothesis of evolution, that man's physical, mental, and moral powers are products resulting from a long succession of acts of attention and expression throughout countless generations, we must admit that by attention the afferent nerve tracts were created and developed; that by expression the efferent nerve tracts sprang into being and power; and that the great central ganglion, the brain, is the product of continuous acts of both expression and attention.

If we are not prepared to grant this comprehensive working hypothesis of evolution, but prefer some other theory for the beginning of man, we must still admit that attention and expression have played most important parts in the development of the individual and of the race.

These two modes of human action, attention and expression, are organically related by motive. The motive for attention is found in the motive for expression; the demand for an act of expression is a demand for attention and reflection.[1]

Attention and expression together are the action and reaction of the whole being in mental and bodily movement.

Expressions may be generally defined as the manifestation of thought and emotion through the body by means of the physical agents. The modes of expression are:

Gesture	Making
Voice	Modeling
Speech	Painting
Music	Drawing

Writing.

All the works of man's hand and brain are the products of these forms of expression, of thought manifestation through the body. Language is by far the greatest outcome of thought and expression, and is at the same time the best means of studying human development in every phase; each word, each idiom, tells its marvelous story of the strife and struggle of the being in the effort to express thought. The language of a people is its ethnographic body created by its composite soul.

Next to language may be placed the tools and instruments which man has used through all the ages in manifesting his needs and his aspirations to others. Art products which manifest higher thought may be placed next, followed by construction, or building. From the latest modern edifice to the oldest ruin, we trace the growth of man's skill and intellect. Through these creations that have sprung from human life and human spirit we interpret and understand man in each and every stage of human growth and development. Language gives us the longest vista for interpretation; implements and instruments of use, the second; art, next; and last, the products of imagination expressed by building. Morgan, in his great work, *Ancient Society,* marks the transition from one stage of savagery or barbarism to another—the successive steps of lower civilization—by certain definite creations of the human mind. Thus the middle stages of savagery "end with the invention of that compound weapon the bow and arrow";

from savagery to barbarism, the transition is marked by the invention of pottery; and from barbarism to civilization, by the invention of a phonetic alphabet.

The aim of the ethnologist is to discover the products of man's skill all along the line of human development, in order to measure his physical, mental, and moral power in each and every stage. What has been said of the race is true of the individual; *all education is by self-effort; the two fundamental modes of self-effort are attention and expression;* the power of attention culminates in expression, and is interpreted by it; self-effort, in acts of attention and expression, results in enhancing physical, mental, and moral power. Sweep all the products of human expression, all the creations of the human mind, from the face of the earth, and the infinitely greater product will remain—the man himself, the developed creator, ready and able to recreate. Thus the history of the evolution of attention and expression is the inner history of the human race.

To include many specific questions into a more general one, we may ask the question: Has the exercise of each and every mode of expression been an absolute necessity in the evolution of the human race? We may contribute in some measure to this discussion by an attempt to investigate each mode of expression, in order to determine the factors which enter into each, and also, if it be possible, to understand the results of the exercise of each upon the whole being.

"Necessity is the mother of invention"; it is indeed the impelling influence to most human action. We can interpret the evolution of the modes of expression by understanding the motive which gave rise to them. *Motive* is the impelling power of all action, controlling and directing the will. The general content of motive is necessity, and necessity may have a physical, mental, or moral cause. Fundamentally, the motive of human action is self-preservation; a higher motive is the preservation of family; a still higher one, preservation of community, and desire for the best good of a nation; and highest of all, self-abnegation, the desire for the best good of all mankind. Out of the instinct of self-preservation probably all the motives for human action have arisen. Self-effort, impelled by motive and under the direction of the will, is intrinsic to development. Motive, the impelling power of all human action, is the main factor in human development. Human growth is measured by the quality of the motive— the higher the motive, the higher the human action. Motive determines method and controls result. The inner secret of all education may be found in the development of motive; motive which determines the kind and quality of thought, the method of action, the physical functioning, and the externalized thought. Expression, then, is fundamentally the means of developing that which is noblest in a human being—the impelling power to action. In all action under motive, the executive power of the ego, the will is brought into continuous exercise. In short, we can say with truth that there is nothing to be developed in the human being but motive; that everything else follows as a sequence; and, with equal truth, it can be said that unexecuted motive is negation of action, disintegration of thought processes.

Every act of expression must be preceded by certain definite thought processes; without thought, there can be no expression. The motive determines the intellectual action, and inspires that continuity or persistence of will which impels execution.

All acts of expression demand corresponding physical exercise; a particular agent of expression is called into play and is enhanced by the action of the whole body. The inward impulse finds expression in outward form; as the Creator manifests Himself to man through forms and qualities of matter, so man manifests himself to his fellow men by formal creations.

The externalization of thought is by means of the physical skill, whose developing influence upon the being may be briefly stated: First, the cultivation of motive, the intrinsic quality of the soul. Second, the demand for certain definite mental action; the intensification of that action as a preparation for expression; the enhancement of conscious activities by the reaction of the physical exercise upon the mind; and also by the continual conscious and unconscious criticism of the forms in the process of expression, leading to a reshaping of forms. Third, the continuity of will-action in the execution of motive. The will depends fundamentally for its power and continuity of action upon expression. Fourth, the exercise of the physical agents in acts of expression. This exercise is brought about by the striving of the will to make skill in expression adequate to thought; the health, growth, development, and elaboration of the body as an instrument of attention and expression depends mainly upon the variety, kind, and quality of acts of expression. Fifth, expression demands either reflection or attention, or both. Attention has for its basis the motive of expression. This implies that the trend of all human thought is toward expressive action; that thought which does not end in action dies or stagnates.

We have, then, as guides to the study of the developing influence of the modes of expression upon the race: *motive; thought and emotion; training of the will;* the perfection of the body as an instrument of attention and expression; relation of expression to the evolution or development of psychic power are elements operative in development of expression by the race.

Changes of the body which manifest mental states may be classified under the general name of *gesture.* Gesture comprehends what is usually called pantomimic expression, for lack of a better term; it includes, in fact, all the movements of the body, aside from the production of voice, which do not require artificial addenda or a tool, such as pen, pencil, brush, or other implement. Gesture, no doubt, was in the human race the primitive mode of expression. It marked the first glimmerings of intelligence, the dawn of mental power; its development has characterized each step and stage of progress; it is the one universal mode of expression common to all consciousness. And while its forms present definite limitations, it can still be said to have an almost unlimited range in the manifestation of conscious activities.

Out of this primitive mode of expression it is probable that all other modes of expression, with the exception of voice, music, and speech, were evolved. We can very easily understand how a gesture, a form in the air, might suggest a more enduring form traced in the sand or soft earth. As touch is probably the primitive and fundamental sense, out of which all the other senses have been evolved, so gesture, the primitive reaction of touch, is the germ out of which were developed making, modeling, painting, drawing, and writing. The actions of the conceptive modes of expression are the effects of touch upon a medium of sufficient density to retain the impression. It is an easy step from a form traced in the air to a form traced upon paper, or molded in clay.

At first, gesture enhanced the expressive power of the inarticulate voice. The rudimentary, inadequate speech of the savage is accompanied by descriptive gestures. Gesture supplies the missing link, enhancing at every step and stage the development of articulate voice, and remains to-day the greatest means of explaining and emphasizing speech. As a means of enhancing thought, it is comparable only to the voice emphasis itself. From the manifestation of the crudest thought to the emphasis of the highest intellectual action, the development of gesture as a means of expression may be traced. That which was the rude movement of the untutored savage has become the mode of expression that distinguishes the highest culture.[2]

The relation of gesture to *music* is exceedingly intimate. Gesture may be used to express the lowest possible acts of intelligence, but, like other forms of expression, it is capable of a development coördinate with the evolution of the highest thought and feeling. *Dancing* may be called the physical accompaniment or the gesture of music. It is a well-known fact that all religious music is savage, barbarous, and the early civilized stages of man was accompanied and emphasized by rhythmic bodily movements. I have already intimated the close relation of gesture to the art or conceptive modes of expression. It is but a slight step from a pure gesture to the expression of thought by means of an instrument—a stick, brush, or pencil; the same laws of physical movement which control gesture are equally applicable to the expression of thought in painting and drawing. The influence of gesture upon the development of the body is of the highest significance; ease, precision, equilibrium, the essentials of grace, are necessary to freedom of movement, and to mental and physical well-being. Gesture has a marked reactive influence in this direction upon the physical organism, enhancing skill, developing higher and more subtle coördinations. Grace, the economy of bodily action, by the nice adjustment and coördination of the agents of the body, is the main educative physical product of this universal mode of expression.

Voice may be classed in the same category as gesture; it is an open question which developed first. Voice, like gesture, is common to all consciousness, and both were probably the earliest, the best apprehended, and the best interpreters of human desires. Indeed, gesture and inarticulate voice, out of which were evolved all the other modes of thought expression, to-day remain the most effective means of expressing pain or pleasure, interest or indifference, attraction or repulsion; universal mediums by which the finer subtilties of human thought and passion stand revealed. Probably inarticulate cries and pantomimic movements of the body had a common and simultaneous origin, or at least immediately succeeded each other. Voice is in its very nature rhythmic, subject to inflection or cadence—the reflection of conscious action; the inflection of voice corresponding to the inflection of thought,

or emphasis. Gesture supplements the action of the voice, and
voice in turn supplements gesture. Out of inarticulate voice the
qualities of articulate sounds were developed; or, to state it better,
out of the crude qualities of inarticulate voice was evolved human
speech or articulate voice.

The instinctive rhythm of inarticulate voice led naturally to
the more pronounced rhythm of cadenced or metrical expression.
Rhythm is the inflection of sound; melody is the mode of inflection; and harmony is the unity of inflections. Vocal music is
voice, in which inflection, melody, and harmony are metrical in
a higher degree, with more pronounced intervals, than in voice
proper. Music is the means by which joy and grief, pain and
pleasure, ecstasy and woe, when all other modes fail, express
themselves.

> Thoughts hardly to be packed
> Into a narrow act,
> Fancies that break through language and escape,

find expression and voice in this most divine of all God's gifts
to man.

We are told that savages take the greatest delight in rude
attempts at vocal and instrumental music. Schweinfurth relates
that the cannibal in the heart of Africa will sit with a rude instrument of two strings and thrum all day long, filled with the
keenest delight. Music from the beginning has been used as
the distinctive mode for the expression of the deepest religious
emotions and the strongest sentiments of patriotism. The educative function of musical expression is to cultivate and enhance
those emotions which influence, in the highest degree, the motives
of man.

The relation of music to language is of the closest nature.
Music explains, interprets, and glorifies poetry; it is the natural

medium for the manifestation of poetic thought; it blends, harmonizes, and enriches the whole being. The highest formal beauty of *speech* consists in its rhythm, melody, and harmony. Vocal music, in the cultivation and development of the voice, plays a most important part, and its influence over speech is of immense value. When language fails, when argument is useless, the marvelous power of music comes in, with its persuasive, controlling, and compelling influence, arousing flagging zeal, developing enthusiasm, cultivating the highest religious feeling, and enhancing courage and heroic endurance.

That which is best for the soul is ever and ever the best for the body. Exercise in vocal music finds its highest physical outcome in the rhythmic articulation and adjustment of the agents of the body, one to the other, blending, harmonizing and strengthening them, furnishing, through reflex actions, a means for the development of their correspondence in all modes of expression. The rhythmic adjustment of the bodily agents or members is an important element of grace, and true grace is the highest indication of mental, moral, and physical power. The normal exercise of the vocal organs in music has a marked reactive influence in the development of the whole body, not only in rhythmic adjustment, but in the development of the lungs and heart. The utterance of musical sounds demands the perfect ease of bodily action, the unrestricted use of the lungs in breathing, and the normal circulation of the blood. In short, the exercise of the voice in music demands perfect physical freedom; the slightest tension, through dress or other restrictions, interferes with and prevents the free action of the voice.

In this brief outline of the educative effect of music, it may be said that an absolute necessity for the cultivation of the higher emotions is apparent. Without emotion man is nothing. What man is, depends upon the nature of his emotions. Music has ever been used effectively in arousing in him the highest aspirations

and the deepest reverence. The history of music is the history of
the development of the emotions of the human race from the
beginning. Music has, then, for its function the cultivation of the
spirit, or the higher development of the soul of man. We do not
mean by this fact that the highest may not be utterly degrading.
In fact, the rule is that the more effective any one means becomes,
when properly used, the more degrading that means may be
when it is used to incite in the human soul that which is low
and sensual.

It is a long step from the discussion of the purely spiritual
manifestation of thought through emotion to that manifestation
of thought which we term, though ambiguously, *making*. Making has for its general motive self-preservation, health, and the
general comfort of man; it supplies the great underlying needs,
which form the indispensable basis of his spiritual life. In short,
making is the material basis of life and living, the function of
the object made being essentially the practical use of that object.
Making may be defined as the complete externalizing of individual concepts—concepts acquired either by observation or constructed by imagination. When derived from observation alone,
the process of making is called imitation; when making is a
manifestation of an individual concept constructed by the imagination, the term creation or invention is used.

Attention has been called repeatedly to the products of man's
hand and brain—tools, instruments, buildings, and all the countless objects that have been evolved in human minds and expressed by human hands. The motive in making is the use of the
object made. The maker is impelled by necessity to realize the
function of the object made; his method of action is dominated
by the adaptation of the thing constructed to use. Such motives
are the most easily appreciated, most freely comprehended, and
therefore are adapted to the lowest orders of mind, the most
primitive stages of mental action.

The necessity for shelter stimulated invention. We can picture the early savage, from the suggestion of overhanging bank or hollow tree, digging a cave with his hands, or tearing off the dry bark for a rude refuge from sun and rain. The necessity for food led to the construction of a sling; the use of a stick suggested the manufacture of a club and a spear; and out of these evolved the still more highly developed weapons, the blow-reed and the bow and arrow. All these necessities of invention in making demanded exercise of the body, the mind, and the will, and were so many steps toward a higher development.

A brief analysis of making may be stated as follows: (1) the arousing of motive by means of necessity; (2) the concentration of thought in an individual concept to be expressed; (3) the steady exercise of the will in continued acts necessary for the externalization of the individual concept; (4) the physical exercise or use of the whole body in executing the demands of the will; (5) the continual criticism necessary for the exact adaptation of the object to its function. "The slightest change in form, or the slightest lack of the proper adjustment of parts, will," reasons the maker, "destroy or damage the design." The bodily exercise obtained by this complete externalization of individual concepts is of the most marked character. Aside from the motive of obtaining bodily sustenance, the human race, without doubt, owes its physical strength, its powers of endurance, its skill—in fact, that which is necessary as a basis of development—more to the exercise of the body in making than to any other cause.

Making, as a primitive and fundamental mode of growth, is close to the heart of man. Its motive is clear and most distinct; it acts for the preservation of self and the preservation of others. The intellectual action is in the beginning the simplest, most clearly appreciated, and the plainest product of observation and imagination. In fact, *making is the natural beginning and foundation of all the conceptive modes of expression.* It is nature's primary method of human growth, laying and building a sure foundation for higher action.

Making, modeling, painting, and drawing may be called the conceptive modes of expression, because individual concepts in each of these modes constitutes the bases of the expressive acts. In making, the concept is completely realized in an external object. By the other conceptive modes, the concepts are partially realized. In *modeling,* the concept is expressed in outward form of three dimensions; in painting, by colors; and in drawings, by lines and shading. Modeling, painting, and drawing are the art modes of expression. Making has for its motive practical use. The design of art is entirely limited to the expression of thought, the individual concept is a mental means or medium of thought expression; the motive and thought are embodied in an individual concept.

Man in the early mythical stage believed that all nature, and indeed all external objects, were animated like himself. He believed that sticks and stones, trees and streams, stars, moon, and sun exercised spiritual power over him—power that he must in part possess for his personal weal, else disaster would follow. He believed that the forms of objects embodied invisible spirits; therefore, in his first attempts at art, he endeavored to imprison and command the unseen powers which surrounded and controlled him. A model in clay, a rude paint-daub, to the savage's dawning intelligence, took away the invisible strength of the object. Certain Alaskans carved pictures of powerful animals upon their clubs to endow their blows with corresponding strength. Many savages, to-day, will not allow themselves to be painted or photographed from a fear that the picture will take away their power, or, indeed, kill them outright.

The claim that art sprang from the myth or elementary religion is a reasonable one. The main function of art expression in the past, and, indeed, until modern times, from the ugliest idol that ever frightened a poor savage into obedience, to the manifestation of redeeming love in the Sistine Madonna, has been the cultivation of fear, reverence, adoration, and love for invisible and divine power. The development and nature of the religions of the past are interpreted more through art than by any other means. The earliest use of secular art was the expression of character in individuals; the statues and pictures of statesmen. Then followed the representations of heroic deeds in order to stimulate patriotism, and lastly, the interpretations of nature and natural objects. True art has no other use than the manifestation of the invisible: in religion, divine power and love; in statues and pictures, character; in pictorial descriptions of heroic deeds, patriotism; in paintings from nature, the invisible life and power that animates all and breathes through all. Following and perhaps preceding speech, the pictorial mode of thought expression may be numbered among the earliest acquisitions of the race; out of pictorial expression was evolved a system of hieroglyphics, the beginning of *writing*.

In the relation of art to human evolution, there must be made the strongest discrimination between intrinsic art and mere imitation. Any imitation of a work of art, such as the modeling of idol or statue, the copying of painting or drawing, is essentially making; it is not art expression in any sense; it lacks the highest thing that is cultivated in art expression—motive. An Italian marble-cutter may copy the model of a great artist with complete accuracy, may chisel marble with the greatest skill, and never for an instant thrill with thought or emotion kindred to that which moved the soul of the artist; he may, indeed, work long years with the utmost faithfulness, and without a suspicion, even, of the motive which prompted the creation. Here imitation of art has no relation to art itself, and no educative influence. Imitation, whatever its kind or quality, is essentially making, minus the best thing in making—motive.[3]

In manual training the one motive of making is the function of the thing made; in art the one motive is to give to others a controlling thought, to embody this thought in an individual concept, and to externalize that concept by skill. The nobler the thought to be expressed, the higher the motive, the greater is the striving to make the expression adequate to the thought:

> The presence fair
> Of unachieved achievement, the high task,
> The struggling unborn spirit that doth ask
> With irresistible cry for blood and breath,
> Till feeding its great life we sink in death.

The difference is world-wide between the artisan and the true artist in the reflex action of thought power and skill upon the soul. A serious delusion regarding art lies in the belief that the mere mechanical expression of concepts is art. The modeling of cubes, spheres, and other geometrical forms is not art expression; it is mere copying, manifesting no thought except that expressed in the representation of a thoughtless concept. In the method of drawing, which consists of the imitation of flat copies, there is no art. Indeed, the teachers of such drawing are themselves, rarely artists. If they were, they would inspire their pupils to express educative thought—thought acquired by attention and reflection; they would understand better the organic relation between art and the central subjects of study; would see that the study of geography, of myth, and of history, furnish countless opportunities for its expression. The teaching of art is in its infancy; when it comes to its own and is used to reinforce and intensify the highest thought of the soul, its preëminence as a means of education will be no longer a matter of doubt.[4]

There may have been great artists who were educated through the technically accurate imitation of works of art; but, so far as I know, history fails to name one such artist.

To summarize: First, the strongest common factor in art is found in motive—the motive of manifesting the highest spiritual power, the complete expression of intrinsic personality. That which controls the being is the desire to make known to others cumulation and climax of thought.

Second, individual concepts are the mental means of embodying art ideals. Just so far as man manifests his thought to man through qualities of matter, just so far is he a creator; these creations of the artist finding their intellectual realization in units of elementary ideas, the creations and correspondences of external elementary energies. The individual concept is a means to an end; it is the symbol or medium of thought, and not the intrinsic thought itself. The fatal delusion of art in education lies in the belief that the mere mechanical expression of concepts is art.

Third, in art, thought is manifested through partial symbols, or the partial externalization of a complete individual concept. In modeling, the form corresponding to the concept is fully expressed, without regard to color; in painting, the expressed form consists of shades and tints of color; drawing is the modeling of form, in two dimensions; making is the complete manifestation of the concept. The external products of the four conceptive modes of expression have form in common; the differences consist in the kind and nature of the forms. In making, complete material is used in construction; in modeling, clay or similar plastic material needed to express form; in painting, color alone is used; and in drawing, the material is limited to crayon or pencil.

The variation in materials used demands an immense difference in mental power, or power of concentrating thought. The thought itself in each mode of art expression is similar, if not identical; but the less the quantity of material used in realizing thought, the greater must be the concentration of thought. The thought must be clearer or more distinct, the concept more definite, and the skill or physical exercise of a higher quality. The will, also, must be in more steady and continuous action.

The mere expression of the concept in itself has little to do with art; it is the character, the life, the power expressed by means of this thought embodiment that is the all-controlling motive. Clay, color, line are means to an end—the means of arousing in those who may observe the work of art certain thoughts and emotions, definite ideas of character, religious, heroic, patriotic. The true landscape painter reveals more of life and beauty in a landscape than a common observer gets from the real landscape itself. He interprets the hidden beauty and hidden power of nature to others. There would be no reason for art if art did not translate and transcend nature.

> "We're made so that we love
> First when we see them painted, things we have passed
> Perhaps a hundred times nor cared to see;
> And so they are better, painted—better to us,
> Which is the same thing. Art was given for that;
> God uses us to help each other so,
> Lending our minds out.
>   —From Robert Browning's, *Andrea Del Sarto.*

Art shows things to man which he cannot otherwise see. The true function of art is revelation and inspiration. Works of art have marked the highest spirituality in each stage of human evolution; they rank as the highest interpretation of human life.

In art an individual concept is a mental means of thought embodiment. In making, as I have already said, the individual concept is fully manifested in the expression; in modeling, the form corresponding to the individual concept expresses the thought. Plastic materials, like clay and wax, are used as the material for thought manifestation, and form is the result.

Through form invisible character is manifested. Next to making, modeling is the nearest adequate mode of expression; for form is the highest manifestation of energy. The physical training induced by modeling is the development of the tactual sense. Recalling the discussion of the place the sense of touch holds in its relations to intellectual power, it will be seen that there is no possible training of the tactual sense that equals this means of expressing thought.[5]

In painting, the medium of thought expression is color; that is, the expressed thought corresponds to the individual concept in colors alone. Probably painting followed modeling in the evolution of the primitive modes of expression.

We find in these four conceptive modes of expression a beautiful sequence in the means of thought evolution; when the concept is weak, and the being undeveloped, the means of thought manifestation must be the greatest. This condition is found in the materials for making; the next step in lessening materials is in modeling; still less, in painting; and least of all, in drawing. The hypothesis which I believe to be a sound one is, that the less material used the stronger must be the motive, the more concentrated the thought, and the more continuous and powerful the influence in acts of expression. All conceptive modes are related to each other by the common bond of individual concepts.

The physical training in art expression is of the highest and most delicate quality. It can all be comprehended in the word grace. Adequate skill in the manifestation of thought is the most exalted function of the human body. Skill is acquired by exercise in thought expression. The nature of the conscious activities to be expressed determines the quality of the skill. In the striving of the soul to make the expression adequate to the thought lies the highest possible and most educative exercise of skill.

Making requires the exercise of all grades of physical strength; the art modes demand the finest delicacy of touch. Modeling exercises that great intellectual sense—touch—in an incomparable way; painting requires still finer handling; and drawing, the most skillful of muscular power. Grace is diffused strength, diffused from a physical center of strength; the greater the central physical power, the greater the possibilities of delicate touch at the extremities. Delsarte's principle may be applied here: "Strength at the centre, freedom at the surface, is the true condition of being." The exquisite touch of the artist is applied grace, applied in enduring gesture. Grace requires the coördinated action of the whole body—the entire energy of the being acting in harmony—thrown into one act.

We can trace in the conceptive modes of expression a natural and indispensable sequence of human evolution—a harmonious evolution of the mind, body, and soul. Can one of these modes of expression be omitted without loss to the development of character?

The particular educative use of the art modes of expression is the concentration and idealization of thought; the expression of the most exalted states of the soul in the most defined way, appealing directly to that which lies in other souls. In speech, not only concepts, but judgments, sequences of reasoning, generalizations, classifications, are expressed. The intimate relation of the art modes to speech is obvious; art tends to concentrate thought in speech, keeping it from diffuseness and dissipation.

Speech is articulate voice, which no doubt was evolved from voice itself. Like every other product of the mind of man, it began in exceeding crudeness.

I have called the language of a people the ethnographic body of a composite soul. Words are pure symbols; they have no correspondence whatever to the thought expressed, unless we accept a few words that retain suggestions of onomatopœia. The individual finds a language ready-made for his adoption and mastery. Oral words are functioned by the hearing of language, and speech by their use in expression. Inflections—other than accent—emphasis, harmony, and melody, are spontaneous qualities of voice.

Speech, its acquisition and mastery of, is the most common and, at the same time, the most marvelous product of human energy. The mechanical obstacles to be surmounted exceed in difficulty any and all the other forms of thought manifestation.

The mechanism of speech is wholly a product of imitation; not the imitation of the movements of the vocal organs, for a child cannot observe them, but the imitation of elements in words, and the units of words in sentences. The acquisition of speech requires an immense amount of mechanical practice, but this incessant practice takes place, beginning with spontaneous, preliminary babblings, under the immediate impulse or desire to express thought. The indomitable energy that springs continuously from the ever-impelling desire to express thought, carries the little learner triumphantly over all the tremendous obstacles—tremendous in analysis—which lie in his path.

Speech has one predominant advantage over all the other modes of expression, with the exception of gesture, and that is the continuous and countless demands for practice. "Uebung macht den Meister," say the Germans. If other modes of expression, making and drawing, for instance, had as many demands and opportunities for exercise as speech, the skill in these modes would be as great as in oral language.

The speech of a child ever conforms to his thought power; words and sentences, subjects, predicates, and modifiers in all their varied forms and relations, simple and complex, spring directly from the exact nature of the conscious activities to be manifested. No words or sentence is ever learned solely for future use; step by step, language is acquired with thought and for thought. Any attempt of a mother to lay up in her child's mind a stock of language-forms for use, when perchance the fitting thought should come, would be futile.

As the language of a people is the positive indication of growth and of the stage of growth, so the language of an individual is a distinctive mark of culture. By this is not meant accuracy and polish of speech, but its power as a medium of thought expression. The motive of speech is the immediate conveyance of thought to others; the controlling impulse is to move others to a complete understanding of one's thought.[6]

Back of articulate voice which is strictly mechanical, impelling, enforcing, explaining, and emphasizing, lies voice itself, with its qualities of rhythmic inflection or melody, its unity of inflection or harmony, its major inflection or emphasis. Accompanying speech is gesture, or pantomimic movements of the body, emphasizing, supporting, and supplementing articulate voice. No argument is needed to prove the reflex action and influence of speech upon the whole being, mind, body, and soul.

Writing was the last mode of expression in order of evolution. The phonetic alphabet marked the transition from barbarism to civilization. Writing is an evolution from drawing. Picture-writing, or hieroglyphics, was the first graphic mode of expressing thought. Along the line of economy, hieroglyphics were gradually modified until letters were evolved.

The mechanics or forms of expression in penmanship are the simplest and easiest made of all the form in any mode, being a modification of the simplest lines of gesture. The forms of letters consist of straight lines and simple curves. The physical agents of writing, the hand and the arm, are the most complex and best developed joint-organs of expression, and, as a rule, are the most exercised, being used in all the modes of expression except vocal music and speech. In the conceptive modes, the forms of expression are governed by the concept; in writing, the simple forms of expression are fixed and ever recurring. The making of simple curves and straight lines is a very easy matter; the making of the words correctly, or the spelling, constituting the principal difficulty of writing. To English-speaking children the useless and monstrous incubus of unphonetic spelling is a needless and senseless barrier in the way of education.

It is true that devious methods and devices for teaching penmanship make this mode of expression often exceedingly hard to acquire: but here again the difficulties are not in the writing itself, but in the abnormal methods and devices used to teach it. Of devices for teaching writing, there is no end; and most of them cripple the mind and deform the body. Thank God, the method of teaching children to speak was invented before the schoolmaster appeared!

The main difficulty in writing is found in the nature of the thought to be expressed. In speech there is an immediate demand for expression, the impulse being quickened by the desire to make the person or persons addressed understand; in writing, this immediate stimulus is lacking. Speech may be fragmentary and disconnected; writing demands connection and relation. Speech may be brief; writing calls for sequence of thought. The motive in speech is immediate understanding; the written page is to be read after the work is done. The speaker watches the effect of his words; the writer must imagine the effect. The motive in writing is, in general, far stronger than that in speech; in the former there must be a steadier and more continuous action of the will in controlling thought power. Speech is strongly enhanced by the attributes of voice; writing stands alone in dead, cold forms.

The controlling motive in writing is that those not present may be reached by the thought expressed. Writing admits corrections and changes; vocalized breath dies on the air, and nothing but its immediate effect remains; writing may remain for ages. Speech and writing mutually enhance the power, each of the other. Speech may be enthusiastic and diffuse; writing, deliberative and concentrated. Speech affects writing by earnestness; writing influences speech by its slower and more cautious mental action. Speech springs, in the main, from loose or immediate thought; writing, as a rule, demands the closest study and preparation. Far fewer opportunities, as a general thing, present themselves for writing than for speech; therefore the latter is much more slowly acquired and less used by the masses. Speech has had a mighty influence in the development of the whole race; writing, of the few. The action of both has developed language.[7]

I have spoken of the relation of the modes of expression to attention and reflection. Expression is essentially doing; it is that toward which all human action moves, and, indeed, should move. Expression is ethical action; it should be the application of truth. Expression concentrates and focuses the soul; it reveals personality. The motive that controls attention and reflection is the motive to make others feel, think, and act in accordance with personal ideals. The motive of expression impels the soul to its best effort in observation, study, and reasoning.

The nine modes of expression have a most powerful influence each upon the others, and all upon each. Gesture, the initial mode, carries its influence over to the conceptive modes, enhances their power, and ever remains an incomparable means of discriminating the more subtle distinctions of thought and feeling. Voice is embryonic speech; its finest qualities are displayed in vocal music. Music, in turn, makes speech beautiful and breathes its rhythmic sweetness and power through poetry. The conceptive modes of expression develop concentration of thought; speech and writing expand and broaden thought; the art modes of expression—modeling, painting, and drawing—are three great steps in the evolution of man.

The proper and educative exercise of all the modes of expression presents the most vivid illustration of what Froebel meant by the "harmonious development of body, mind, and soul." Expression ever acts to develop motive; it makes the highest demand for thought power, and requires the most healthful exercise of the body. From the standpoint of race evolution each mode has been an essential factor in human advancement. It is hardly possible to imagine the omission of the influence of one mode without serious detriment to progress: Each mode is capable of almost infinite development. From thrumming on two strings to magnificent orchestration, music makes its way; making reaches from the cave to the palace; art from the rude daub, or the frightful idol, to the Venus of Melos.

From the race we turn to the individual; from general development to personal education. The exercise of all the modes of expression has been and is a necessity in the promotion of civilization.

The ideal of education controls both method and means. A republic can logically hold but one ideal and that is to make of each individual all that he possibly can be. Any stopping short of this ideal is impossible in the development of a people that shall rule itself. Personal freedom in the sense of personal struggle, in the sense of "working out your own salvation," in the sense of "The truth shall make you free," must from very necessity be the ideal of all who follow the Golden Rule, and find its application in true democracy. The high ideal of personal freedom gained by self-effort includes and comprehends all other and lower ideals—the practical ideals, the bread-and-butter ideals. Citizenship, in the best sense of the word, can be attained only by striving toward the highest goal. Those lower ideals are merely steps on the way to immortality. "Seek ye first the kingdom of God and His righteousness, and all these things shall be added unto you."

The manual arts have done more for the human race than

any other mode of expression. They are absolutely indispensable to normal, physical development; they have made for intellectual growth and have cultivated ethics as a basis of all moral growth. Handwork should be made an organic factor in all education from the kindergarten to the university inclusive.

We may profitably appeal from the theoretical side of this question to the lessons derived from experience and history. It is a well-known and oft-repeated fact that most successful men—bankers, manufacturers, inventors, ministers, lawyers, authors, and statesmen—received their primary education in the shop, or on the farm. Our country is full of examples of this kind. Handwork on the rocky farms of New England has given as much of moral power, sturdy integrity, and indomitable perseverance as have her famous universities. Follow the history of any family, rich or poor, the members of which disdain handwork for a few generations, and you find steady deterioration. War was once the resource of aristocrats; athletics is now taking its place. Without these substitutes for honest labor, poverty would have its perfect revenge. The erstwhile curse of man, "In the sweat of thy face shalt thou eat bread," becomes, in the light of fuller comprehension, his greatest blessing.

Sound health, a strong body, a persistent will, a logical mind, are some of the marked results of that manual training which springs from stern necessity. On the other hand, the world is filled with liberally educated incapables—men who have studied much and done little; who have never learned the lessons that lead to success—lessons of responsibility, persistent action, of direct application of effort to real conditions. There are ministers with an immense stock of words and phrases, lawyers without cases, physicians fortunately without patients, teachers helpless before work that requires original thought and invention.

Laziness is not the cardinal sin of the world—selfishness occupies that place; but laziness is the negative cause of many

evils which degrade and debase mankind. Laziness is an acquirement, a state of mind and body induced by wrong education, or
the lack of any. The child is a born worker; activity is the law
of his nature; helplessness is the product of too much help.
"Alas for the man who has not learned to work," says Channing.
The foundation of education consists in training a child to work,
to love work, to put the energy of his entire being into work;
to do that work which best develops his body, mind, and soul;
to do that work most needed for the elevation of mankind.

Education is self-effort in educative work. It is impossible to
do all-sided educative work without training in handwork.
Manual training is the most important factor in primary education and must remain a prominent factor in all education. Contempt for labor is an inheritance and a suggestion from the
ruling classes. The mere isolated study of textbooks induces and
enhances this contempt: the product is legions of men whose
main problem is how to avoid handlabor. Contempt for labor
is in the highest degree dangerous to society and to the cause
of democracy. Manual training cultivates love and respect for
hard, persistent work; and thereby it tends to cultivate a contempt for all human beings whose main purpose in life is to
avoid labor.

In large cities, vast numbers of children have nothing whatever to do—no farm, no workshops; children of poverty run
in the street and learn its awful lessons. The apprentice system
is a thing of the past; workingmen, to-day, generally do one
thing—make some one part of a machine. This monotonous
work is anything but educative. If a manufactory closes and
these laborers are thrown out, they are helpless generally; their
trade habits are fixed—they can do nothing else, and they fall
a burden to charity or a prey to hunger. Educative, all-round
manual training develops the habit and skill for all-sided work;

it makes the worker capable of doing new tasks and attacking new conditions.

Manual training has a moral tendency. Vice, intemperance, and crime are the fruitful products of laziness and contempt for work. It may be said that many children have plenty of manual training at home. Then I say, exalt and dignify it; enhance skill by recognizing and emphasizing handwork in the schoolroom.

There is not time for such work when so much unrelated spelling and isolated arithmetic must be learned. *There is time for but one thing, and that is to form habits consistent with the highest type of manhood, and to supply the most pressing* needs of society. The shorter the time a child spends in school, the better the quality of work he should do. Compare the boy who steps from school with the ability to read a little, to cipher fairly well, and to write legibly, but who has never learned to work, with one who has formed habits of work, who has learned to observe, whose curiosity is whetted, who has acquired something of manual dexterity, and is controlled by a deep love for expressing thought with his hands. The boy with the words, number-tables, and penmanship may read himself to ruin, write himself to Canada, or cipher himself to perdition; while the boy who loves work and knows how to work will be apt to educate himself, and at the same time give society the benefit of a life of hard and useful labor.

There is no conflict, really, between manual training and the so-called fundamental studies. The energy and vigor, moral, mental, and physical, acquired in manual training, may be carried into all studies. Education is not so much a matter of times as of quality. In manual training there are the best lessons imaginable in form, geometry, and practical arithmetic. Manual training is primary logic, so much needed in speech and writing. Manual training trains the will by persistent effort, stimulates the critical faculty, and, above all, develops ethical motives.

The reason why manual training makes its way so slowly into schools is plainly that many teachers have spent their precious time in preparation for verbal examination, and therefore have never been trained themselves to skilled habits of handwork.

In regard to the art modes of expression, I have already suggested the arguments. On the practical side, there is much to say in favor of modeling, painting, and drawing. There is never a day in a useful man's life when the skill, taste, and critical power acquired by the exercise of one or all of these modes is not called into practical use. There is no trade, business, or profession in which the results of art, skill, and study do not essentially and practically assist. What are distinct concepts of color, form, symmetry, proportion, to the carpenter, architect, designer, shoemaker, tailor, dressmaker, gardener—in fact, to every namable trade in this world? Reading, writing, and arithmetic are called the tools of learning; but educative practice in art is learning itself.

Mistaken vocation is one of the saddest results of mistaken education; there is always ideally some vocation for which a person is best adapted. To find that calling is blessedness; to mistake it is misery. Education should be the unmistakable guide to vocation. There is many a minister who could pound hot iron on an anvil to far better effect than he pounds the pulpit-cushions; and there is many a sturdy blacksmith who could make an audience thrill with love of God and man, if he had found his way to the pulpit. Countless young men leave the free life of the farm to become counter-jumpers and writing-clerks. Education turned their eyes away from the possibilities of the soil and the advantages of handwork and fixed them upon the city as the land of promise. Education with low ideals has a hypnotic effect upon its victims. The varied yet unified work which the proper exercise in each and all the modes of expression gives will have a strong tendency to lead the worker to the right vocation—that vocation in which he will be of the greatest use to the world.

Through expression, the teacher studies the pupil, his thought, emotions, willpower, special aptitudes and controlling motive. Verbal memorizing offers very meager opportunities for this extremely instructive study—a study which directs adaptation to individual needs. Exercise in all the modes of expression opens the child's soul to the fullest and freest inspection—an inspection to a keen-sighted teacher which leads to correct judgment and the most useful adaptation of means.

We must conclude that the use of all the modes of expression is an imperative necessity in all-sided growth, in the realization of the highest possibilities of manhood and character.

The reasons for this conclusion may be summed up as follows: First, true education makes a human being of the greatest possible use and benefit to mankind. The central-point and sole purpose of education is to make the highest motive a fixed habit. Motive is cultivated by righteous action. "He that does righteousness is righteous." All righteous action culminates in expression. Skill in each mode of expression gives a person greater power to do good. Ethical training consists in doing the right thing in the right way under the right motive. Expression is the supreme means of developing motive, and motive determines the right method.

Second, the intellectual effect of acts of attention is to intensify consciousness—indeed, all the power of the mind. Each mode of expression has an especial and indispensable function in intensifying thought. I have characterized thought intensity, given an educative subject, as the highest moment of educative action. The demand for expression is a demand for attention or reflection, or both. The central subjects of study present the conditions for study; the different modes, the conditions for the expression of the thought thus acquired. All subjects of expression may be limited to the study of the central subjects; taking anything outside of that wide range is unnecessary, and a waste of time.

Third, physical training has for its sole end and aim the development of the body as the most perfect possible instrument of attention, reflection, and expression. There is not, neither can there be, any physical training comparable to exercise in acts of expression under all the modes. Steady exercise in one mode limits and narrows physical power rather than extends it; the exercise of each and every mode of expression brings into full play all physical agents—thus the conditions and adjustments of certain muscles are enhanced by the healthy exercise of the whole body. Physical training *per se* is too often made a substitute for wholesome play and purposeful effort of children.

On the practical side, the exercise of all the modes of expression prepares the individual to be of the greatest benefit to mankind.

The pedagogical value of training in all the modes of expression may be briefly stated:

(1) The child's individual concepts are very simple and crude; he has no complex concepts.

(2) The fundamental use of exercise in all the modes of expression is to intensify those individual concepts upon which analyses, comparisons, classifications, original inferences, and generalizations depend.

(3) Concepts are developed slowly. The demand for expression should be adapted to the growth of concepts. Any attempt beyond this limit cripples mental action.

(4) The difficulties of technique or skill are very much overestimated. The reason for this overrating is that attempts are commonly made to make forms of expression without adequate

motive and unimpelled by thought—forms that have no thought correspondence.

(5) If, in the studies of the central subjects, all the modes of expression are continually and skillfully used to intensify thought, every child would acquire proficiency in them.[8]

[1] John Dewey, *How We Think* (D. C. Heath), pp. 189, 192.

[2] Rugg and Shumaker, *Child-Centered School* (World Book Co.), Chap. XVIII, "The Children's Theater."

[3] "Creative Effort," Vol. VIII of *Studies in Education* published by the faculty of the Francis W. Parker School of Chicago.

[4] Rugg and Shumaker, *The Child-Centered School*, Chap. XV, "The Copy Book Regime in Arts"; Chap. XVI, "The Creative Artist Enters the Classroom."

[5] *See* pp. 42-44 of this volume.

[6] John Dewey, *How We Think* (D. C. Heath), p. 170.

[7] Rugg and Shumaker, *The Child-Centered School* (World Book Co.), pp. 244-263.

[8] Rugg and Shumaker, *The Child-Centered School* (World Book Co.), Chap. XIX, *"Psychology of the Creative Art."*

XI

UNITY OF EXPRESSIVE ACTS

ECONOMY of energy is the method of evolution in matter and life; economy is the distinctive mark of all progress. The highest outcome of invention, machinery, and scientific discoveries, is the utilization of force. The process of education consists in economizing personal energy; it means using to the greatest advantage, and with the slightest possible expenditure of power, the whole being—body, mind, and soul. Economy of personal energy is freedom, and freedom is conformity or obedience to God's laws. Personal liberty is self-effort unrestricted by anything but the laws of being. Strict obedience to law is the highest economy of self-effort. Every human being is endowed with a definite amount of energy; the problem of education is how to use that energy for the full realization of possibilities.

In education the being moves to higher planes of thought and action by sinking lower planes into the automatic; consequently a useless expenditure of energy upon lower planes obstruct normal upward movement. Over-effort and useless striving keep the mind too long in one stage of development, and cripple its action in higher stages. Education is the economy of self-effort. In the strongest and most effective action conforming to law, there is the greatest economy. We find the supreme rule of self-effort in unity of action—the culmination of economy.

I have already spoken of unity of action in attention; but

this law has a far higher application in acts of expression; higher because the end and aim of human life is expression.

By unity of action in expression is meant the functioning or use of the whole being in one act of thought manifestation in order that motive, conscious activities, physical action, and external form shall follow each other in immediate and uninterrupted succession; that from motive to form, impulse shall follow impulse without the slightest break or pause; that the agent or medium of expression shall not absorb the attention of the ego; that consciousness shall not be divided; and that the body shall act simply as the agent, medium, or instrument of expression. It is the function of teaching to present educative conditions for effective acts of consciousness needed for the highest self-effort. Training consists in presenting the best conditions for the development of the body as a medium of attention and thought expression.

Perfect skill is the adequate manifestation of the soul. The training of the body has for its purpose the complete domination of the body by the ego; when this control of the body is normal, its reactive influence upon the mind is healthy, rational, and effective. The perfection of skill consists in the precise, immediate, and automatic response of the body to the mind; any failure in such response requires undue effort to overcome obstacles in the agent, and renders the act partially or wholly abortive. In unity of action, the particular agent of expression never acts isolated and alone; it is reinforced and energized by the entire organism, under the direct and full command of the ego.

Grace is the outcome of physical and mental strength. It has its source in the depths of being; it diffuses itself through the extremities and is manifested in lines of beauty and power. The elements of grace are ease, precision, and equilibrium. Ease is the greatest economy of physical action consistent with the most effective expression; precision is exactness and accuracy in skill; equilibrium is the diffusion of that energy which conduces most strongly to the enhancement of a particular act of expression. Ease, precision, and balance make adequate skill possible. They are the physical conditions under which the ego is enabled to concentrate or throw all its energy through the agent functioning the thought, thus economizing to the full, self-effort. Restriction, tension, or effort to act renders poise impossible, and is indicated by the absence of grace, or awkwardness.

Illustrations of the beautiful law of ease and equilibrium are abundant. Some of them may be given:

(1) Self-poise in danger is the infallible sign of courage, enabling one to reflect with lightning-like rapidity, and to throw energy where it is most needed.

(2) The more easily the rifle rests upon the arm or is held in the hand, the better the aim. The same fact is true in the use of all tools and instruments.

(3) The plowman in a stumpy field lets the plow handles roll in his hands in order to meet shocks and control the implement most effectively. If he tries to hold the plow itself, his strength is quickly exhausted.

(4) The first lesson a mower must learn is to hold the snath nibs with the least possible pressure; undue pressure reacts and weakens the center of strength.

(5) The blacksmith swings a heavy sledge

With measured beats and slow.

He holds the hammer handle loosely in his hands, and is thus able at the exact moment to concentrate energy.

The illustrations in this direction are unnumerable and universal; the wood-chopper swings his ax with the slightest muscular tension; the skillful driver holds the reins with the least possible exertion; the skillful penman lets the holder rest in his hands; in walking, the whole body must be mobile and elastic. Untrained, awkward novices in handwork are generally lacking in harmonious action and waste a vast amount of energy in overstraining and exhaustive muscular tension.

Grace is the product of unity in continuous acts of expression; awkwardness results from broken unity. It is not possible to secure true grace by mere physical training; grace has its source in the soul, and must spring from that center. The order of succession in development is first equilibrium, then ease, and last precision. Equilibrium is the indispensable condition of ease, and ease, of precision. Rhythm is the harmony of ease, balance, and precision. If habits of precision are made the initial steps in training they must be broken down before there can be any successful cultivation of grace. The thoroughly trained soldier is an example. A Prussian officer is generally a perfect illustration of trained precision—stiff, ungainly, and abnormally precise—a machine rather than a man. Precision aims at training the extermities, the limbs, legs, arms, hands, and head. Delsarte's statement of expressive power is: "Strength at the center, freedom at the surface, is the true condition of being." External grace or power is a product of the whole. From brain to spinal cord, physical power by proper exercise is gradually diffused over the whole body, reaching the efficient agents of expression last. Attempt to train the extermities—the fingers, for instance—before there is due strength at the center, and the result is a knotting and a tension of muscles that compress efferent nerve tracts. The inevitable result is the obstruction of free action from the center, and the body is thus weakened by abnormal reaction. A person who learns to write by the finger movement must later overcome a fixed, unnatural habit, before he can ever make a smooth line, the infallible indication of ease.

Precision as preliminary training isolates agents of expression, cuts them off from the reinforcing action of the whole body. We have seen singers trained to use the organs of voice alone and isolated, and penmen who wrote with cramped fingers. The imperative rule for an adequate act of expression is that the whole body, every muscle and fiber, is concentered upon the act; a person should sing, write, speak, by means of the freest action of the entire physical organism. When agents are isolated by premature attempts at precision before poise and ease of body become habitual, the inevitable knotting and tension of muscles react, cripple the body, and constrain the mind.

One marked indication of unity of action in expression is genuineness. In genuineness, the forms of thought manifestation are recognized as the direct reflex of the mind; no matter how crude the expression may be, there is not a superfluous word, a line too many; there is no waste of breath, ink, clay, or paint; words are used to reveal, not to conceal, thought. Genuineness means a transparent, truthful soul, and a body through which the soul shines.

Little unspoiled children are the best illustrations of unity of action. Listen to children's voices while at play—perfect melody, harmony, emphasis, and inflection, the pulsations of their joyous souls. Watch their movements in walking, running, skipping, hopping and dancing; their gestures are in broad lines, full of unconscious grace. The agents of expression and locomotion are harmoniously adjusted and coördinated. Indeed, that which the child acquires spontaneously and instinctively, the orator seeks to acquire by long and arduous training. The best of our orators, under the impulse of a dominating motive, have the ease and power of expression that is characteristic of childhood. This spontaneity was the great charm of Wendell Phillips. I have seen him stand upon the platform with perfect poise and perfect ease, every muscle flexible, mobile, under absolute control, and still the whole being so abandoned to thought and feeling that the throbbing of his great heart, instinct with an all-controlling motive, found instant and complete expression.

The actor as well as the orator strives for this same unity of action on the part of body, mind, and soul. Indeed, many seek for this, the perfection of art, "but few there be that find it." "The highest art is to conceal art." And among actors Salvini may be cited as a nearly perfect exemplification of the actor's part.

A person under a strong impulse to do a courageous deed will suddenly acquire unity of action. The cry of fire is heard; the brave man forgets himself, he acts under the highest impulse, using his powers to the greatest advantage. The untried soldier marching to battle often presents the very opposite. He is dominated by fear; his soul seems separated from his body, and his thought is riveted upon the danger which will come in deadly wounds or immediate death. But if this terrible fear is overcome, as it will be if the soldier marches straight ahead, then comes the soul again, the full command of the body, and heroic, almost superhuman deeds are the result; death is nothing, victory is everything.

One can present far too many illustrations of broken or impaired unity of action. I once knew a school that was famous throughout New England for its so-called copperplate writing. The children spent much time during six years in making the forms of writing. Their motive and their intellectual action were absorbed in one purpose—that of making painfully accurate forms, slowly drawing these forms by single letters, words, and meaningless sentences; and in this they really had succeeded. Their writing was the wonder and admiration of all who saw it. A devotee of that plan myself, I proposed to test its efficacy still further. I read to the pupils of the eighth grade a simple, interesting little story of about one page, gave them paper, and then asked them to tell the story, themselves, in writing. The result was disastrous; the writing was nearly illegible, and the spelling wretched; in fact, the whole execution was disheartening to any teacher who had toiled and moiled for long years to train pupils to make these so-called beautiful forms. The reason for this terrible waste of energy is not far to seek. There had been no unity of action on the part of the pupils, and when that was required it was not forthcoming. The teaching had violated the first principles of Mother Nature, under whose skillful training the children had been from the first babble to the mastery of the common idioms of the language. *Writing had never been used as a medium of thought expression.*

Experience brings home the crippling effects of broken unity. Too often the end and aim of oral reading is the perfunctory pronouncing of words, to which is often added an arbitrary, unnatural, and worse than worthless emphasis. In the very tones of the child's voice, in its artificiality, the wide departure from the normal is apparent to all teachers who love genuineness. The child's whole being is absorbed in the pronunciation of words, and poverty of thought and imagination results.

The broken unity so fatal to education, reaches its climax and culmination in many of our so-called lessons in elocution, in which enunciation, emphasis, pauses, pitch, stress, and all the countless contrivances and devices to depress and distress the souls of children are unmercifully used. To add to this misery, gestures are taught! Heaven save the mark! A "made" gesture is a frightful caricature of thought. It is enough to make Delsarte turn in his grave to hear his name used in connection with such ignorant, unpedagogic teaching. A child never makes the slightest mistake in emphasis or gesture when his own thought controls the action. Emphasis is the spontaneous discrimination of thought; thought emphasizes itself.

The verbal recitation of memorized words and pages is another extremely successful device to break down and destroy unity of action; and when this dull drudgery is stimulated to the highest degree by fear of punishment or hope of reward, its destructive influence is most complete. The entire being is concentrated upon the physical exertion of pronouncing and repeating words recalled from an otherwise barren mind. A student who has had twelve or more years of this process, wasting energy in this terribly extravagant way, has little power to relate words to thought. Ask him a question, and if perchance it falls within his verbal horizon, he fishes it out; otherwise, he is helpless. This is true in a marked degree of students who have been eminently successful as word memorizers.

The normal healthy action of mind and body is damaged, often irretrievably, *by concentrating attention and effort upon the acquisition of forms of expression, without relation to thought*. A brief and partial list of the devices for dead-form learning, selected from a much larger list, may come in place here:

(1) The alphabet-, phonic-, and phonetic-methods applied pure and simple, with the least possible regard for thought.

(2) Penmanship acquired by drawing, letters, words, and sentences, followed by long and painful exercises in copy books.

(3) Flat copy drawing—or better, imitating with painstaking accuracy meaningless forms made by machines upon paper.

(4) Modeling spheres and cubes without adequate motive.

(5) Oral reading which consists in pronouncing words with the addenda of artificial and false emphasis.

(6) Formal exercises in elocution, of pitch, quality, emphasis. Dramatic expression taught through affected gesture and poses given to music.

(7) Learning *verbatim* number-tables, and "doing sums" disassociated from activities which demand judgment and reason.

(8) Page learning and word repetitions disassociated from thought.

The pupils to whom I have alluded as models of acquired skill in word-form drawing were called upon to think a little, and force the thought over unused and therefore unrelated nerve tracts. The word forms vanished like the mists of the morning, spelling acquired by years of practice failed to rise above the plane of consciousness, and the undesirable result was but an added proof that unity of action must be preserved in all acts of expression, else time and energy is wasted in an unnatural and useless struggle. The conclusion is inevitably forced upon us, that forms of thought expression, or skill, can only be economically acquired by the united action of the whole being; and that intrinsic thought must be the impulse, and controller of the agents, and the true basis of form in criticism.

Self-consciousness is the sad result of making forms for forms' sake. I do not use the term self-consciousness in a strictly psychological, but rather in a popular sense. True consciousness of self which leads to self-confidence and a proper self-assertion, is the antipodes of self-consciousness in its popular meaning; the latter either utterly damages and destroys confidence of self, or leads to the equally undesirable emotion of self-conceit. Self-consciousness, so-called, is the partial or complete absorption of mental energy in attention to the physical agents and forms of expression in attempted acts of thought manifestation. A "made" gesture is a striking illustration of self-consciousness—a speaker watching the movement of his arm in the air. The orator who listens to his own voice, and admires it, has an audience that listens to empty sounds. Screaming, yelling, and bellowing in public speaking are means to calm the fears of a speaker, all too conscious of himself. Pronounced rhythm or sing-song is a rut into which a scared orator glides, to keep himself from "going to pieces." Affectations of all kinds—lisping, drawling, overstraining, and the like—all spring from an over-attention to agents of expression. Cant and hypocrisy lead to fixed facial grimaces, habitual attitudes and bearings, constant muscular tension, the outcome of effort which strives to impress the "truth of a lie."

All the physical features and traits of pedantry spring from an overpowering desire to impress others with a belief in one's profound erudition and intellectual superiority; many men are marked and scarred by steadfast and continuous efforts to bear silent witness to others of personal piety or unlimited wisdom. The distinctive indication of this is precision of muscle; fixedness and habitual tension of the whole body devoid of grace, and expressive of a soul devoid of harmony. Such pedants too often find a ready market for their wares; the world is apt to take men at their own valuation, letting the men who think and doubt— doubt because they think—wait for centuries.

Self-consciousness is very easily cultivated. A little girl comes in; her voice is music, her movements poetry, her body responds to her soul like the strings of a harp to an artist's touch. Some thoughtless person exclaims, "Oh, what a lovely girl! What an exquisite voice!" The sharp little one hears, alas! and understands. "I am lovely, I am lovely," rings in her ears and sinks into her soul. The reaction is over-attention to body; she listens to her own voice; she watches her own motions; unity of action is destroyed; self-consciousness, affectation, cant, and awkwardness mark the awful transition. A boy, owing to his divine nature or unconscious growth, does some genuinely good deed. "What a good boy!" is his reward. "I am a good boy; if I do good people will notice and praise me; I'll do good for approbation." Genuine goodness moves out, and pious cant moves in.

Public declamation by little children is another fearful cause of self-consciousness. Too early public declamation has given to the world some frightful specimens as orators, and deprived it of countless good ones. I know a highly educated man of noble heart, whose soul is full of human kindness, but whose manner and conversation is often brusque and even coarse; the secret of this manner is timidity. We often deem a loud-voiced public speaker self-conceited; too often he is struggling with self-consciousness, striving to drown his fears in billowy waves of sound.

Why should it not be as easy to speak in public as in private? The answer is "Fear!" We think of the attitude of our bodies when we stand, are painfully conscious of the forms of speech; attend to the expression alone, until we repress, paralyze, and stultify all freedom of action. An otherwise graceful person may be overcome with fear on entering the presence of some person of exalted position. The moment the room is entered attention is entirely directed to personal appearance; how the hands shall be used; how the head shall be carried; the tongue loses its cunning; the feet refuse to move; in short, body, mind, and soul are paralyzed. I suppose there is no one who has not at some period in his lifetime experienced this woeful lack of dignity, this quailing of the soul before some bugbear of the imagination. The reason why many teachers' meetings are fruitless and flat, is that those present painfully strive to formulate thought, fail, and decide to let others do the speaking. "We are modest, we are! Let bolder ones speak; we will sit still." "Do not deceive yourselves, my brothers: it is pride, not modesty, that controls you. You fear that you will make a mistake, and therefore you are modest."

The evil effects of self-consciousness may be particularized: The most common effect is an abnormal fear before expressive acts that are in themselves exceedingly simple, a fear which induces temporary constraint of body, and inhibition of mind. We are all more or less victims of this form of self-consciousness; illustrations are not far to seek. Did you ever go to the blackboard to write a word—"received" for instance—and suddenly doubt whether the form is "ei" or "ie"? Have you ever taken a written examination upon which much depended, and for a moment forgotten all that you ever knew? Did you ever come before a person in authority and wish to explain something of great importance to yourself, and have your tongue cleave to the roof of your mouth? Were you ever suddenly asked a question in company which your very anxiety to answer prevented your answering? Were you ever asked the name of a person whom you knew intimately and however you might struggle to recall it, the name refused to come? Were you ever speaking in public, and all at once wonder if you were making a favorable impression?

Most stammering, stuttering, and hesitations of all kinds are results of an over-attention to forms of speech; there is also stammering of the mind from the same cause. Self-consciousness breaks the connection between thought and action. Constant repetitions result in lack of control of the hand or vocal organs, and induce an unnatural habit of action; attention is entangled in the functioning; the difficulty of making the required forms constrains the mind, and fear, the most perilous of all emotions, not only hampers and hinders expression, but through continual failure lessens activity and renders our best efforts abortive; in short, "makes cowards of us all." We do not dare to read aloud, to speak or sing in public; we shrink from writing and drawing because thought of such action suggests mistakes and failure; the form of the thought is ever before us, a terrifying specter. Fear that is a direct product of self-consciousness obstructs growth and diminishes personal influence.

A still worse outcome of self-consciousness is self-conceit. There is a certain and common type of mind sparsely endowed with original talent, that has, as a poor substitute, great facility in memorizing and repeating words. Such verbal wonders are the delight of teachers whose ideal is quantity of knowledge. They are filled with flattery; but they find their fatal mistake when the stern problems of active life confront them. Fear may be overcome by persistent effort, for fear is backed by conscience, but self-conceit well-nigh seals the doom of its victims.

It is hard to reconcile the demands of some of our schools with the demands of life. Many of the most successful men in real life, it is well known, were looked down upon as hopeless dullards in school, frowned on by the teachers, driven out by per-cent examinations, and mourned over by loving parents. Such boys are called stupid or worse, because a divine instinct prevents them from trying to learn words and "do sums" which to them are meaningless. Blessed are geniuses who find the thought in everything, no matter how much "the method" stands in the way!

Too many prizes, rewards, and high per-cents, are given for this mind-stupefying work. Practices in each and every mode of expression is too often made the means of developing self-consciousness—that self-consciousness which is the greatest obstruction to human development, and its fearful products of fear, or self-conceit.

"Keep back thy servant from presumptuous sins; let them not have dominion over me: then shall I be innocent of the great transgression."

The subject of overburdening school-demands has been much discussed of late. Students, we are told, break down with overwork; ambitious girls suffer from nervous prostration; indeed, until physical training came to the rescue, few young women left high school or college without impaired health. Genuine educative work is the healthiest exercise, both for mind and body, of which the human being is capable; the power of endurance in unity of action is simply marvelous. All-sided educative work stimulates the healthful action of brain, nerve, and muscle. The laws of compensation, of interaction and reflex action, of coördination and adjustment, bring about a constant refreshment, building up the physical agencies of the mind, that would be otherwise weakened through one-sided or partial action. The prolific cause of overburdening is not genuine work, but mental drudgery; one-sided and partial action of the being, in which there is no continual wellspring of joy in the discovery and expression of truth. Excited by the glittering baubles of reward, of per-cents, of place in class, of victory over others, ambitious students struggle for the mastery of dead forms until nerve power is exhausted, sympathetic organs fail in their functions, and the muscular system collapses. Motive sinks to the lowest plane in this senseless and selfish striving for rewards and approving smiles.

Self-consciousness is an incipient disease. An expert physician will tell you that the continual attention of the mind directed to the body and its organs leads to a change in these organs, to morbidness, and to the inhibition of healthy action. Awkwardness, stiffness, cant, affectation, and such abnormal manifestations, are simply indications of that which, if the processes which lead to undue consciousness of self are continued, will be followed by results of the most serious nature—may lead even to insanity.

I believe that I have not overstated the dreadful consequence of self-consciousness. The question is, whether this unity of action, begun spontaneously and instinctively in childhood, this marvelous power which is sought for by all artists, this genius, this centering of self, cannot be continued to the end; whether all expression may not be under the immediate impulse of thought controlled by the will, and dominated by right motive; and whether it is not possible, under the proper training, to educate children without fostering and inducing that which is abnormal.

There are two hypotheses in education, the prevailing hypothesis may be stated as follows: It is an absolute necessity to take the greater portion of schooltime in training pupils to learn and imitate forms of expression, with the avowed purpose of using them in the future, when, perchance, they may be needed for the manifestation of thought. This is, I believe, a fair statement of the motive which controls much of our school-work.

The second hypothesis states that it is possible to acquire all the technical skill needed for the adequate expression of thought, in each and all the modes of expression, under the immediate impulse of intrinsic thought, controlled by the will and dominated by the right motive. I place these two hypotheses side by side for your consideration. We have had a long experience in the former and a very slight experience in the latter; but the question should be asked most earnestly: Is it possible to devote all the time of the child in the most economical way in the search for intrinsic thought? I have presented phases of this same question in other relations over and over again, but this latter question is undoubtedly the most important, for it is the center of all educational problems.

I cannot leave this subject without a brief discussion of a question which is of profound interest to us as teachers. Is it possible to overcome habits of self-consciousness when formed, with all the defects involved? It is possible; but the one who conquers will no doubt learn to comprehend the depth of the divine words—"Blessed is he who overcometh." It is safe to say that much of the scientific teaching consists of attempts to eradicate defects and change bad habits, which are the negative products of unscientific teaching. These habits, comprehended in self-consciousness, with its two baneful results, abnormal fear and equally abnormal self-conceit, stand as effectual barriers in the path of personal education; there is no way around them, they must be overcome, must be broken down, else education becomes a farce and a delusion.

The sin of wasted and misdirected energy has small place among current discussions of human ills, but it is an evil of evils, a sin of sins. To keep a soul in utter ignorance may be called the

greatest waste of energy; but with the direct purpose of economizing energy by education, to deliberately waste it in
abnormal obstructions, is a terrible loss to humanity. *True
education frees the human spirit.*[1] It stimulates to most effective
action—that action which reveals inaccessible heights still to be
attempted. " 'Tis not what man Does which exalts him, but what
man Would do." A personal ideal that can be attained in this
life must, of necessity, be low.

> All, I could never be,
> All, men ignored in me,
> This, I was worth to God, whose wheel the pitcher shaped.

Common experience abundantly proves that students may
spend long years in the most laborious drudgery and never develop the power of original imagination, inference, and generalization. That power of the mind which is the supreme test of
true education—the power to understand new phases of thought,
to discover and to adapt new conditions to new needs—is lacking.
History is replete with, and society full of, such sad examples
of defective teaching; indeed, pedantry to a great extent to this
day controls public opinion. Whittier's lines,

> Of all sad words of tongue or pen,
> The saddest are these,—"It might have been.'

may be applied to memories of wasted energy—energy wasted in
struggling to do the impossible, while leaving vast possibilities
unrealized.

Sedulously cultivated habits of fear destroy self-confidence.
The child is afraid to read, to write, to spell, to cipher, to recite,
on account of the cruel specters of fancied difficulties. No one
can teach long without observing that many children are ab-

solutely crippled by timidity; such children have a longing to do what they see done, but having an overweening respect for the accomplishments of others, their minds and bodies are paralyzed by the emotion of fear—fear of making a mistake if they try. It is needless to recount the many devices for the cultivation of this perilous emotion. They may be generalized in one sentence: "Here is something difficult, something you must try very hard to do; give attention, study, strive, and perhaps you may conquer." The "something very difficult" is the acquisition of dead forms. The exercise of that mental energy which makes forms of expression immediate and imperative necessities sweeps away seeming difficulties as light dissipates darkness.

Self-conceit is not self-confidence, the true consciousness of self, self-conceit is the overweening, unwarranted self-satisfaction in a certain facility of action—for instance, a glibness in recitation and a fertility of barren verbal memory which bad teaching demands and ignorant teachers praise. Add to constant approbation the complex and effective machinery of rewards, per-cents, prizes, and promotions, and the means are complete for making a conceited donkey of a child. Prizes put a premium upon superficiality and frighten the fearful children (fearful because they have a great reverence for knowledge) into outer darkness.

The common experience that dull boys often distance in real life their high-per-cented competitors, is easily explained. Reputed dullness in many cases, as I have already intimated, is the result of an absolute refusal to learn words without understanding them. "I think," began a bright little girl. "We don't want any thinking here: tell me what the book says." This is an actual reply, a typical command from an unscientific teacher. The pedagogics of defect should constitute a main branch of the general subject.

I can best illustrate means and methods of remedying defects in education which are the products of defective teaching, by appealing directly to those teachers who catch a glimpse of the unlimited possibilities of scientific teaching. The effect of such a glimpse is often a discouragement which amounts to despair. "Conviction must precede conversion." A true teacher feels deeply the immense influence of his own knowledge and skill or lack of them, upon his pupils. There is practically no limit to the instinctive ability of pupils to imitate their teacher in every detail of thought and expression, extending even to gestures, movements, and manner.

Great skill in penmanship—the ability to write rapidly, legibly, and beautifully upon both blackboard and paper—renders the task of training pupils to write a very easy matter. It is perfectly safe to say that proper skill on the part of the teacher saves three-fourths of the time of pupils in this direction, when compared with the results of training by teachers whose penmanship is poor. A teacher who can exercise upon his pupils the enchantment produced by excellent oral reading has at command the best possible means of teaching oral expression. A teacher skillful in drawing arouses, by the exercise of this art, a strong desire on the part of his pupils to do the same thing in the same way. No method in vocal music, however good, can begin to compensate for a teacher who cannot sing. The real grammar taught in a schoolroom is the language of the teacher. In fact, "As is the teacher, so is the school," may be truthfully interpreted, "As is the skill of the teacher, so is the skill of his pupils." There can be no efficient substitute for lack of skill in any of the modes of expression; the best makeshift comes from the teacher's frank acknowledgment of his weakness, and the practical expression of desire to improve, by courageously working with his pupils in acquiring the needed skill.

Failure in knowledge itself, failure to command subjects of thought, failure to understand relations, inability to present conditions for mental growth, lie at the root of most imperfect teaching. The very teachers who make quantity of knowledge the end and aim of teaching are generally those who themselves have lost all zest and love for knowledge; they are fully convinced that they have enough on hand for present purposes. It seems a curious paradox, that many teachers whose sole aim is to "impart knowledge" are not real students themselves. If genuine exhibitions of skill have such an influence over pupils, how much greater is the influence of the teacher's attitude toward study!

A teacher who has not a profound appreciation of his responsibility and influence, who does not earnestly long for greater skill and more knowledge, cannot be counted with the efficient members of the profession. A teacher should realize that this influence over immortal minds is eternal, that whatsoever he is goes into the immortality of his pupils; their true success depends, to a great extent, upon him, upon his knowledge, skill, and character. What the teacher is, his pupils will be.

The highest motive is alone sufficient to break down the barriers of fear and destroy self-conceit. What the wrong motive produced, the right motive, the love for humanity, must destroy. As is a teacher's love for his pupils, so is his work. It is blessed for a teacher who has had his own mind stiffened and stupefied by word—cram "to hunger and thirst after righteousness." But if love leads the way, miracles will be performed.

To change the motive is to overcome habits of fear or self-conceit. Undue consciousness of self is the direct product of wrong motive; it may be changed to righteous self-confidence by changing the motive. Self-conceit is shattered when actions are controlled by high aims. Timidity vanishes when the courage of duty and high purpose enters.

Most children read orally as if they were unconscious of auditors; oral reading is generally a sort of muttering to one's self. No lessons in force, pitch, stress, or emphasis are sufficient to cure such habits. The efficient cure is to make a child very anxious to be thoroughly understood in what he reads. In that struggle all the arts of oral expression will find a place—under an all-controlling desire to make others think, feel, and appreciate the thought and emotion of the reader. Lead pupils to forget themselves and their fears under the dominant stress of motive.

The motive of learning forms for form's sake always and invariably leads directly to the dire evils of overconsciousness; the only remedy for these evils is to reinstate the highest motive in supreme command, and with it unity of action. The altruistic motive is the intrinsic quality of the soul; it controls thought and expression; it directs method; its one criticism is: Are the results of expression adequate? Do they have the proposed influence upon others? This motive directs action out of one's self toward others, and the false self sinks out of sight. "He who would save his life, must lose it."

That which is lost of time and struggle cannot be regained; but there can be a conversion—a new start, under which abnormal barriers may be overthrown, and the way to higher development opened. A low grade of insight and a high grade of pedantry, spring from low motives; but inspiration, revelation, and prophecy come only to souls devoted to the weal of mankind. That which is true of humanity in general must be true of children. Self-consciousness may be overcome, but genuine economy is found in preserving the unity of action from the beginning; in sedulously cultivating the altruistic motive, self-confidence and the most educative self-effort.

---

[1] "True Education Frees the Human Spirit." This is the quotation chosen by Charles Hubbard Judd to be carved upon the fireplace below the bust of Colonel Parker placed in the School of Education of the University of Chicago. This school was founded by Mrs. Emmons Blaine to carry out the educational philosophy of Colonel Parker, and Colonel Parker was its director until his death.

XII

ACQUISITION OF SKILLS IN THE MODES
OF EXPRESSION

IN THE previous chapter we considered two hypotheses regarding the acquisition of forms of thought expression. The first hypothesis held that the forms of expression could be taught without relation to the thought itself, which the forms express. Much teaching of art, language, and number are based upon this hypothesis and its tenets are too familiar to repeat.

This mechanical work upon the means of thought manifestation takes, generally stated, more than two-thirds of the time spent by pupils in the elementary school—a course of eight years. There can be no reasonable motive for this vast expenditure of time, toil, and money except anticipated gain in the power to express thought, when, in some future time, it may be evolved.

The second hypothesis is of tremendous import to education. It holds that the technical skill necessary for the adequate expression of thought in all modes of expression may be thoroughly acquired under the immediate impulses of intrinsic thought, or thought evolved in the study of the central subjects.

The propositions involved under this second hypothesis are worthy of detailed study and may be stated as follows:

(1) That the entire time and power of the pupils in school may be *concentrated upon intrinsic thought,* the thought embodied in the central subjects and in social living. By intrinsic

thought is meant the free action of the mind toward truth along the shortest line of resistance.

(2) The function of educative expression is ethical; it determines and develops the motive for the concentration of the mind upon intrinsic thought.

(3) Each and every act of educative expression intensifies intrinsic thought, develops the body as an instrument of expression, trains the will, and enhances motive.

(4) That the personal energy engendered by the necessity and desire to manifest thought is sufficient, when scientifically directed, to overcome the technical difficulties of form.

We may apply this specifically to school work as follows:

(a) Writing, including spelling, punctuation, and capitalization, may be gradually and surely mastered by successive attempts to express thought.

(b) Technical grammar, with its modifications of etymology, syntax, and prosody, may take enduring form and shape, when welded under the white heat of absorbing thought.

(c) Efficient arithmetical power and skill may be acquired by the continual exercise of judgment and reason in the necessary application of numbers essential to a knowledge of the central subjects.

(d) The cultivation of the voice in music and public speaking should be immediately controlled and governed by thought and emotion.

(e) Art forms in modeling, painting, and drawing may be best acquired under the immediate stimulus of the ideal to be manifested.

Seen in the light of economy of human action, these are significant propositions. All the schooltime of a pupil is concentrated upon intrinsic thought; every act of expression intensifies that thought. The forms of expression are adapted to the needs of the child at every step. They grow with thought, conform to the thought, and are therefore genuine and adequate means of expression.

Finally every moment in education will be an *ethical moment*. Every act of the body, mind, and soul will be a unit; the body will be developed and immediately responsive to the soul's action along the line of the slightest resistance.

It is then of vast importance for us to discuss this hypothesis with the greatest care, for if it be true, its acceptance means infinite changes in the direction of higher development. It means the realization of possibilities undreamed of in the common ideal; it means an acquirement of skill and technique in the direction of adequate expression far exceeding any known results.

In considering this hypothesis it is well for us to ascertain if there be anything analogous to it in human development outside of designed education.

Speech, that mode of expression which presents the greatest mechanical difficulties, is, and always has been, acquired under this general hypothesis; but with this exception, that thought, expressed by oral language and intensified by expression, is far from being intrinsic. A child acquires the forms of speech under the immediate impulse to express thought. It is true there are spontaneous preliminary exercises, "baby babblings," instinctive actions on the part of the child, which bring in time the various muscular coördinations of the organs of speech under the control of the will; but the main work of learning oral language is done entirely under the desire to make others understand one's own thought. Forms of speech are learned by imitation, but the incentive to practice speech comes entirely from a desire to express thought. The countless difficulties and obstructions found in learning speech are steadily overcome by constant practice in the expression of thought. Vocal music and the gestures of a child are acquired in precisely the same way.

Making, or the complete realization of individual concepts in external forms, presents the fewest difficulties in the application of the second hypothesis. If making be controlled by the functions of the object made, all details, skill, and technique may be acquired with comparative ease. If, on the contrary, parts of an object are made without direct relation to the whole, parts that have no function in themselves, that are of no use except when adjusted or united with the whole object, then the motive, especially with a child, is not definite, and the mental action consequently weak. The child will easily overcome difficulties—for instance, the making of joints, of measuring and adjusting part to part—if he is controlled by the *motive of function;* that is, his action at every step will be stimulated by the desire to have the article made adapted to its use.[1]

In physics and chemistry ingenuity may be taxed by the invention and construction of simple apparatus. An experiment is to be made, and the pupils must show the proper and exact conditions. This leads to the drawing of each piece of apparatus, followed by its making.

In botany, the modeling, painting, and drawing of leaves and flowers, of trees and shrubs—indeed, of all kinds of plants—afford infinite opportunities for effective art expression, stimulating and guiding observation as in no other way.

Art should have a very prominent place in the study of botany. Leaves, bushes, and trees, to the eyes of the child, are patches of color; outline is not definite, but color is. Nature tells beautiful stories by color, shade, and tint. To draw a definite outline of a leaf or flower is not an initial step in art; through color the life of a plant is revealed to the child, and he should give it back as he receives it. The result may be a crude, unrecognizable daub to the artisan teacher, but it is beautiful to the teacher whose aim is to arouse self-effort, whose purpose is genuineness, and who feels "the future in the instant."

Everything in education should be judged by its tendency—
not what it is at the present moment, but whither it is going.
The courage to be crude is the only path to success. The point
of criticism with the teacher should always be, "Did you tell by
the picture what you wished to tell?" Modeling and painting
are the initial steps to drawing. An effort to force a child to
make an accurate drawing of anything at first is absurd, not to
say wicked.

In order to fully discuss the second hypothesis, and prove, if
possible, its truth and capability of application under adequate
teaching, certain questions must be considered.

If the central subjects of study, and sciences, geography, history, and literature, are made the essentials of school work for
eight years, and the various modes of expression are used whenever and wherever they are needed to intensify the thought, will
there be practice enough to aquire the technique of speech,
writing, modeling, painting, drawing, etc.?

The products of observation are used in apperception for the
construction of mental pictures which lie beyond the material
horizon. Here again is a wide field for the exercise of art. If
the teacher admits no effort that is not genuine, the pupil must
imagine the general nature of the thing that he models or draws.
The mere copying of maps, like all copying, has the lowest
educative influence, and worse than that, prevents a real study
of surface by the interposition of conventional forms. For instance, geography is the study of the present appearance of the
earth's surface. It is a study of form by direct observation in
field lessons, or by imagination where the forms lie beyond the
sense grasp. As an initial step, there are no other means as
effective as an effort to model in sand that which a pupil has
observed. A child's concepts are, of course, exceedingly crude.
An attempt to model in sand or to chalk-model upon the blackboard makes a child aware of his need for more careful obser-

vation and for more accurate knowledge. An arbitrary demand for an exact map or correspondence to external forms (copying) destroys the springs of art—of spontaneity and genuineness. An art critic—and every teacher should be one—can detect instantly the vast difference between pure products of the constructive imagination, and the base alloy of typical forms and barren imitations. The field for art in the central subjects is practically unlimited, and furnishes no end of objects for initial practice.

Closely related to geography is the drawing necessary for geology, or the expression of thought gained by observation of the changes in the earth's surface through erosion and other causes—drawing of river or brook cuttings, pictorial descriptions of the action of the wind and water upon the earth's surface; in a word, the effects of the action of the elements and forces continually changing the earth's surface by wearing and building.

The study of minerals makes modeling, painting, and drawing a necessity; the closest observations of the forms and colors of minerals can be brought about by a demand for conceptive expression.

Zoölogy, in this essential work of preparation, presents many, and excellent, opportunities for modeling as well as painting. What a child intuitively recognizes in an animal is character, revealed to him by its attitude or bearing. With a lump of clay he will express, very crudely to be sure, the character as he conceives it. This is the beginning of true art; if rightly guided, it will steadily grow; but if the demon of accuracy enters at first, talent flies, and genius is "cribbed, confined."

Geographical drawings in relation to history are indispensable. Any attempt at a knowledge of history without a clear image of its geographical setting is well-nigh fruitless. In history, architectural drawings and paintings which illustrate the art of given periods or peoples are essential.

The proper study of the central subjects will present opportunities without number for the expression of thought through the conceptive modes of expression. There is indeed no limit to the opportunities, and every effort may be made a means of enhancing thought. I believe that these facts will be granted on the part of every one who understands the relation of art to the discovery of truth.

Contrast the results of isolated drawing lessons two or three times a week under a special teacher who has very little knowledge or sympathy with the work of the central subjects, with the results that may be obtained when art is related to all the central subjects, and effectively used to reinforce them. Under the former plan we have comparatively little practice in art; under the other, the necessities of the main studies make the practice continual. The great advantage speech has, in mechanical execution, over other modes of expression is that it is in constant use; and it may well be argued that the partial failure of art in education is due to the fact that its relation to other subjects has not been understood, and consequently few opportunities presented for its use.

Granted that the opportunities for art practice are unlimited when they are made a continual means of acquiring knowledge in all studies, the conscientious teacher next considers: *Is the modeling, painting, and drawing growing out of the study of the sciences, geography, history and literature best adapted in technical execution to the growing abilities of children?* Are not the difficulties too great in this direction, and will not the child's efforts be swamped in them? We meet here the prevailing argument that springs from an apparent necessity for a logical arrangement of difficulties, sequences of adaption to energy. History is full of illustrations of supposed logical sequences as:

The names of the letters must be learned.

Words must be learned before a sentence can be read.

The child must make the sounds of letters before he can read a word.

It is necessary to make elements, such as lines—straight and curved—and single letters, before a sentence can be written.

Addition must be acquired before multiplication.

In drawing, straight lines, curves, triangles, squares, rectangles, must be made as indispensable preliminary exercises.

These are only samples of the many illustrations of logical sequence claimed to be paramount necessities in teaching.

This principle of logical arrangement for learning is fundamentally wrong; it fails to recognize the spontaneous powers of the child.[2] It leaves out of the reckoning what the child has already acquired. It shows a complete ignorance of a child's method of acquiring knowledge and skill. That which is ignored constantly in the child is *motive, thought, previous development, and the unparalleled energy with which it overcomes difficulties and acquires skill*. Untold energy is wasted upon the acquisition of dead forms. Under the theory of concentration, each act of expression springs from, and is dominated by, strong desire to express thought. The sequences in technique are adapted and conform at every step to the thought to be expressed; the mechanics of gaining skill in expression is adequate to the conscious activities to be expressed, the sequence of difficulty is thus made perfect, and the development of skill will be in the highest degree economical.

The only way in which one unskilled in these forms of expression can appreciate the extreme crudeness of a child's individual concepts is to attempt to model, paint, draw, or even to describe accurately some familiar object. When a child paints a leaf, for instance, the result is a daub, a blotch of color—not in every case, perhaps, an exact correspondence to his concept, but the best indication of it. The child is pleased generally with his work; any dissatisfaction, however, shows that the correspondence of the "daub" to the concept is felt to be inadequate, and that a desire to do it better is aroused. This felt inadequacy is true, yes, the only, line of criticism. Through the expression the teacher watches the action of the pupil's mind; he judges whether the expression equals the concept, and thus infers whether the pupil is lacking in skill, or in thought. In this process, genuineness, the intrinsic quality of art, is developed.

Under the theory of logical sequence of form development, the principal demand is for an accuracy and an exactness which conform in no wise to the concept. The results of this are a straining after an effect that does not correspond to an adequate cause and a lack of genuineness that kills art feeling.

The only excuse for drawing from copy is the false demand for abnormal and mind-crippling accuracy. True accuracy has only one normal relation, and that is its relation to adequate expression of thought; constant effort in the direction of adequate thought expression is the one way and means by which adequate skill is acquired. The false assumption that a child must be accurate or nothing, leads to the abnormal demand for minutely detailed forms, and is a preparation which never prepares.

Did you ever see a little child go to the blackboard to illustrate a fairy story, or to give free rein to his budding fancy? His self-confidence only equals his delight to express what he feels. With broad free lines, he draws hills, valleys, trees, bushes, houses, and people; no fear of mistakes, no apprehension of crudeness. Here is unity of action, self-confidence, and childish freedom.

Remember that ease and equilibrium must precede precision, that the child is telling the story as he feels it, and that he will feel it better and tell it better if you give the help that he needs —help that will not destroy his beautiful self-confidence and crush out his delight in the work. The moment is a dangerous one for a child—indeed for anyone—when the critical faculty

surpasses skill. That is the reason why we, you and I, do not
learn to draw, my fellow teachers. If we could become "as a
little child," we might acquire a skill that has hardly an equal
in teaching power. Pace by pace, the critical power should keep
step with skill, and both steadily move to higher levels. Recognize weakness, sympathize with it, and lead it with a loving
hand toward the full strength of complete maturity. Remember,
above all things, that it is not the rude sketch on the blackboard,
but the growing power of the child which you are observing;
not what he has done with chalk, but that which happens within
the child, under a strong desire to express his thought. Pestalozzi
said, "Education is the generation of power." Develop that power
as you believe in God and eternity.

The normal movement of mind is from particulars to generals, from crudeness, obscurity, toward clearness, distinctness,
adequacy; this movement is inductive. Deductive movement is
from generals to particulars, when it is possible; that is, when
general notions become mental powers through processes of
induction. With a child, it is a long road from the crude concept
to the clear, and the distinct.

There are no typical forms in nature, the great storehouse of
art studies and the realm of the beautiful; here every shape de-
viates from perfect form; it is irregular and individual; it
expresses a definite character which differs from all other characters; *it is art to find that character and express it.* Form and
color are manifestations of the invisible; true art transcends
mere imitation of either. No matter how crude the child's in-
genius modeling or drawing may be, you see in his work an
attempt to express something more than mere form or color,
you are struck by the motive or feeling; the drawing may be
out of joint, and the perspective wholly bad, but there is an
indefinable something that makes you certain of an attempt to
express thought.

This indication of feeling is the germ of art; be careful not to crush it by injudicious criticism, either of blame or praise; nourish it, give it countless opportunities for exercise, make it the center of well-considered suggestions that will lead the young artist to be a true critic of self—of his own thought and skill—and art may thus be made to take its true place in education.

If genuineness is made the *sine qua non* of training; if crudeness, daubs, and even blotches, with a faint show of feeling, are gladly accepted because they are genuine expressions of the child; if art is made a principal means of intensifying the thought continually evolved in all the central subjects; if pupils strive to express thought adequately, and in the striving become acute self-critics; if nothing is expected or demanded of pupils except the honest manifestation of that which they feel; if development of thought demands of itself development of skill, then the way is open and the method plain; by no other plan of teaching will the demands of technique conform to individual ability, and consequently present the efficient means for ever-increasing skill. Of all the shallow, heartless sayings, "Art for art's sake" seems to be the culmination and climax. "Money for money's sake," "Knowledge for the sake of knowledge," are comparable phrases. There is nothing in this universe that is not for the sake of human souls and their salvation.

The theory of concentration brings art home to every child; makes it an incomparable means of personal education; discloses hidden springs of beauty; turns its vast influence upon intellectual power; cultivates the most exalted emotions and the noblest motives; leads to an absorbing love of the beautiful in nature and art; unites it with all other conditions of educative work; but best of all, it takes art from its isolation and renders it a blessing to every man.

I have not the slightest doubt concerning the direction of art in education: It is to be made the strongest aid to attention, the mightiest help to observation, and the most powerful stimulus to the imagination; it is to become an indispensable auxiliary to all study.

Drawing was introduced into our schools for the purpose, not of intrinsic value as a means of education, but as a means of training skilled artisans; the end determined the means and the method, the road to artisan work seemed to be through artisan training. This motive isolated drawing from all other subjects; special schools were established for it; special teachers were trained to do the work. The special teachers degraded art through misdirected attempts to exalt it; and on the other hand, the regular teachers, failing to see the relation of drawing to every other subject, have had little sympathy with it and, besides, little or no skill to teach it.

I would not have you understand that I do not appreciate the earnest, honest efforts that have been made by the pioneers of art studies all over the country; they have done the greatest of works—they have made progress possible. There must be beginnings; still it should be remembered that beginnings, like majorities, are rarely right. Very little has been done, as yet, in the new direction; indeed, everything is new relatively in that education, whose purpose is to set free human souls. The principles are nearly nineteen hundred years old, but the application still awaits the teacher.

Art awaits teachers, teachers inspired by the truth, with some insight of the marvelous possibilities of this subject; teachers who, with an understanding of its great value in education, will have the courage to carry its inestimable blessing to every child.

---

[1] This is the fundamental principle of Sloyd. Dr. Salomon, founder of Sloyd, insists that the controlling motive in making any piece of woodwork is the use which is to be made of it. The incentive determines the quality of effort of the worker.

[2] *See* John Dewey, *How We Think* (D. C. Heath).

XIII

SPEECH AND WRITING

EDUCATIVE thought governs all expression. All the conceptive modes of expression stimulate and direct observation, exercise imagination, and concentrate mental energy. Each and every mode has its special educative function. Of the discussions of the mechanics and function of the various modes of expression, speech and writing alone remain to be discussed.

Until recently, speech and writing have been almost the only expression recognized as potent means of education; nevertheless, it remains for us to inquire whether they have been used to the best possible advantage and whether improvements cannot well be made in their use and development.

Back of articulation in speech is voice—a mode of expression parallel with, and as spontaneous as, gesture. The instinctive attributes of voice, are pitch, force, and quality, with the varying elements of stress, inflection, rhythm, emphasis, etc. By instinctive attributes are meant the direct reflexes of conscious states. These are projected and become essential qualities of acquired speech.

The mechanics of speech are acquired by imitation. Whatever language, dialect, pronunciation, idiom—correct or false—a child hears becomes his habit in the use of oral language, and once sunk into the automatic, fixed in habit, is changed with the greatest difficulty. In pronunciation and syntax, the child imitates only sounds and unities of sounds; it cannot copy the placings and positions of all the vocal organs, for the good reason that all cannot be observed; they are hidden from view.

Hearing or understanding language must of necessity precede the effort to speak. The correspondence of oral words and sentences must be associated in consciousness with their appropriate ideas or activities.

From the awakening of conscious life, the process dates: First, a period of ten months or a year in hearing-language. This period is marked by "baby babblings," the instinctive use both of voice and the organs of speech; the daily and hourly practice by which the infant finally learns the use of both, bringing them under control of the will, is often unmarked by parents and educators who see in it merely the baby's delight in "making a noise." This constant and persistent effort to enunciate and articulate leads naturally to the higher processes, to the making of words, the joining of words into phrases, later into sentences. Two years' practice is sufficient with the average child for the mastery of the elementary sounds, the pronunciation of a limited vocabulary, and practical use of simple idioms. There is probably no acquirement in after-life that equals this overcoming of the difficulties of speech on the part of the child. The method of this wonderful acquisition, did we but know it, is a perfect method of learning all languages; and the closest study of this method of nature should not, because it is so common, be undervalued by parents and teachers. It is, as it were, "catching Nature in the act." It is safe to assume that if a child acquires so much in so short a time, during the undeveloped state of infancy, this natural, instinctive method should be taken advantage of and used in later acquisition of language.

Imitation is the absolute basis in acquiring mechanical forms, but imitation in itself is only a secondary and subservient factor in learning language. Behind every mechanical effort is an energy that directs and controls the action of the organs of speech. That energy is the motive to make others understand, directed by the thought to be expressed, and the exercise of the will in control of that thought and its expression.

The thought and emotion which impel vocal expression manifest themselves in emphasis, rhythmic cadence, melody and harmony, varieties of force, pitch, and quality, by which the thought is discriminated, and the character of the emotion demonstrated. These factors of voice are instinctive and spontaneous; they are the direct reflex of conscious activities, and *can be cultivated only as thought and emotion are developed and expressed.* To attempt to imitate melody, emphasis, and harmony, is to caricature thought expression. These are dominated and impelled by the desire to make others understand. The movement of the spoken language in its development with the child is along the exact line of the movement and growth of his thought; the language conforms strictly to the thought, and keeps pace with it in coördinate exercise. The unity of action is perfectly maintained at every step; this is shown by the melody, harmony, and perfect emphasis of the normal child who seldom makes a mistake in emphasis.

Is it possible to continue this unity of action in all the future steps and stages of education? The child enters school usually with physical, mental, and moral powers developed by six years of constant action. "It has learned more in the first six years of its life," says Hegel, "than it ever afterwards can learn." All improved methods of teaching that have never been discoverd spring from a study of the spontaneous activities of the child—his knowledge and power, his methods of learning and skill—before entering the schoolroom. Right methods in school are simply the continuation of nature's methods. An unnatural method obstructs or deflects energy; for whatever intellectual power a pupil acquires is best acquired through natural methods—those methods which spring from, and are guided by, the inherent tendencies of the being. The method under which children acquire the power of speech can never be improved; but it may be enhanced by new matter and changed conditions.

Another mode of expression confronts the child at the door of the schoolroom—that of *writing*. Its influence upon education may be made as potent as that of speech. When should a pupil begin to write? This question, then, must be answered for each child. When a little child exhibits a desire to write, let him try; if the attempt is successful, the time has come. There is nothing mysterious or essentially difficult in the act of writing; the mechanics of penmanship are exceedingly simple; under a normal method, penmanship is more easily acquired than any other mode of expression. In fact, compared with the complexities of enunciation, the results of the almost infinite adjustments of lungs, larynx, and the organs of speech, the adjustments of hand and arm in writing seem simple indeed. Previous preparation, moreover, assists here, for the arm and hand have been so constantly exercised in functional use in making, drawing, and writing.

The pupil comes to the work of learning to write usually with about six years' active use of the whole body—six years' exercise of the mind, and six years' practice in speech. Although mechanical difficulties of writing are very much less than those of speech, speech has the advantage of a more continuous practice, and of a stronger and more instinctive impulse.

Self-consciousness is the explanation, nine cases out of ten, why, given the same facilities for practice, one mode of expression is so much more at command than another. In speech, because of youth and a more natural environment, children generally preserve unity of action. Unity of action requires the minimum expenditure of physical energy for intelligible expression. The vocal organs are instinctively adjusted; in writing, however, the muscular coördinations, the adjustment of the body and its agents to unity of action require the highest art of the teacher to make necessary habits sink quickly and unconsciously into the automatic. The question of the perfect attitude and position of the body, and the movement requiring the least possible physical energy for legible writing, is one of first importance, because the unlearning of a bad habit is a much more serious thing than the acquirement of a good one.[1]

A smooth line is an infallible indication of ease in writing. The first point to be settled is: In what position and by what movement can a smooth line be made with a pen?

(1) Place yourself before a desk of the proper height; rest the forearm easily and lightly upon it. There should be no tension caused by raising the arm too high, or dropping it too low.

(2) Sit in a chair that will allow you to rest the feet flat upon the floor, the legs forming an obtuse angle at the knees.

(3) Sit square to the front of the table or desk, providing the full forearm can easily rest upon it; otherwise sit at the slightest possible angle that will allow you to rest the forearm wholly upon the desk.[2]

(4) Have the forearm form an obtuse angle at the elbow with the upper arm.

(5) Place the forearm parallel to the right and left edges of the paper, and in moving the forearm from left to right, keep it parallel with the right and left edges.

(6) Let the wrist rest without pressure flat upon the paper.

(7) Let the pen rest between the thumb, the index and second fingers.

(8) Let the pressure of the pen upon the paper be equal upon both nibs.

The whole body should be in the easiest possible position for the required action; the energy should be withdrawn from the arm, which should rest upon the desk with the least possible tension of muscle.

In this position, draw the arm down, with no purpose but to make a straight line; the angle thus made will be between 51° and 52°. This movement following the prescribed position requires the least expenditure of energy to make a smooth line; indeed, it may be doubted whether smooth lines in writing can be continually made in any other way. A smooth line requires a rapid movement of the pen. The movement across the page from straight line to straight line is made in curves.

I am giving in detail the fundamental principles of the American or Spencerian handwriting. Its discoverer found the law of the easiest movement consistent with legibility, and, at the same time, with the greatest economy of physical action.

All written forms consist of simple—straight and curved—lines; in the small letters there are thirty straight lines in exactly the same relative position—eighteen of the same length, and twelve of varying lengths. These straight lines constitute the principal parts of all the same letters except "e," "o," "c," and "s." The straight lines are connected by simple curves in five or six different positions. All the capitals consist of ellipses, compound and simple curves.

The slant required (51°-52°) is perfectly adapted to the arm-movement, but wholly unnatural for the finger-movement. The finger-movement, when natural, is perpendicular or vertical. The renaissance of the old-fashioned English "pothooks and hangers" is a strong protest against the body-crippling struggle to make slanting lines with the fingers. If the fingers must go up and down in writing, by all means allow the children to move their digits as easily as possible.

The strong reaction in favor of perpendicular penmanship, I repeat, has its origin in long-continued attempts to make slanting lines with the up-and-down movement of the fingers. The sole reason for the slanting line is that it is made with the least possible expenditure of physical energy.

The strongest reason why the finger-movement should not be used is given in the talk upon unity of action. Nerve currents, according to the latest authorities in child-study, are distributed very slowly from the spinal cord to the bodily extremities. This fact gives us the reason why children move more freely and naturally in broad lines or curves, and why the attempts to train the extremities and lead them to make short lines and curves before due strength has been received from the center, reacts upon that center, weakening and crippling the whole body. Slate-writing, or the painfully slow movements of the fingers in pushing the pencil over a resisting surface, is a common illustration of the manner in which the body is ignorantly weakened. But the crippling of the physical organism does not tell the whole of the sad story; the muscles of the fingers and forearm become more and more tense and contracted; the wrong habit becomes fixed, and where constant use of the pen is demanded writer's cramp is the inevitable outcome.

Advocates of vertical penmanship point to the unhealthful positions of pupils. They say: "The disease to be attacked is bad writing and bad health, the twin children of sloping writing." The bad positions and consequent deformity of the body are due to the attempt to make the slope by the up-and-down movement of the fingers. Making the slant with the fingers causes them to be twisted to the right, thus inducing unnatural tension and constraint. The vertical line requires the least effort on the part of the fingers. The sloping writing was looked upon merely as a "fashion," a "fad," for the time; no regard was paid to the principle which underlies it, and the poor children were taught to do a right thing in an unnatural way.

There is one insuperable argument, if true, brought in favor of vertical writing, and that is the supposition that the slant affects binocular vision unfavorably. If this be granted, it is a sound argument for vertical writing, but no argument against arm-movement, because it can be shown that vertical writing, as well, is best made by the arm-movement. Change the angle of the paper to the forearm, and the thing is done; vertical writing is there, and the arm-movement remains. Indeed, every argument goes to prove that writing with the whole arm, reinforced by the easiest and most natural position of the body, is the only normal, healthful position.

But the argument for the arm-movement is by no means completed when the mechanical and optical difficulties of writing and reading are shown to be in its favor. There are two hypotheses that may be applied to penmanship, the first one is that: All forms of writing, including spelling, punctuation, spacing, and capitalization, should be acquired in a purely mechanical way, with no relation to thought, so that in the future, when thought is to be expressed, these forms may be ready for use.

The methods, devices, and details of mechanical work, under this hypothesis, are well known to most teachers of experience; they have many variations, improvements, and changes that are not improvements.

The second hypothesis, that of concentration, is as follows: All forms of writing, including spelling, punctuation, spacing, and capitalization, may be adequately acquired under the immediate impulses of intrinsic or educative thought.

Educative original thought is developed, throughout the course of eight years, by observation, reading, study of the natural sciences, geography, myth, history, literature, form and number. The sources of continual interest are the discovery of facts, the making of original inferences, and the delights of observation and imagination.

The main thing and the true thing is that there is personal

energy, personal motive, and intrinsic thought, impelling every attempt in expression.

First-grade children enter at once upon the study of science, number, literature, and history; speech, modeling and painting are freely used to develop thought. In observation, comparison, or inference, a child wishes to express an idea and *one word* will do so adequately. For instance, when a group have been examining stones to detect the presence of lime, those children who found it, wish to record the fact. The word is then written by the teacher rapidly and well upon the blackboard; those children who need it give a concentrated effective glance at the blackboard, the word is erased—and the children write the word. The results will be crude but beautiful, the writing will be characterized by broad, sweeping lines; the work will be done rapidly; a mental picture of the word will be closely held and quickly expressed. If the children are allowed to copy the word, the writing will be much slower and less effective. The children read aloud with delight the word they have written. This is the beginning of reading, writing, and spelling. I should have said that some lessons in reading from the blackboard should precede the first attempts to write, the written words springing directly from the thought. After a few words written upon the blackboard, the children try a whole original sentence. In a very short time children under skillful training will acquire a wonderful power of writing original sentences. They then tell what they have written! If the lessons written upon the blackboard are afterwards printed, the children will read as readily as they do from the board.

From these initial steps on, writing is made a potent means of intensifying and relating thought.

If I have made this method seem unnaturally easy for the teacher, I must correct the mistake. First of all, the teacher must be an excellent penman and blackboard writer. Pupils will imitate their teacher with the greatest accuracy, not only her writing, but her manner of writing. Clear, legible, and rapid writing on the part of the teacher is more than half the victory in training beginners to write. Important, however, as is the skillful penmanship of the teacher, this is but a tithe of the influence which must be exerted. The even more significant matters are *the tact and ability to stimulate interesting related thought* in the minds of the children and *the recognition of the psychological moment in which to help the individual to express that thought.*

Enough in this direction cannot be said. Arouse the energy and set it free; "complete the organic circuit," as Dr. Dewey says. When the child writes a word, he gives back what he has received and just as he received it; it passes over the optic-nerve tract, and is immediately "discharged" through the arm and hand.

It was a great discovery in the art of teaching when it was found that children can write words upon the blackboard with the same power and ease that they pronounce them. By the skillful application of this discovery, the major part of the painful and painstaking drudgery of carefully drawing elements and letters and of slowly copying words and sentences becomes unnecessary. The fact is proved beyond a doubt that a child is capable, impelled by intrinsic thought and guided by skillful teaching, of writing rapidly and easily whole words and original sentences. The first results, as I have already said, will be crude, just as the first attempts at speaking are crude; but under thoughtful direction they may be steadily improved. The true inwardness of this simple device is that the child takes great delight in expressing his thought with the crayon, and practices as naturally and unconsciously under the desire to tell his written story as in previous years he lisped, in imperfect numbers, his spoken story.

In the first steps in teaching reading, writing may be made a far more effective means than oral reading. As I have already said, the child gives back the thought just as he interprets it.

When writing a word under the impulse of thought, the acts of association are made continuous and effective. No device for the first steps in writing has ever been found more satisfactory than writing upon the blackboard. Blackboards, it goes without saying, should be constructed so as to present the least possible resistance to the movement of the arm, and at proper height from the floor for a child's easiest use. The crayon should be of the best quality. The child writes with his whole body; he stands with perfect ease; the arm moves with a broad, easy swing, rhythmic and beautiful. When the word is written by the teacher and immediately erased, one glance of the eye is often sufficient to mirror the word in consciousness; the child holds it by an act of the will and immediately reproduces it. Thus, rapid writing is made a necessity. The same can be said of the making of original sentences; the movement of consciousness is very rapid; the thought is discharged through the arm as soon as it is felt in consciousness.[3]

Slow writing cannot be the expression of immediate thought. In slow writing the whole energy of the mind is absorbed in the recollection and reproduction of words alone or part of words. Writing, to be the immediate expression of immediate thought, must keep pace with the movement of consciousness. The slowest movement of consciousness requires comparatively rapid writing. In speech, the activities of consciousness are instantaneously "discharged" through the vocal organs, and the reflex action of the expression upon thought is perfect. In slow writing, written words are recalled, or speech is slowly translated into written forms. In either case, there can be no immediate or intense thought action. Strong, vigorous thinkers can rarely write slowly. Readers and compositors often are driven to their wits' end to translate their scrawls. If such persons should attempt to write slowly enough for legibility, thought action would be greatly impeded.

The proposition is, then, that writing should be made educative from first to last. By educative writing is meant—first, intrinsic thought; second, its immediate expression through the arm-movement upon blackboard and paper. Such acts of expression react upon the thought expressed and intensify it. Educative writing is an economical means of sharpening and directing observation, of cultivating imagination, and of developing the power of original inference; slow writing is not educative, or is at least only indirectly educative. The arguments in favor of rapid writing seem to be unanswerable.

By freedom of movement, unity of action, unity of consciousness, brain and hand may be perfectly maintained. This unity of action is an absolute necessity to freedom of thought; when energy is absorbed in physical action, it is withdrawn from thought action; therefore the thought action is greatly impeded, if not altogether stopped.

To sum up, rapid legible writing may be easily made an exceedingly efficient means of mental and physical development. By it all the forms of language and of grammar may be economically acquired, and writing made just as efficient a means of education as speech itself.

The function of speech and writing in education is to intensify educative thought, and to enhance its quality. The motive of speech and writing is to interpret self to others. The stronger the motive, the more intense will be the thought action, and consequently the more intelligible the expression. All forms of language are most economically shaped and molded under the white heat of thought in the act of expression.

Speech and writing are the direct complements of each other in their respective functions; each has an office which the other does not perform with equal effectiveness, and which, in turn, mutually enhances the other.

Speech is generally more fragmentary and unconnected than

writing. Writing may be effectively used to relate lines of thought in general descriptions, summaries, recapitulations, and comparisons.

Rapid writing should be freely used in all recitations. To Illustrate: Writing materials in good condition always should be ready for use; the teacher leads up to an original inference or a generalization, then asks the question; and their response shows that the children are ready for answers. "Write it," says the teacher. The written answer will be a test of both the pupil's personal power and the teacher's skill. At the beginning of the lesson, perhaps the teacher requests a brief summary of the previous lesson. In laboratory work, writing may be effectively used in taking notes. In all cases, the point is that to use this mode of expression constantly is to minimize difficulties and to create power.

It is not my purpose to present methods and devices in detail; I wish rather to show by principles how efficiently speech and writing may be used as a direct means of mental development.

Eight years' constant work in experimentation, investigation, observation, and study of the central subjects and their auxiliaries; eight years spent in processes of reasoning and collecting data for correct original inferences; eight years in the discovery, assimilation, and application of natural laws; eight years in the continual use of speech and writing as an indispensable means of educative thinking! The proposition is that from first to last, throughout the course of eight years, speech and writing in the study of the central and auxiliary subjects may be made a powerful and influential means for the development of the whole being; that the unity of action may thus be preserved; that all the forms of language, pronunciation, spelling, punctuation, capitalization, etymology, and syntax may be thoroughly and economically mastered.[4]

These claims are indeed great, but they demand thoughtful

consideration because the theory seems sound, and because they have been partially proved by careful and critical teachers.

Contrast this scheme with the custom of devoting the greater part of the entire elementary school period to purely formal studies. Consider, if you please, the precious time saved and the power gained if all the countless opportunities for the expression of thought in the study of geography, science, and history are taken advantage of.

There remains another important question for closer discussion, and that is the much-mooted subject of methods of teaching grammar. Grammar has two functions in education, namely:

(1) The correct use in speech and writing of the conventional forms of language, those forms which are sanctioned by the best usage.

(2) The cultivation of the power to understand, to gain a clear and close insight into meaning, the ability to "penetrate thought." Thus grammar, properly taught, should enhance the power to study, to read, to write, and to understand speech. In a higher sense, grammar is the elementary study of English and of philology, and is a substantial basis for the study of psychology.

Although the English language offers technical difficulties, still functional grammar should be thoroughly mastered; it should be taught in all grades of the elementary school. The question is simply and solely: *How* should it be taught? It should become a part of the warp and woof of all teaching; every lesson in every subject should be a lesson in grammar.

The child, when he enters school, may have acquired inaccuracies in speech by imitation of patterns at home. There is only one feasible plan for changing these incorrect habits, and that is by giving him countless opportunities of using the correct forms, supplemented by hearing and reading the best literature and language. Good, and even elegant, language used by the teacher, whose keen sensitive ear and quick sharp eye detect and correct at once the slightest mistake at every level of education is worth more as a means of teaching than the best textbook on grammar ever made.

The pertinent questions just here are: When, by this plan, should the accidents of grammar be introduced? When should definitions, rules of syntax, and the like, be taught? What place have parsing and analysis in this scheme? One comprehensive answer may be given to all these questions: Whenever and wherever, throughout the course, a part of speech, a fact of etymology, a definition, explanation, rule, or general direction, a lesson in parsing or analysis, will directly assist pupils in comprehending or adequately expressing thought, any and every detail of grammar should be freely presented and freely used.

The necessities in the evolution of thought and language should determine in detail the use of grammar.

Parsing and analysis have very little to do directly with expression. Analysis, especially, may be used throughout the course as an excellent means of comprehending printed language, providing always that the language is worth comprehending and is directly correlated to the subject studied. The power to read and study text with intensity, to understand quickly and thoroughly, is of the first importance. Analysis, properly used, will enhance this power, when the child is old enough to have an analytical interest in language.

Writing, as I have already argued, is the best possible means of teaching the first steps in reading; the next best to writing as an efficient means of developing the power to read is speech or oral reading.

Oral reading differs from ordinary speech only in the use of the words of another; the chief difficulty in the use of writings of an author lies wholly in the peculiarity of idiom—the spontaneous factors of speech, rhythm, and emphasis, remain the same.

The motive in oral reading is the main thing to be cultivated; it consists in developing a strong controlling desire on the part of the oral reader to make others understand his thought. This motive should dominate all action in reading. The method of oral reading should be directed entirely from the standpoint of motive, and this standpoint should determine all criticism. The one question from first to last is: Do you make yourself understood? Pronunciation, emphasis, attitude of the body, in fact, everything, should be controlled by this motive; without it, there can be no effective teaching or oral reading. The end and aim of oral reading is to sink the mind into the thought to such an extent that the action in reading becomes unconscious and automatic. When a criticism brings attention to a fault, that fault should always be in relation to the effectiveness of the reading in the minds of the hearers. The intellectual purpose of oral reading is, as in all other modes of expression, to enhance thought in the mind of the reader. The demand for oral reading should be a demand for intensity of thought action. Under the motive of making others understand, the thought action will become more intense.

If, however, the reader's motive is to pronounce words, the ethical reaction is lost sight of. If the intellectual action consists of mere correspondence to the forms of the words, there is no adequate intellectual action; the whole being is controlled by one purpose—the pronunciation of words. The attitude of the body is constrained, unity of action prevented, and energy wasted. To sum up the whole matter, the serious fault in the teaching of reading consists in making oral reading an end in itself.

Leaving in abeyance any mistakes the child makes through defective speech and models which he imitates, the child's voice is well-nigh perfection. No human being in ordinary speech makes mistakes in emphasis. In a child's voice, the unity of action is absolute; its rhythm, melody, harmony, and emphasis are well-nigh perfect, because of the unconsciousness of the child in regard to forms of expression. His speech is the result of automatic action.

By following one rule in teaching oral reading, the unconscious beauty of automatic speech may be preserved; never require a child to read anything that is not intensely interesting to him, and never allow a child to read a sentence orally until he has the thought. By following this simple rule, the freshness and vigor of the voice may be maintained and the expression of oral reading have its fullest effect upon thought itself.

If the unity of action in oral reading is once broken, complete restoration of true freedom is extremely difficult. Loss of time and great skill in teaching is necessary to overcome the division between thought and form when in the first year of a child's training in the art of oral reading his conscious activities are absorbed in the forms of words.

The value of the oral language when properly used as a means of developing mental power cannot well be overestimated.

Questioning is a mighty power in the hands of the teacher if properly conducted. A good question is one that arouses the right desire in the minds of the pupils, and leads to intensity of thought. It is a direct means of awakening in consciousness certain definite activities. A teacher watches with great closeness the action of the pupil's mind. This action is watched by means of oral expression. A question quickens that action, corrects any mistake, leads a pupil to concentrate more closely upon the subject. If the pupils use words that they do not understand, a right question immediately makes them aware of that fact. Questions are used to relate thought. The teacher should always have a definite purpose; that purpose, generally stated, is to lead the pupils to make original inferences. If in the answer the proper inference is not made, it may be that the pupils have not observed enough, have not read enough to make the inference; then the question leads them to desire to make further investigation.

In concluding these discussions of the modes of expression and their educational values, allow me to say that the principal obstruction in the acquisition of forms of expression in all the modes, is caused by an over-estimation of the seeming difficulties presented in the acquisition of skill and technique. Methods of teaching expression, to-day, are replete with formal details to be overcome with little or no regard to the powerful impulses of intrinsic thought. When the vast resources of the central subjects and their intellectual and social auxiliaries are scientifically used for personal development, and practice in each and every mode of expression is brought to bear upon thought intensity, skill and technique will be acquired with great facility.

[1] This chapter on "Speech and Writing" in the original book is particularly full of repetitions which have been largely eliminated in the present edition. The editing committee originally planned to place Colonel Parker's arguments for *Arm Movement* in an appendix as *historical matter* but a large majority of the advisory committee believed that it should have its place in the body of the text. Therefore all the important statements concerning it are included in this edition.

[2] Desks and chairs that can be adjusted to children are very much needed.

[3] A child who does not reproduce a word after one glance is not made conscious of failure. The teacher expects to rewrite and erase words constantly for children beginning to write. She encourages them to ask for help as often as necessary. But when the child is ready, he writes rapidly the word or sentence which expresses his thought. A habit of rapid writing is established in this way.

[4] If a child has difficulty in coördination or does not observe the formation of individual letters well enough to reproduce them, his attention is called to correct letter form—as a means to an end he welcomes *drill*. This is not done while the child is attempting to express his thought on blackboard or paper. But his individual errors in formation of letters, in spelling or in grammar, are brought to his attention and are material for drill for which the child understands the need.

XIV

SCHOOL GOVERNMENT AND MORAL TRAINING

THE purpose of a school is educative work. By educative work is meant self-effort in the direction of personal development. School order is that state or condition of a school in which the best educative work is done in the most economical manner. The process of education consists in presenting conditions for educative acts on the part of the individual. Method is the special adaptation of educative conditions to individual needs. Teaching is the presentation of conditions for educative self-effort. Training of the body consists in the presentation of conditions which develop the body, and make it a more efficient means of receiving and manifesting thought.

A school is a community; community life is indispensable to mental and moral growth. If the act of an individual in any way hinder the best work of the community, he is in the wrong. The highest duty of the individual is to contribute all in his power to the best good of all. This principle is the sure guide to all rules and regulations of a school. How much noise shall there be in the school? Just enough to assist each and all to do their best work. How quiet shall it be? Just quiet enough to assist each and all to do their best work. How much whispering? What shall be the rules for coming in and going out? For punctuality? Every rule of a school, in order that it may be of educative influence and be felt to be right by each pupil, consists in carrying out this motto—"*Everything to help and nothing to hinder,*" The first essential to true manhood is to feel the dignity of life, and that dignity comes from a sense of responsibility for the conduct of others.

There is but one test, one genuine test, of a school, which may be explained by two questions: First, is every individual in this school doing educative work in the most economical way? Second, is that work the best for the whole, and at the same time the best for each individual? If the answer to these questions is in the affirmative in regard to any school, then it can be said to be in order. The prefect ideal of order is that each and every minute shall be filled with that work which best assists each and all in growth and development.

The initial steps in inducing the government here defined are indeed the most difficult. Children enter school with marked habits of inattention, with a cultivated dislike for work, and frequently with the feeling that the teacher is their natural enemy. The question, then, of first importance, is: How can habits of work or self-effort be induced? This question cannot be easily answered, but certain marked factors in it may be mentioned. The highest qualification of a teacher is a dominating love for children, manifested by a strong desire to assist them. The second qualification, an outcome of the first, is that a teacher must be a persistent, close student of the subjects taught. Third, must be a persistent, close students of the subjects taught. Third, he must have power and skill in the manifestation of thought. And, fourth, he must have the courage of his convictions.

It is common to humanity to worship power, and children, above all other persons, have this inborn tendency. A teacher who has a high grade of skill in singing, in drawing, in oral reading—in fact a skill in any or all of the modes of expression—has a rare opportunity to initiate and cultivate habits of work on the part of pupils. The influence of the teacher's personality,

moral and intellectual power, and skill, never can be overestimated; every act of the teacher is perpetuated in the conduct of
his pupils.

A knowledge of each pupil's individuality, gained by intuition and the study of psychology, is a necessity with a teacher.
Tact on the part of a teacher means the presentation of conditions adapted to the individual effort. Next to tact, and dominated by it, comes the courage which is born of a high ideal,
great love for children, a clear conception of what they need in
growth, and the power and persistence in a skillful presentation
of the right conditions.[1] Children feel and admire courage in a
teacher. Courage manifests itself in quietness, in poise, in the
appearance of reserve force, never threatening and never yielding
to wrong. Children know instinctively, from a short study of a
teacher, what stands before them in the way of work. The highest duty of a teacher is to direct the energies of the pupils, and to
this task he must address himself from the outset.

One very important suggestion may here be made, a teacher
should never lose a moment's time in trivial things, but go
directly to the most interesting work. Children, however, indifferent at first, soon appreciate a demand for educative work. Prejudices and purposes which tend to disorder may be overcome by
an immediate demand on the part of the teacher for such action
as will lead the pupils to forget all their bad intentions. No matter how much courage or intuitive tact and skill a teacher may
have, if the children are not led immediately to work, if the
conditions are not adapted to the absorption of the mental and
moral powers of the child, then control must be gained by arbitrary means.

Order limits personal energy to educative work. Educative
work is that self-effort needed for the education of the whole
being; body, mind, and soul. This question still remains, and
will remain as an everlasting and unsolved problem: *What is*

the work which educates? One general answer may be given: The exercise of the mind in the acquisition of that knowledge most needed for personal power and present use.

But knowledge is boundless, and your pupils can get but a drop of the ocean. What knowledge shall you present them in the years you have them under your care and guidance? What rule shall govern you in the selection? The answers are not far to seek: Your selections can be entirely governed by what each individual pupil needs for his personal development. He needs that knowledge which will enable him to best serve the school and world. The two answers are one: The needs of the school and the world are the needs of the individuals. The child should study history. Why? Because history is the record of the struggle of the human spirit to acquire freedom. He is to go through a like struggle if he would be free. History is the path to freedom, over miseries untold, over battlefields, over wretchedness and woe. The child is the inheritor of the experience of the past, and history presents him with that inheritance. This rich inheritance is to be given to all; the child may be a mediator. Who can understand history without the love of all mankind in his soul? Love is an interpreter of history.

Much is said about the development of patriotism in a child, and much more should be said. There is a kind of patriotism which may be called family love, and which limits efforts to the good of the family alone. There is another kind of patriotism which limits efforts to the community in which one lives, without regard to the good of others. There is a national patriotism, a love of one's own country, in which the main question is: What is the immediate good of my people? But, under the light of truth, under the highest ethical motives, there is no patriotism in this world worthy the name, no true religion, that does not embrace every child born under the shining sun. And in proportion as this motive controls the being, so will be the desire to study and know more of all humanity, its past history, its present conditions, its prospects for the future. Indeed, history, properly studied, has for its product a deep and profound sympathy throughout with the struggles of mankind for higher conditions.[2]

But history is vast and time is short: What particular history should a child study in the eight years? The history of American life, and the genius of American liberty; not, indeed, the history that dates from 1776 or 1492, but that history which reaches away to the Magna Charta, to republican Rome, to Greece, to the hills of Palestine, to all the heroes and martyrs who have lived and died to make men free. The child should be led to feel the heartbeats of liberty in all ages; to feel in his soul the pricelessness of his inheritance; that he is bought with a price—the suffering and blood of untold millions. Why? That he may feel the responsibility of living; that he may put himself, a courageous influence, into human life; that he may understand when he casts a ballot that he is choosing the right for his people and for the world.

History properly taught joins the individual to the whole race, past and present, with bonds of sympathy and love. One can learn in no other way than by unprejudiced study of history the breadth and depth of Christ's words: "Blessed are the merciful, for they shall obtain mercy." Biography should instill lofty motives, high aims, and the duty of heroic action. The student who knows something of the past, and from its lessons draws righteous inferences, is able to judge more correctly of the present needs of humanity. *The immediate outcome of the study of history can be applied every hour in the community life of the school.* What subjects in history should be selected? Those subjects that have the strongest influence over right action in the schoolroom, in the home, in life.

Why should children study science? History is the path but

science is the guide to freedom. Let it be remembered that science is the knowledge of creation, and therefore of the Creator. The application of science is the economizing of energy, the secret of all progress. What science does a child need? That science which makes home better—better cooking, plumbing, better air—and improves all the means of health and sanitation; that science which improves the fertility of the soil; which binds a nation together—nay, the world—by railroads and electric wires; which can be put to immediate and continual use. Science gives us inspiration, because it presents the means for a higher condition or development in the light of true motive. "All are needed by each one," and it can no longer be argued that the development of motive is narrow; it is as broad as humanity, as deep as the ocean of truth, as high as the throne of God.

It is the present, the immediate use of knowledge acquired, that arouses in children the highest zest for learning.[8] The adaptation of subjects to immediate practical needs is the sure guide to the selection of materials in the teaching of elementary science: The weather of each day, the vegetation of spring, summer, and autumn, the needs of winter, the geography of home, in fact the earth that pupils walk on, the air they breathe, the water they drink, their food and clothing, present an endless number of interesting and profitable subjects. In every lesson function or use leads the way. The lesson of lessons the child will learn is that God gives the universe to man, and regulates it by wise laws. Science is the essential means of cultivating an intelligent and all-controlling love for the Creator.

Civics, when properly taught, enters into the child's life as a most essential factor; it is the science of mutual relations and duties. *The little community called the school represents the best possible conditions for the cultivation of these relations and duties.* There is never an hour in schoolroom life that does not call for positive exercise of every article in the positive code of morals universally acceded to by mankind. Why should a pupil study with all his might? To satisfy his own need and because his example in work has the highest influence for good upon a whole class. The individual should feel that the influence of each one is important, and that there is no means more potent than by doing whatever he has to do in the best possible way. His perserverance, his struggle in overcoming difficulties, all have the strongest power to induce the same earnestness and zeal in others. Why should he desist from making undue noise, from distracting the attention of others, and preventing them from doing their best work? The answer is plain: He is hindering the work of the whole school. Why should he not whisper? Why should he be punctual and prompt? Why should he be attentive? The feeling on the part of the child will be perfect if right conditions are presented in this direction; if he can be made to fully realize his relation to others and the rights of others.

In a recitation the *teacher* is there to present conditions for educative efforts on the part of each pupil; he watches every mental act with absorbing interest; he is very careful not to allow his own prejudgments to interfere with free mental action of his pupils, still holding them, however, strictly to the subject in hand. In open discussions individuality will show itself in a strong light: no two pupils will think alike, have the same concept, or draw identical inferences. The chief value of a recitation consists in each individual contributing his mite of self-effort for the good of all, attrition of mind with mind changing and modifying the point of view. A teacher who is a genuine student will receive far more from his pupils than he gives—just as a reflection of a landscape will bring out points and perfections that are not felt in the general outlook. The sole motive of the teacher is to assist each pupil to put forth his highest efforts; and that which is true of the teacher is just as true of the pupil, whose sole motive, however unconscious, is to assist all his mates in the best possible way. This is, and will be, possible under the right conditions; but, *per contra,* when pupils are working for a mark, a per-cent, a promotion, or to surpass others, their thinking powers are lamed and crippled, and their best energies are wasted. In the former mode of recitation there is a consensus of opinion, a comparison of views brought about by a determined search for the truth, in which all earnestly participate. The effect of such a recitation is independent study, arousing interest and directing economical research. School life can thus be made ideal life—a unity of individual lives under one purpose, that of interesting, educative, and therefore profitable, work.

The predominant condition, then, for moral training is community life, the society of the school. The social factor in education stands far above all other factors—higher than principles, methods, subjects, and the teacher. It is not possible to educate a child at home by private tutors. "The greatest study of mankind is man." By attrition of mind with mind, knowledge of other characters, perception of weakness and strength, feeling of duty, generous competition, unselfish giving of one's self for the good of the community, the child acquires lessons more necessary to his well-being than by all possible book study.

The inestimable glory of the common school is that it contains all the necessary factors of an embryonic democracy. With the altruistic motive controlling the teacher and his methods, the conditions are perfect. Here measures and gauges of history are acquired by actual experience; here civics is essentially practiced; the roots of after-life, the springs of action, are all here. Home is the center; the church makes home better; but the common school is the place where the lessons gained in both may be essentially practiced. Here classes learn to respect each other; the children of the rich and the poor; the intelligent and the ignorant are fused and blended by mutual action and mutual love.

The common schools present a perfect means of moral train- ing; order, work, and play all tending to the cultivation of true manhood.

Ethical life is ethical action; this action in school is expres- sion under all its modes. The motive and zest of study are found in the manifestation of thought. Dr. Salomon, founder of Sloyd, insists that the controlling motive in making any piece of wood- work is the use of it. The child is controlled by the emotion— "This is to be for father. This is to be for mother. This is to be for the household." [4] In every cut of his knife, in every observa- tion of his own handwork, the whole child full of zeal and earnestness is concentered upon the use to be made of the object. If the object is imperfectly made, its function is limited, or fails utterly. Under this guiding motive, steady, prolonged work is the result; difficulties that would otherwise seem insuperable are easily overcome.

That which is true of woodwork is just as true of the other conceptive modes of expression. Art is the fundamental means of telling the truth. What words, spoken or written, cannot do, the clay, the brush, the pencil, can do. Art is then an indispensa- ble means of cultivating truth-telling. Any touch of truth in the soul demands expression. The pupil feels that his mates are interested in everything he says or does; the teacher is there to accept nothing but his best efforts. Music, speech, writing, making, modeling, painting, and drawing, are at hand, for the manifestation of thought in all its phases. *Every act of expres- sion under true teaching is made an ethical act.* Every demand for expression is a demand for the discovery of truth.

I have thus presented a glimpse of the educative work with which school-hours and the hearts of children may be filled. There is not, neither can there be, any cause of disorder, except by lack of work which educates. All truly educative work is interesting; no one can ever study anything that is good without loving it. This statement needs no proof, for truth is the design of both study and expression; and truth is beautiful.

True order and moral training are evidently one and the same thing, so that any discussion of moral training comprehends the discussion of school government. I shall not attempt to give anything like a comprehensive definition of morality; my sole purpose is to show that the school is one continuous opportunity for righteous action.

Let us take it for granted that the human being was created and designed for the exercise of the highest moral power; that in each individual there are germs of the divine; and that all education is the outworking of this design of God. However much evil there may be in heredity, however much there may be in the child that is abnormal, notwithstanding tendencies that seemingly point toward evil, I shall take it for granted that the predominating tendencies of a human being are intrinsically moral, and that education consists entirely in the presentation of conditions for the exercise and outworking of moral power. Therefore, moral training, which comprehends all education, consists in that teaching and training which leads to the designed development of the child; the realization of possibilities for good and growth. If this hypothesis be granted, that education is the outworking of the design of God into highest character, into highest possibilities of individual development, then all education is, in itself, intrinsically moral. I repeat that education is the outworking of God's design into character; that all education is by self-effort; that the process of education consists in presenting the right conditions for personal self-effort; and that every self-effort that moves toward the outworking of the design is intrinsically right. Method is the perfect adaptation of conditions to self-effort, and therefore natural method, that which is in conformity to law, is in itself moral.

Education involves the adaption and presentation of all the

conditions needed for personal development; therefore any embodiment of these conditions in a course of study, for instance, is a system of morality and ethics. In education, there is absolutely no separation of intellectual and moral power. Morality is the direction of mental power, the movement of the being upward.

We will assume something which is generally believed and very little practiced—that all growth is by law, by the laws of the Creator. Method consists in the adaptation of the conditions necessary for the educative action of the whole being; in other words, method is the special adaptation of those conditions which bring about the highest action of law. Certainly self-effort in the direction of growth is moral, and method has for its sole purpose the right direction of self-effort. Natural method is the exact adaptation of subjects to the action of law; therefore natural method must be in the highest degree moral.

Education consists wholly and entirely in the cultivation of the altruistic motive; the motive without which religion is a delusion; the motive presented in the life and words of Christ; the motive of making one's own life and character of the greatest possible benefit to mankind. Although this motive is fully recognized as the central principle of all religions worthy of the name, still a practical belief in it is in abeyance; indeed, philosophy has been invoked to deny that the highest mission of man is universal salvation. Personal happiness is defined as the goal of life by the utilitarians, and they present a strong argument in support of their proposition.

I take issue squarely with this, and call your attention to a few arguments that have fully convinced me that the development of the altruistic motive is the end and aim of education. *Vox populi, vox Dei* is true of a civilized people after a long interval between deeds and final judgments. Beyond the blinding glare of famous lives you will find one common standard of judgment—how much love, how much of self-abnegation, how much self-sacrifice for the good of family, the state, the nation, and the world? The memory of Alexander, Caesar, Napoleon—although they were indirectly of great use in progress, and all honor is given them—lie cold and dead as ideals in human hearts; while the exalted lives of Socrates, Pestalozzi, Froebel, Horace Mann, John Bright, Florence Nightingale, Washington, and the greatest of all, Abraham Lincoln, will ever be beaconlights for mankind. If we could discover a scintilla of selfishness in Christ we should reject him. Great force of character or genius, combined with selfishness, inordinate ambition, and all-controlling avarice, leads, often to great political power, to wealth, to bloody victories, but beyond it cannot lead. There never was a bit of true art, music, song, painting, sculpture, or poetry, destined to immortality, that did not spring from inspiration born of love.

"If the altruistic motive assumes entire control," you exclaim, "what is to become of self and self-interest?" "What of knowledge, of physical training, of personal success? Does not self-abnegation mean the giving up of self?" Find answer, perfect assurance, and the "peace that passeth all understanding" in the divine paradox: "He who would save his life must lose it." There is no incentive, no impulse, no spur equal to this sublime assertion. Persistence, endurance, martyrdom, death, the salvation of man, all possibilities of life here and hereafter, are comprehended under it.

All the truth in the world ever transmitted to knowledge by human minds is needed by man. Search for truth gives man power; its application raises the possibilities of the seeking for truth to higher levels. The transcendent motive for the search for knowledge is the clear vision of mankind needing and waiting its application. Knowledge is sweet in itself, "sweeter than honey and the honeycomb"; but the discovery of truth reaches its sublime height when the discoverer feels in his heart of hearts that this is for the dying world, this is for the "millions yet to be," this is for time and eternity.

Thus in developing motive we develop everything; motive is the center, and everything comes to it. It is the application of the profound principle of the Great Teacher—"Seek ye first the kingdom of God and His righteousness, and all things shall be added unto you." Inspiration comes only with motive. Look down the ages, and for every great act of self-abnegation, for every great self-sacrifice, for every thought that lives and burns in the hearts of men, and you will find the motive of love to mankind. It is preached from every pulpit; emphasized in all teaching—practiced where?

That which is the consensus of human judgment, that which is the essence of all divine revelation, should be the center of the education of children. Children enter school with their souls too often clouded by "home-made" selfishness; but long experience proves that the moment they mingle with a community, the deep interest in others, which is spontaneous in all children, may be easily directed by skillful teachers into a desire to help others. Nothing appeals more strongly to a child than the idea that he can be of use to others. This germ is easily developed into a strong controlling motive, a habit of living. At what point in school life will selfishness enter? I answer without qualification—just where it is cultivated!

The power to choose the truth and apply it is the highest gift of God to man. "The truth shall make you free," means that, given the right conditions, the human soul will find that tentative truth which is best for itself. The controlling authorities of past and even present civilizations have everlastingly denied the right of man to exercise his reasoning faculties in all directions; in this denial is the inner secret of human misery. Every step onward in civilization is dependent upon finding and applying the truth. Every step in personal development is through original inference and its practical application. No human being can find the truth for another; the highest aim should be to discover conditions that will enable others to reason in the right direction. The command is, "work out your own salvation." Reason is the supreme faculty of man; its proper exercise is the direct purpose of all teaching. *Teaching consists in the presentation of the best conditions for the exercise of judgment.*

Ideally, the child should choose only the right, and therefore should have only the conditions for right choosing presented. Nothing but the right should ever be presented to the child. The old teaching of evil, so that by knowing evil the child may avoid it, is fundamentally and everlastingly wrong—pernicious to the last degree. Evil is negative, good is positive. The good is true, and the good is beautiful; and nothing but the true, the beautiful, and the good should ever be presented to the child. The principle so often enunciated, that a child should never see a wrong form, should never make a wrong form, is to be applied in all directions. A child should never have anything presented to him that is not in itself beautiful. He should learn to lift his eyes to the true and the good, as the flowers do to the sunlight. But how will the child know the evil if good is always presented? is the pertinent question of some inquiring teacher. He will know all of evil that is necessary for him to know by the shade that it casts over the good; he will be educated above its temptations by the positive root of good in himself; when evil offends the taste and does not arouse inclination or desire, it has lost its most potent influence. If the love, and therefore, the desire, for the true, the good, and the beautiful is "thoroughly informed" in the child, the abnormal has lost its power; it is felt at once to be a counterfeit, and who will ever knowingly choose a makeshift when the real thing can be had without money and without price?

It is said that in China, where there are countless coins of different kinds, counterfeiting is prevalent, and experts are carefully trained to detect bad coins. This is accomplished by requiring them to handle for three or more years good coins, and when thus trained they detect counterfeits instantly. This illustrates a fundamental principle; *spend no time in presenting the wrong; always present the right and the true.* Furthermore, present it for the choice of the child. Evil will always come of itself; civil is accidental; it is a negation for every right deed. When evil comes and the child has no light by which to detect it, then present the positive and let the child choose. Good is always predominant, good is always beautiful, and the nature of the child, where the training has been in any degree normal, inevitably gravitates toward good.

The training of choice through reason is the training of will; indeed, it is impossible to analyze the ego without the will. The will is that which is behind every action, thought, or expression of the human being. The will controls attention, reflection, the acts of expression, indeed, the whole being. The will is the executive of the ego; there is no act of the ego, good or bad, without simultaneous act of the will.

Motive controls, reason chooses, will executes. Will is self-effort; teaching and training present the conditions for self-effort. Motive without execution dies; therefore next to the motive in education stands the training of the will by educative work. Habits of reason, continuity of action in one direction, patience, persistence, courage, self-control, are formed by the exercise of the will, exercise in actual doing of that which is to be done. Training of the will leads to prolonged, persevering, independent struggles to overcome obstacles, to find and apply the truth.

The value of an act of the will consists entirely in its content, or, in other words, the direction of the action determines the power acquired. The most effective discipline is acquired by the action of the being upon those conscious activities needed for the immediate stage of personal development. To step outside of this rule, for means of *discipline,* is to grant that there is not sufficient intrinsic truth for the exercise and training of the will. Teaching has for its central purpose the training of attention. Attention is that power of the being to hold itself in the best possible attitude for the action of external attributes. The will is exercised in observation, hearing-language, and reading, which are modes of attention. Acts of attention should be essentially moral acts, so that reading, the study of texts, and observation should be limited to that which is true and invigorating literature.

Exercises in expression, under each and all the modes, if properly conducted, train the will as in no other way. In the conceptive modes, the action must be steady, continuous, and prolonged; there is an ideal to be realized by action; the concept must be held in consciousness, the hand must be controlled by the will.

Imagination is the heart of the being; the images that occupy the mind and control the desires make man's destiny. Out of imagination springs the ideal which guides and dominates. "The pure in heart shall see God." The content of imagination should be the reflections of truth. Literature should be the interpretation of truth.

Teaching has for its main function the cultivation of the creative power of the mind. Imagination is the norm of creation. Observation prepares for the exercise of the imagination, reading exercises it, study intensifies it. What a child's imagination will be is determined by the subjects and methods of his thought and its expression.

In the education of the child the formulation of moral precepts should be the outcome of his own reflection and experience; these will, and should, come very slowly through induction, the outcome of ethical action. Moral training consists in the presentation of effective conditions for virtuous deeds. The laws of action, or the principles of right doing, should grow out of the doing itself. The ideal of the school should be that all action is positively moral. Keep the child *unconscious of motive,* of the goodness of his own movements, just as long as possible. "The kingdom of heaven cometh not with observation." Should there be a certain portion of time devoted to morals? Should there be textbooks in that direction? Not as isolated, didactic periods but in a larger sense all teaching should be intrinsically moral, and all good books are textbooks of morals.

History, the account of the human spirit, striving through long ages to find the truth; biography, the record of the lives of men and women who have lived and died for humanity; pure literature, the reflection of noble souls and the interpretation of nature; myth, the fire-mist of religion; civics, the science of community life; science, the search for the natural laws revealed through the universe by the All-Loving; mathematics, the weighing and measuring His work: all are moral—shall I say religions? Formal lessons in morals are unwise below the university, where ethics as a science can be studied intelligently and comprehensively.

The demand for teaching morals as an isolated subject springs from the absence of moral effects in all other teaching. If, however, moral precepts are not to be used as guides to action, what are true means of inducing moral and ethical effort? I answer, the feeling of righteousness, caused by educative acts. I have already illustrated this, under education of motive. The child at home feels that it is right to do what he sees done by his parents: the girl wants to cook, to sew, to sweep, and to keep house; the boy, to buy and to sell, to drive the horse, to mow, to plow; in fact, all attempts at imitation are made under this feeling. In woodwork, the pupil feels that it is right to make some article of house furniture, some apparatus which he is to use in experiments. This motive unifies mental and physical action; he puts his whole mind upon the work, brings to bear all his skill, because the article when properly finished is to be of use. In the same work, form and number are acquired; they are necessities in making. All this is essentially moral, because of the strong feeling of right which a child experiences when using all his powers to apply a truth adapted to his present condition. The delight felt in original inference, and in the collecting of data necessary to the exercise of judgment, is a sweet and wholsome emotion, which, constantly induced, will bring lasting good to the child.

In the free expression of thought on the part of children, there is continual pleasure. They will speak, write, model, paint, draw, and sing with great confidence and delight. This sense of right doing is the true interest by which mental energy may be used for its best outcome. The child lives in the present; immediately anticipated pleasure may enchant him; but his experience is so limited that he can have little judgment and less interest in regard to the future values of his studies.

The feeling of right and of interest is the fruitful germ of anticipated pleasure; the day will come to him when faith in the future will compel him to long continuous struggles in study and work. It is too often urged that a child should be given hard, uninteresting tasks, or disciplinary studies, in order to prepare him for close and prolonged application. Nothing can be farther from the truth; if in youth the child has felt the warm glow of interest in all his school-work, the spark engendered will brighten into an enduring flame, will become the inspiration of long years spent in unremitting work and study.

It is impossible to discuss one faculty of the mind without including all. We can say with truth that the proper development of motive, will, and reason is education; one cannot be trained without the others; each is involved in all. That faculty of the mind which has the dominant influence in deciding motive and directing the will is emotion. Joy, happiness, interest, are different names for the same thing; they are synonyms for pleasurable, agreeable, healthful emotions. I need not pause to discuss the inestimable blessing happiness is to man; life devoid of pleasure is worthless. My purpose is to discuss the fundamental principle of true happiness and the method by which it may be cultivated. Permanent happiness is the result of continuous, persistent self-efforts in the normal, all-sided development of the body, mind, and soul. The most effective self-efforts are only possible under the highest motives; therefore happiness is the product of doing the greatest amount of good for humanity.

The two statements are one in content and meaning; education presents the means for the full exercise of the laws of personal development, of which self-activity is the central factor. The emotions of pleasure excited by the most economical, and therefore the most effective, self-effort in the line of self-needs are right—the healthiest, strongest, and most enduring. Emotion is the immediate result of thought; the higher or the more educative the thought, the more intense will be the emotion. The supreme mental act is that of original inference, or the mind in action, searching for law. Original inference is conditioned upon data or knowledge of facts; insufficiency of data makes correct inference impossible.

The central factor of class teaching consists in watching closely the mind of each pupil. Teaching, you will remember, is presenting conditions for educative mental action. In order to judge of the conditions to be immediately presented, the state of the pupil's mind must be known. The standpoint of the teacher's judgment of mental action dominates that action. There is but one true standpoint, and that is of the power of original inference. Original inference is the highest test of that knowledge which is power. If the knowledge is wrong or insufficient, the inference will be wrong. By a skillful question or suggestion the pupil is made to see mistakes, and by the same token is driven to revise his data or seek for new facts. A demand for inference is a demand for knowledge, and at the same time points to the facts to be acquired; facts are the eyes through which we see laws.

Science is acquired by a series of inferences, a process of reasoning, classification, and generalization. A new inference, then, is based upon all previous facts and inferences. Science is an organically related body of generalizations derived from facts; inferences broaden and deepen at every step, and clearer and more comprehensive generalizations spring from the knowledge of relations of sciences to each other. The effort in original inference demands related knowledge.

Self-effort in making original inferences is the highest quality of mental action. If the teacher concentrates all his efforts upon quality of action, the quantity of knowledge will take care of itself. Quality of mental action cannot exist without quantity of knowledge, but quantity may be acquired without the slightest efforts at quality. Quality of mental action is intensity of action; to the conscious center of quality gravitate all the facts and judgments that have ever existed in the mind. This is a fundamental law of psychology.

Original inference exercises the supreme power of the mind —the power to acquire that knowledge which is in itself power. Under this effort, knowledge becomes a dominant necessity and is acquired with the greatest possible ease. The exercise of the pupils' minds in processes of reasoning, enables the teacher to sharply discriminate individual power, and to weigh personal attainment. When pupils fail to reason correctly after the best help and repeated efforts, the teacher will understand that they are beyond their depth; he must go back to a safe starting point.

But the most prominent feature of this genuine teaching is the pure delight pupils will take in the search for truth. That which is best for the unspoiled child gives it the greatest pleasure. The emotion that springs from the search for truth is second only to the purest joy in the world—the application of truth for the good of others.

Self-conceit is not possible to one who has a heart open to the truth; the joy of profound humility which comes when a glimpse of infinite truth fills the soul, leaves no room for egotism.

The possibilities for mental, moral, and ethical action in school are unlimited; opportunities for virtuous deeds are countless. The faculties of the mind are capable of infinite development; true, they await the teachers, as the mighty stored-up energies of steam, heat, electricity, and sound awaited their discoverers. When the teachers come, all the marvels of the nineteenth century will sink into insignificance before the full manhood and womanhood of realized possibilities.

If the application of methods that conform to the laws of the being constitutes moral education and leads to ethical action, what shall be said of methods not growing out of, and derived from, the laws of the being? Are they immoral? Is this too sweeping, too frightful, an accusation? I will draw up the indictment for your decision:

(1) Methods not adapted to the laws of the being obstruct self-effort, waste the pupil's time, and deprive him of the free use of all his powers.

(2) The learning of dead forms, or symbols without thought, not only wastes the time of children, but cultivates self-conceit, self-consciousness, obstructs the action of imagination, and inhibits reason.

(3) That study of history which demands a belief in the views and prejudices of a narrow-minded author or teacher induces bigotry and hate. History, taught from the standpoint

of a creed, a party, or a nation, is often replete with prejudice and false statements. The one-sided teaching of history narrows the sympathies and shuts the soul from the broadcast love of humanity.

(4) The textbook study of science, which consists in the *verbatim* learning of facts that should be gained by observation, and the memorizing of inferences that should be original, hems in a child's spontaneous activities, and robs him of his love for truth.

(5) Drawing from copies, and all mere imitations, weakens the power of observation, and reduces the educative influence of the study of art.

(6) Corporal punishment degrades the soul, and makes children cowards.

(7) Rewards, marks, prizes, per-cents, cultivate selfishness and destroy unity of action, making the altruistic motive wellnigh impossible.

(8) When a teacher controls by sheer will-power, reinforced by corporal punishment and rewards, his pupils have no opportunity to exercise their own wills.

The latter proposition will possibly be misunderstood, and therefore needs some explanation. There are teachers of such strong will-power that they overcome the wills of the children, and so-called order is the product—the order of arbitrary authority, which is in itself frightful disorder. The pupils are still; they study in perfect obedience and under the perfect control of the teacher. If the bare will of the teacher is not strong enough to accomplish this sad result, then arbitrary means must be used —punishment, reward, or both means of controlling or suppressing any exercise of the child's will, or the formation of habits of self-choice. This order, under the control of the teacher's will, to inexpert eyes seems the proper thing. The room is quiet, the children are busy. But this occupation is not educative work;

they are busy, not because of interest in the work, filled with the joy of overcoming; but because they must be, out of fear of punishment or hope of reward.

If the teacher's will is the child's will, and if the child has no feeling of the right of choice, if the habit of choosing is not formed and confirmed in the child, then he becomes will-less, a being to be controlled by others, drifting weakly and helplessly, at the mercy of every strong current that seizes upon him.

There are plenty of examples of home tyranny. Parents, though loving their children as only parents can love, often demand unquestioned obedience, and bend the wills of their children to a rigid subservience, unenlightened by reason. The broken spirits sullenly obey and silently rebel; the opportunities of liberty are awaited to indulge a helpless will in license, and very often vice.[5]

I have seen schools in which discipline had reached the ultimate. The machinery for the entire subjugation of the will was perfect. The pupils stared at the white walls opposite as if their lives depended upon perfect rigidity of muscle. They stood up, recited, sat down, as if moved by springs controlled by electric wires. The teachers exhibited their schools as if wonders had been accomplished. The poor victims of mistaken education were deprived of all right to exercise the slighest liberty of action, not to say reason. When we see a vast multitude of unthinking citizens blindly obeying the orders of a modern tyrant, the political boss, the cause of such awful degradation is not far to seek. Children trained to unthinking obedience becomes the means by which greedy politicians degrade democracy and act for its entire overthrow. *The primary gift of God to man is choice; and education should be the presentation of conditions for choice, for the exercise of reason.* We may take it whichever way we will, if we say the outcome of education is to be a true citizen,

then the citizen's highest influence is right choice for the whole
people.

Here is the difficulty: The shortest road to so-called order,
which is very generally understood to mean stillness and the
delusive appearance of educative work, is the result of the immediate will of the teacher; the children are wrenched into line;
they are forced into habits of quietness. On the contrary, if the
child's will is to be educated, if the order and the industry of
the schoolroom is to be the outgrowth of his own self-control and
self-interest, there will be, it goes without saying, in the initial
steps some apparent disorder; children must have a chance to
choose, and given such chance, will exercise the judgment to be
expected of such immature minds. If a child commits a crime
against the school, an immediate punishment may settle the case
and bring quietness, if this is the end to be worked for; but it
does not educate the child; he has no choice, he is not led to rule
himself, he is compelled to comply through fear.

I grant at once that there are times in life when the mother's
will should be the child's will; that there are times in school-
work when the teacher's will should be the pupil's will; but
any exercise of authority on the part of parent or teacher which
does not contain the reason for the order, or any exercise of the
will which does not bring the exercise of the child's will to coin-
cide with the parent's or teacher's (and in every instance the
child should be made to feel the justice of the demand), is fundamentally wrong; is the perpetuation of that mode of government by which tyranny has kept the spirit of man for ages from
seeking and finding the truth; is varying oppresive and suppres-
sive methods, so effective in the past, into the embryonic democracy, into the central hope of freedom, the common school.

In the past, corporal punishment was the principal means
of enforcing the will of the teacher. Corporal punishment has
for its basis the working hypothesis that children are bad by

birth, by nature, and by tendency, and that this badness must be surpressed; that children do not like educative work; that it is necessary to discipline the mind through fear. Corporal punishment has for its basis the idea that children will not do right unless they are forced to do it, and because of this the horrible anticipation of continual punishment is placed before them. The child gets his lesson and does his work under the controlling emotion that if he does not do it he will be punished. Few of us who live to-day have any appreciation of how far this principle was carried only a few years back. Some older person can tell the story of corporal punishment. Oliver Optic (William T. Adams), well known to children, once said to me: "If I left out even the smallest word in my page recitation, an 'and' or a 'the,' I heard the stern call of the master, 'Adams, come to the desk!' and I knew what that meant." "Fear is the beginning of wisdom, but perfect love casteth out fear."

The change from punishment to another great auxiliary to the will of the teacher is reward—presents, prizes, promotions; from an appeal to cowardice, to love of approbation or avarice. The change from fear was the hope of some extraneous reward, some special mark of approbation on the part of the teacher, something that could be heralded as a triumph on the part of the pupil. Bad as corporal punishment has been and is, the substitute of a system of rewards is infinitely worse. Fear of punishment is bad enough, indeed, but the systematic development of selfishness is damnable. The infliction of corporal punishment is degrading to the mind, but the hope of extraneous reward for study destroys the highest motive and sedulously develops its opposite, selfishness. I would place corporal punishment and reward-giving as in the highest degree criminal; as criminal as lying, stealing or swearing. I know it is not generally understood in this way; but I ask of you, my fellow teachers, to look at it with the greatest care.[6] Why is it that the sordid nature of man is so highly developed in our country? Why is it that man looks upon his fellow man as a means to his own selfish ends? Why is it that we doubt almost every man who seeks for office—doubt whether he loves his country more than he does himself? To-day, one of the most prominent products of our schools is the systematic cultivation of selfishness—want of an interest in public welfare, public interests, the best needs of the commonwealth. Do you question this? Study the situation with that courage which dares to doubt!

"Would you not cultivate ambition?" some one says. "Are not Webster, Clay, and Calhoun the products of ambition?" Continue the list and include many modern statesmen! Is it not true that if we as citizens could go to the polls and vote for public servants, with a complete or reasonable conviction that our candidates love their country more than they do themselves, we should be profoundly happy?

Were not the few really great men the products of the "old education" you ask? They were certainly saved from that education, but who can count the lost? Bought at home, bought at school, with merits, per-cents, and prizes, bought in college and university by the offer of high places, the young man with a finished education stands in the world's market-place and cries: "I'm for sale; what will you give for me?"

What is prize-giving and what the results? Each child is born with personal power. He owes physical, mental, and moral power, and its foundations, not to himself, but to his ancestors, taking strains of strength or weakness from the remote past. One child comes into the world with the inborn power to do incomparably better work than another child. A prize is offered; it is genarally known from the beginning that the getting of that prize will be confined to one among two or three children. Prize-giving is the rewarding of an ancestor; rewarding a child for the virtues and mental power of his great-great grandfather.

A child dimly feels this, and if constantly led to accept honors which come so easily, his sense of justice is warped and blunted; you have developed an aristocrat keenly alive to his own rights, not a citizen regardful of the rights of all. But that is not the worst of it! The child with inborn weakness looks in despair upon the mark of approbation to his mate, and in his despair he sinks, his confidence is gone, his manhood is degraded, and the loss to one soul is a loss to every soul in the community. The only safe thing to reward is *self-effort*—self-effort measured by the capabilities of the individual. True teaching discriminates individual power. Each child is different in character from all other children; the weakness and strength of each child are understood and appreciated, and then the self-effort is measured by the child's personal capabilities. True, children come into competition with each other, but that competition should be generous, should be the recognition of each other's powers, each other's weaknesses, and a desire to help or to be helped, a mutual giving and taking.

The same general criticism may be made upon presents and rewards, promotions and rankings. It is a very easy way to arouse abnormal activity on the part of children, this hope of reward; but it quickens and stimulates undesirable results. A child is dominated by one desire, controlled by one motive—"I wish to succeed; I am glad when I excel my classmates, when I arrive at the head." The boy rushes home, filled with the joy of a conqueror. He flies into his mother's arms and cries, "I am at the head of the class! All the others are below me; I have beaten them!" No Christianity, no religion on earth, can eradicate this monstrous tendency of selfishness, which parents and teachers are ignorantly and prayerfully fostering. The cultivation of the reward system in our schools is the cultivation of inordinate ambition, the sinking of every other motive into the one of personal success. The reason why education to-day is looked upon with such narrow views, the reason why the learning of dead forms is forced upon the community, is that selfish man, living for self and in self, effectively excludes inspiration, does not study or care to help the wretchedness and woe of mankind. Men so trained are filled only with an ambition that controls them, narrows them, deprives them of all aspiration and reflection; they live and die for themselves. This is a severe arraignment against reward-giving, so common in our schools; but it is true, and the pity of it is that it is all so useless.

Corporal punishment is the enduring power of the old and long-tried method of making man utterly subservient to human authority; it is the living relic of dungeons, torture, police, standing armies, used to force human beings into unreasoning obedience and fixed beliefs; it suppresses the divine aspirations of the human soul in its struggles for the liberty to become free.

Reward-giving had its origin in bribery, the purchase of a bit of liberty enjoyed in the early republics; its effectual purpose was the reëstablishment of despotism.

Does not God grant rewards for virtuous deeds? Yes, He alone knows all the circumstances, the conditions, of individual life. His discrimination of self-effort is perfect: The thief upon the cross received a sweeter reward than the selfish rich man. His reward is love, and the more you give of that the better. School rewards propose to do the impossible—to measure desire, emotion, and motive, and to weigh character. There is no scale invented, no measure, however exact, that can give in numbers the value of effort. With effort you must weigh heredity, home surroundings, health, and vitality. All that rewards, per-cents, and prizes can measure is quantity learned and recited.

The only reason for the existence of corporal punishment and rewards is unnatural uneducative drudgery. They are the effective means of quantity-learning along the shortest line of resistance; order and quiet can be easily maintained by fear or reward, and an all-controlling ambition cultivated by the same auxiliaries. I have no hesitation in saying that the development of fear by punishment and of selfishness by reward is radically immoral. There is absolutely no necessity for either. Real genuine educative work, real search for truth and its ethical application, needs no other stimulus. Drudgery must be driven by fear of the unnatural incentive of rewards; but all-around educative work, work for the brain and hand, for the mind and body, work that best develops the whole being, work that is most needed by all the members of a school, brings its own sweet, joyous reward.

I shall not wonder if you more than doubt every word I say in regard to this subject; but I ask you to point out a school to me in which the needs of the whole being are met by perfect conditions. I can point out to you schools by the thousands in which hungry souls are never fed; in which the body shrivels and dwarfs; in which the "three R's" are the idols, worshipped until the soul is prostrated and the faculties benumbed. It is no fancy, no dream of the imagination, that children's souls are starved to death, while the universe is full of the bread of life. The doctrine of total depravity is man's excuse for his ignorance of the divine nature of the child. The fundamental reason why children do not act right is because they do not have the conditions for right action.

The talk of the Holy Spirit and all the comfort it has given us by the sense of the presence of God in our souls is well; but when it comes to some realization of His truth in nature, His truth in history, the expression of that truth, and its power to make for righteousness, we have absolutely no faith; we are infidels. Even in Sunday School rewards are offered, dinners are given, and children swell the numbers only to be more strongly directed and fortified in greed and selfishness. Educative work brings its own reward. No one can search for the truth without being touched as with a live coal from an altar. The cry of

"Eureka" has rung down the ages from the lips of the searchers for truth and from the hearts of reformers. It is possible that each and every child may quicken with this inspiration, the Holy Spirit of the highest life. Truth is not to be relegated only to the exceptional few; every child on this earth must have the conditions of finding the truth and feeling the truth for himself. "The kingdom of heaven is within you." To doubt this is to lack faith in the infinite possibilities of human growth, and the infinite means at hand to nourish them. This lack of faith in humanity is the greatest infidelity.

It is not a vision that I have presented; it is not a barren theory. Are there not bounteous means by which human action can be made joyous, exhilarating, both in the present and in anticipation? The answer is yes, and again, yes! The purpose of word-learning is a well-defined purpose to limit the human being to human authority. The purpose of seeking the truth is to find God, the Author of truth, and to be controlled entirely by Him. I have already said that all truth is God's truth. We sometimes make a difference between scientific truth and sacred truth, but there is no difference. God manifests Himself through the universe to human souls. He differentiates His all-efficient energy so that His manifestation may touch every mind from the weakest to the highest, that "he who runs may read."

I have argued in previous talks that there is but one study, and that the study of law. All law is truth itself; therefore all search for law must be intrinsically moral in itself. An honest, unprejudiced struggle of the soul to find the truth is a moral action—is second only to the highest moral action, which is the application of truth; therefore I can say with perfect confidence, that all real study is in the highest degree moral, and all application of the truth found, by the manifestation of thought through the different modes, is in the highest degree ethical when controlled by the motive for the good of others. There is nothing in physical or intellectual work that is not in itself intrinsically moral, a moral action at every step.

I know that there has been much discussion upon this particular point, and fear has been expressed that there is little or no moral training in our public schools, and a general verdict has been formed that there must be more specific moral training, that textbooks with moral precepts and moral directions must be introduced and studied. The solution of this problem is simple and plain; every bit of teaching should be intrinsically moral, and that teaching which has not a moral element in it, that teaching which is not prompted by the highest virtue, is not right teaching, and should be so branded. Special moral training in schools is a suggested remedy for that which need not exist.

The most fruitful cause of all the evils of school life is the lack of educative work. Most corporal punishment has its root in the righteous rebellion of children against mind-stupefying and disgusting drudgery. The brightest and best children refuse to toil when they see no reason for it and feel no pleasure in it; rebellion, alas, is their only resource. Prizes, rewards, per-cents, and all the means of stimulating selfishness, and that ambition which ends with self, spring from a profound unbelief that educative work, and right doing, brings its own sweet and sure reward.

Children are lost from total neglect. They cry for bread, and we give them a stone. Their whole nature seeks for the truth, and we give them the lie, in dead forms. The greatest proof of the divinity of the child is that he can meet the ignorant methods of parents and teachers, overcome them, and persist in goodness. The day is come when the grand positive precepts of the greatest sermon in the world, the Sermon on the Mount, are to be applied in depth and breadth throughout school life; the center of that sermon will be realized—"Blessed are those who hunger and thirst after righteousness, for they shall be filled." The Savior said these words because He knew that in human souls there is a depth of love and a breadth of desire which, if the right conditions were presented, would be developed into the highest moral and spiritual power.

[1] W. H. Kilpatrick, *Foundation of Method* (Macmillan), pp. 56-59, concerning "laws of learning" and the personality of the teacher.

[2] Edward Yoemans, *Shackled Youth* (Atlantic Monthly Press), pp. 26-46; the article entitled "A Teacher of History."

[3] John Dewey, *How We Think* (D. C. Heath), p. 11; "Demand for the solution of a perplexity is the steadying and guiding factor in the entire process of reflection." Also Thorndike says: *Education Psychology*, Vol. II, p. 51, "Purposive behavior is the most important case of the influence of the attitude, or set, or adjustment of an organism in determining

(1) What bonds shall act
(2) Which results shall satisfy."

[4] Caroline Pratt, *Experimental Practice in the City and Country School* (Dutton), pp. 12-14.

[5] Froebel, *Education of Man* (Appleton), p. 14 § 13.

[6] Stanwood Cobb, *The New Leaven* (John Day Co.), Chap. II, sec. 3 and 4 on "The Tyranny of Marks."

XV

SUMMARY OF THE DOCTRINE OF CONCENTRATION

IT HAS been my purpose in the preceding chapters to present an outline of a theory of concentration as a working hypothesis for investigation and study. I now propose to sum up the principal points in this theory, and to discuss some of the many difficulties in the way of its application.

First: The being to be developed determines what subjects and what methods shall be used. (a) The environment of the child acts upon it and thereby determines the initial steps of all the studies than can ever after be pursued. (b) The personality of the being determines also the action of external energies, and their reaction in expression. The spontaneous activities of the child are the sure and safe guides to finding and applying the conditions of education. (c) The investigation of instinct, intuition, and spontaneity is the scientific means of ascertaining the methods by which the child is mentally, morally, and physically developed. The laws of the being fix absolutely the conditions and methods of education. (d) The application of necessary conditions by perfect methods means the advancement of the being by the shortest line of resistance toward freedom, the goal of human progress. Imperfect methods obstruct and deflect these lines of advance. The highest economy in education, therefore, is found in the application of methods that strictly conform to the laws of development.

Second: The subject-matter found in the child's environment, to be used in its development, is classified under the head of central subjects; (a) geography, geology, and mineralogy—the sciences of inorganic matter; (b) physics and chemistry—the laws of movement and change of inorganic matter; (c) botany, zoölogy, anthropology, ethnology, and history—the sciences of organic matter and life; (d) physiology—the physics and chemistry of living organisms.

There is no classification in nature. The classification of the central subjects is, like all other classifications, only a means of study, an economy of mental action. The central subjects are in themselves an organic, inseparable, interdependent unit. The relation of a subject in itself to any one or to all the other subjects is as intimate as the relation of the part of any one subject to the whole subject. A tree, for instance, is as closely related to meteorology, geography, physics, and chemistry as a leaf to the twig or a limb to the trunk.

A child comes in contact with all these subjects in its environment, and begins instinctively its investigations in each and every one of the directions indicated by the central subjects. The doctrine of concentration proposes that these subjects be continued as a child has begun them, until there arrives that period of mental development when a specialization of subjects can most economically grow out of the rich subsoil of the related knowledge of all subjects. The direct study of the central subjects, by observation, investigation, imagination, and original inference, furnishes an inexhaustible means of educative mental action.

Third: All knowledge of externality depends absolutely upon that action of the ego called judgment; all acts of judgment or original inference depend as absolutely upon sense-products, elementary ideas, individual concepts.[1]

Sense-products are interpretations of external energies differentiated and expressed through qualities of matter—matter, in turn, being known by judging of the differentiated energies which act through it. All study consists in investigation of the changes brought about by energy acting through matter, organic and inorganic. The quality of energy creating or differentiating qualities of matter, in relation to time, space, and motion, demonstrates law; therefore all study is a study of law, of law under which energy acts and is acted upon. Form is the supreme manifestation of energy. Its correspondence in mind is the foundation of all knowledge. It is the product of the fundamental intellectual sense—that of touch. It is plain, then, that there can be no knowledge or interpretation of knowledge without a corresponding knowledge and interpretation of form. Form study is the indispensable basis of all knowledge of the central subjects. The mental process of direct form study is observation. The sense-products, corresponding to external forms, are reformed by the imagination. The science of form under the action of the imagination is geometry. Geometry is the science of imaging forms that lie beyond the sense grasp, that exist beyond the horizon of the senses, imagination being absolutely dependent upon the products of the senses. Form is the elementary science of geometry; they both have to do with the superficial limitations of objects and bodies of matter in space. It follows, therefore, that they both are integral factors of all study, indispensable to all knowledge.

Fourth: Form is the superficial limitation of objects and bodies of matter in space. Size is the exact limitation of objects and bodies of matter in space. A knowledge, consequently, of both form and size is the basis of all approximately adequate concepts, corresponding to objects and bodies of matter. Through the judgment, the mind measures size by lines, areas, surfaces, and volumes. Number is the special mode of judgment by which an exact knowledge of size is acquired. Weight, that mode of motion we call gravity, is another essential property of matter. Density or compactness of particles or atoms is closely related to weight and size. Knowledge of weight and density is acquired by mathematics. Therefore, the numerical relations of objects and things to each other are products of the same mode of judging.

The proposition of the doctrine of concentration is that the exercise of that mode of judgment called numbering is essential to the acquisition of all knowledge of externality; and also that this mode of judgment may be most economically acquired by measuring and weighing matter, and in all exercises intrinsic to the direct study of the central subjects.

Fifth: Attention is the vital process of intellectual creation, induced by the action of external attributes upon the brain and consciousness. The laws which govern attention are, in themselves, the natural method. Teaching is the presentation of conditions for educative attention. The power of attention is most economically developed by the study of the central subjects. Observation, hearing-language, and reading are modes of attention. Observation has to do with the concentration of external attributes upon consciousness and the results of this action are intrinsic. Hearing-language and reading are processes of thinking by the action upon consciousness of spoken and written words. They are educative processes when the subjects for such thinking are immediately needed for mental action, and when the acts of attention are intense.

Sixth: Observation, with its factors of experimentation and investigation, is made the elementary, preliminary study of the central subjects. These subjects furnish countless opportunities for the effective action of that mode of attention. The products of observation furnish the psychic foundation for all efficient acts of the imagination. The end and aim of both observation and imagination is *original inference,* the essential element of reason.

Seventh: The oral language which a child has acquired before entering school is enhanced and developed by the enhancement and development of thought power. The rule of concentration is that oral language should conform to the immediate necessities of consciousness.

Eighth: Reading is thinking, brought about by the action upon consciousness of written or printed words, arranged in sentences. Reading is the same process in kind as study of text; the latter, however, is more intense, and in a higher degree educative. Under the theory here presented, the power to read and to study text is acquired through use in the study of the central subjects. Words and idioms are to be associated with intrinsic thought from beginning to end. In other words, there is to be no reading or study of text which does not directly and immediately enhance the subjects taught. All reading presented to pupils, from first to last, is to be the best of literature.

In using the three modes of attention—observation, hearing-language, and reading—instinctive unity of action is to be steadfastly maintained.

Ninth: All the modes of expression—gesture, voice, music, speech, making, modeling, painting, drawing, and writing—are to be continually used throughout the elementary school as efficient means to intensify intrinsic and educative conscious activities. The theory is that each mode of expression has its special and indispensable function in education, and its special reactive influence. All forms of thoughts expression under each and every mode are to be directly acquired under the impulse of intrinsic mental action. Unity of action is to be preserved throughout.

The best possible physical development of the whole body as an instrument of thought and expression is brought about by continuous natural exercise of the body in the expression of thought under each and all the modes.

Tenth: Music cultivates those emotions which determine motive and control the will. Rhythm, the basis of all melody and harmony, is a powerful means for the adjustments of the body in graceful supple movements, rendering it a more and more perfect instrument of the soul.

Eleventh: The pantomimic use of the body as distinguished from its functional use develops higher muscular coördinations, which conserve energy and render the body a more skillful agent of the will. This all-sided action is conducive to health, beauty, and grace; it is, like voice and speech, an immediate response to thought; it is a universal medium of expression, and has a direct organic relation to writing and the conceptive modes of expression. Rhythm, which is the successive flow of the parts of the body in time to music, links gesture, dance, and music.

Twelfth: The conceptive modes of expression have a strong reactive influence upon all the modes of attention—observation, hearing-language, and reading—and are also the most efficient means of developing imagination.

Thirteenth: By speech and writing all conscious activities may be most completely manifested. I have presented the argument to prove that all forms of speech and writing may be adequately acquired in the evolution, and expression of thought; that all the definitions, and rules of grammar and their exceptions may be thoroughly mastered in the development of thought power by speech and writing.

Fourteenth: All forms of thought manifestation under each and every mode of expression may be adequately and most economically acquired under the immediate impulse of intrinsic thought, which means, in turn, that every act of expression shall have its full reflex action upon educative thought.

Fifteenth: The main proposition of the theory of concentration is comprehended in the statement that all true education is inherently moral and ethical. Education is the development of the attitude of the being toward truth. All acts of expression consist in the manifestation of truth by each and every mode of expression. The fundamental principle of education is the development of the altruistic motive, under which the highest and best mental action may be acquired. Education is the economizing of physical, mental, and moral energy in the direction of development. Economy of energy is the conformity of the being to divine law. Freedom is obedience to law.

I have thus briefly summarized some of the main points in the theory of concentration. The center of all movement in education is the child. We must grant that human beings are absolutely governed by immutable, ever-acting, all-efficient laws of growth and development, and that all development means conformity to the laws of being; non-conformity is decay, degradation, and death. Ideally the process of education consists in the presentation of conditions, and all the conditions, for the most complete action of the laws of the being. The central law of education is self-effort, that action of the ego, which, when normal, either consciously or unconsciously conforms to law. The constant adjustment and fulfillment of the laws of being ever condition the action of higher laws and form the ever-moving path of educative action.

The supreme intellectual effort of the ego is original inference.[2] Original inference is an active attempt of the ego to find the truth; essential truth is law. A résumé of the argument already made may be here presented. The universe is the manifestation through matter of all-efficient energy. Matter, both organic and inorganic, is differentiated by energy, and thus manifested to the human soul. These differentiations are adapted to personal power of apprehension. Differentiated matter is the visible, tangible manifestation of creative thought; just as words convey the thought of man to man, so differentiated matter conveys the thought of God to man. The universe, with all its contents is undergoing continual, everlasting, change. These changes are controlled by immutable laws. These laws are invisible; they are as invisible as consciousness. One central law controls both man and the universe. The laws of the universe reveal the ego to itself. All law concenters in the law of being, is manifested for the being; all life is for one life. We are made in His Image, and we approach that Image through the effort to know the truth or the law, and to apply it.

It seems plain that there is one absolute goal of self-effort; that observation, investigation, and knowledge of books have one aim and one purpose, namely, the knowledge of ever-changing nature, and the progressive movement of man. Study of change would be of no value were not the mutability of matter governed by immutable laws. Through all the avenues of changing matter, through history, science, language, and art, the intellect has one ideal action—search for law; one ideal purpose—its ethical application. Why do we study the leaf? We wish to know its relation to the twig, the twig to the limb, the limb to the trunk, the trunk to the roots; the leaf, the limb, the trunk, the roots, to earth and air and water, and to the universe; everlasting convergence is the law of approach to central truth.

The objection to this proposition may be that it is indefinite; that it is too remote, that we know so little really of law, that we cannot effectively make it the end and aim of all education. I answer that the human being in his weakness and power has one mission, and one alone, and that is to reach the truth that shall make him free. If we know little, comparatively, of law, we can have an all-controlling faith in law, in that law which is in its essence love. If we cannot comprehend, we can apprehend; we can move forward tentatively; we can see through a glass darkly; we can turn our faces to the light of truth and hold ourselves under the influence of its power.

When we think of it carefully, we are all instinctive believers in the law and doers of the law. Behind whatever we do in our daily lives and vocations is an intuitive knowledge of law; whether we walk, eat, sleep, or work, our belief is fixed and firm that in so far law governs us; that in so far there is nothing left to chance. I ask, as I have asked before, in regard to the spontaneous activities of the child, what is this instinctive belief in law but the spontaneous beginnings of our advance toward law? If chance had any place in this universe there could be no science, no confidence in study, no faith that would impel upward and onward. The scientist in his laboratory, the geologist in the field, and the astronomer gazing through his telescope believe in law as they believe in God; every effort is governed by a belief that law can be discovered.

A still more difficult and everlasting problem is the arrangement of material for adaptation to steps and stages of human growth. An ideal course of study is a thing of the future, to be approached by continual adaptations to changing circumstances. What material is best adapted? Shall we find it in this subject, or in that? For instance, is elementary science or history preferable? What shall decide? What lies nearest the child? What does he love best? What does him the most good? We will all agree to the powerful influence of nature upon the child, of earth and air and water, of plant and animal life. Shall that which is already so well begun continue? Human life has just as strong an influence, perhaps a stronger affective power than nature; shall we choose human life, the foundation of history, for the initial steps? Nature acts upon the child's soul with irresistible power; earth, air, and water sing in his ears their songs of sweetness and beauty; plant life entrances him with color and change; animal life enters into his being; the child is as near the brute as he is to man. Shall the child study nature?

There can be but one answer to these questions: Continue that which is begun, and continue it by such measures and such means as are directly and essentially adapted to the harmonious growth of body, mind, and soul—the means God has chosen in His creation of the human spirit. It is for us to study these beginnings, these germinations of human growth; we are not to affirm that soil alone is good for the plant, or water alone, or air alone, but that all concenter upon the growth of the plant. The child stands in the center of a circle; around him is the environment of the universe, man, and nature. Everything in its elements touches the child's soul; the child's soul goes out toward everything, reacts upon everything. We must not break or distort the circle if we would have it extend and grow upward in the spiral. The base circle must ever widen, and with it, each spiral as it tends upward in its way toward the light and the truth. We, as teachers, must avoid placing undue emphasis upon that which we know best, and that which we love the best; we must remember we are not educated as we desire to educate the child. We may love history, and see in literature an all-powerful influence for mental and spiritual growth; equally we may fail to see, because we do not know, the potent influence of nature. We must remember that the making of a course of study completely adapted to the needs of human growth would require infinite knowledge; it can only conform to the finite in its approach to infinity. The beautiful thing, the sublime thing, about education is, that we can never find the end; that we can never fully know the means; that we can never comprehend the center, the human spirit.

Some one has said truthfully that "suspended judgment" is the greatest discovery of the nineteenth century. We walk by faith and not by sight; faith in God and faith in His highest creation. Our work is to continue creation, is to furnish the conditions for creation; and when we apprehend this, and include in its apprehension the fact that whatever we do to exalt the human soul is eternal in humanity, eternal in its influence upon humanity, we begin to get a slight glimpse of the sacred calling of teaching. The dignity of life is the feeling of eternity behind and before; that the soul is one with eternity.

All that can be done is to point the way toward that which is better and higher for humanity. The rule is, the more exalted the art, the more difficult it is to understand its principles and to apply them. The great advantage of the doctrine of concentration is that its application absolutely requires the art of teaching. Let us look practically at the propositions presented. I have urged that all subjects taught in any university shall be begun in an elementary way, with the little child, and that exercises in all the modes of expresison shall be continued or initiated, through school life.

We have had a great deal of discussion in regard to overcrowding courses of study; that there is not now time enough thoroughly to acquire the "3 R's," a smattering of geography, and a touch of history. What would be the outlook if all the subjects named were demanded in courses of study?

I answer, from the quantity standpoint, that it would be confusion worse confounded. From the standpoint of quantity, the prevailing studies in primary and grammar schools are all-sufficient. Indeed, expert investigations have shown that after eight years of drudgery the children do not read, write, or cipher well, and understand very little, comparatively, of geography and history. What would become of the schools if botany, zoology, geology, and the other central subjects were introduced? In their present isolation the burden would indeed be greater than either pupils or teachers could bear.

If, then, the theory of concentration be true, it commands a complete reversal of motive in teaching. *It demands that quality of mental action shall take the place of quantity.* This demand is consonant with the goal of all human development and progress—freedom. In other words, the business of teaching must be revolutionized into the art of teaching. Quality of mental action may be summed up in one sentence: It consists in the supreme power of the mind to reason and to choose for itself.

The basic element of reason is original inference; the path of original inference is generalization; the goal of generalization is the finding of law; the basis of original inference is the knowledge of facts, of data, gained by observation, hearing-language, and study of text. The art of teaching consists in the ability to guide self-effort in the direction of original inference. The teacher with light enough ahead to lead, moves on toward truth, hand in hand and heart to heart with the children.

It will be readily seen that the power of original inference imperatively demands knowledge of facts, gained by experiments, investigations, observation, reading, and hearing-language. The emotion resulting from self-effort in these directions is the highest inspiration the mind can have to acquire facts. The power of original inference develops the power to grasp truth. Original inference is that knowledge which is intrinsically power in itself; it demands summing up of facts, relation of ideas; it tests the truth of offered conditions.

The main reason why children, after struggling through the elementary and secondary schools, know so little is because the ideal of their teachers has been the acquisition of quantity. Reason demands quantity, but quantity is subservient to reason; reason leads, and quantity follows.

The crucial test of the theory of concentration is found in the doctrine of quality of mind-action, as opposed to quantity. The motto is, "Take care of the quality, and the quantity will take care of itself."

Some of the infallible indications of quality teaching are:

(1) The artist-teacher watches with the greatest care and assiduity the character of each pupil; watches mental action through all modes of expression.

(2) A course of study is a means to an end; from the course of study the teacher selects that material immediately needed for the advancement of personal, mental, and moral power.

(3) The artist-teacher is everlastingly studying pupils and seeking for better means to assist them in genuine self-effort. Close, persistent, indefatigable study of the child and of subjects for the child is a marked indication of the quality teacher.

(4) The artist-teacher has some apprehension of the infinity of means directly at hand for the development of pupils.

(5) All quality teaching concenters in immediate manifestation in character; history lives in the child; civics and ethics mean daily life; science is applied in school and home. There is no waiting for future effects in quality teaching.

(6) Quality teaching excludes all competition, rivalry, and the cultivation of sordid ambition.

(7) The essence of quality teaching is love; its one aim, the truth.

We have tens of thousands of teachers, but we have few earnest, enthusiastic students of education. Genuine progress on the part of the great majority of teachers is scarcely perceptible; after a few years of school-keeping their work becomes routine; and in it their souls seem buried. It is an exceedingly difficult thing to introduce methods founded upon universally recognized psychology. The reason of this is apparent: Quantity teaching, teaching that can be measured by line and plummet, and weighed in the scales of per-cent examinations—such teaching does not admit or require the application of educational principles. We have reached the ultimate in the direction of quantity; devices and so-called methods have been multiplied to the point of surfeit. A teacher not governed by sound principles is an easy prey to the countless devices and methods which infest the educational market. Given honest, persistent students of education, the movement onward in education will become general and effective; each teacher would contribute something of value to the common good.

Some plain facts in the theory of concentration may be easily understood and applied. It is by no means necessary to master the whole theory before the first practical steps in its application may be taken. Indeed, most courses of study, now, involve unification of studies to some extent; geography, for instance, comprehends in a vague way history and most of the sciences. The particular virtue of this theory is that it admits of tentatives. A teacher may see that educative thought has a direct influence over the acts of word-association, and with any method in teaching the first steps of reading may introduce the thought factor.

In all textbooks on arithmetic there are concessions to the practical use of number in a few of its countless applications to the central subjects; the main line of study may be enhanced by relating arithmetic to geography and science, and the drill work still be continued.

Although drill work in penmanship still be maintained, attempts may easily be made in the direction of thought expression. A teacher, while following assiduously some "system" of flat copy-drawing, may find place for free-hand drawing in connection with botany, geography, and the other central subjects.

In the same line, structural geography may be more effectively coördinated with geology and mineralogy, and history with geography. A glimpse makes way for a gleam, and a gleam broadens into a full blaze of light through honest striving in right directions. "He that doeth righteousness is righteous."

This doctrine of concentration will serve intelligently to suggest, guide, and control study on the part of teachers. Many teachers study persistently; but very much of such study is groping in the dark, is blind, but honest, stumbling. The theory of concentration presents a distinct plan for economical study on the part of teachers, and at the same time demands increased and progressive movement. It proves conclusively the absolute necessity of knowing the central subjects and their auxiliaries thoroughly, and it proves also that the teacher should have masterly skill in the modes of expression. This direction of study and practice is the application of the theory. A teacher must know the subject he teaches; must know far more than he teaches; must have great skill in all the modes of expression.

"The realization of the ideal," you say, "is an utter impossibility." Certainly, for us, the victims of quantity teaching, this is true; but the thing to do, the thing that must be done, if we are true to our sacred work, is to move steadily and unfalteringly toward the ideal, along the infinite line of unrealized possibilities. I firmly believe that the theory of concentration throws a strong light along the path of progress; and although in that light difficulties stand out clear and distinct, difficulties multiplied do not produce doubt; to know is to conquer.

The application of this theory gives teachers most favorable means for a comprehensive insight into personalities, the individual powers and social relations of pupils. Individuals are studied through the action of various modes of expression, which reveal the particular attitude of the mind toward all subjects. Thus weakness and strength may be perceived, right tendencies understood and encouraged, and wrong ones corrected The art of teaching discriminates the individual, distinguishes him from all others, and applies the means needed for personal development. The steady, ever-brightening glow of enthusiasm in the teachers' soul inspired by the study and application of a far-reaching theory, is the most potent, indeed the paramount, influence to inspire pupils with a love for work. When a teacher loves a few subjects and ignores all the rest, the pupils are apt to follow suit. Concentration demands that a teacher shall see truth and beauty in all subjects, because all are in nature and purpose one and the same.

The prominent weakness of education is isolation of subjects; reading by itself—first steps and consequent ones; writing in copy books; arithmetic with an occasional application; geography without history; history without geography; "art for art's sake." Indeed, it seems as if the universal tendency has been to separate subjects as widely as possible; to completely ignore organic synthesis. Isolation is analysis gone to seed. No truth is more striking than the essential relation of all subjects to each other. One can scarcely make an effective generalization without going outside of the subject immediately in hand. Philosophy, the science which groups all sciences into one science, proves that the normal action of mind is ever toward unity: relation is strength, isolation is weakness. Convergence, not divergence, is the law of normal movement—meeting lines that concenter in the heart of things.

Concentration is utterly opposed to one scheme that has been utilized by some very intelligent teachers. I allude to special or departmental teaching in grammar schools, the arguments against which can be briefly stated:

(1) The value of teaching to a pupil is determined by the teacher's personal knowledge of the character of that pupil. Character in its complete analysis is revealed by the study of all subjects and through all modes of expression. Any misunderstanding of a pupil, however slight seemingly, is apt to lead to disastrous results. A special or departmental teacher in a school where all work is unrelated, cannot possibly know individual character, for two reasons—lack of time and failure of means; a character cannot be revealed through any one isolated subject.

(2) Special teachers, as a rule, study but one subject, and therefore do not apprehend in the slightest the buttressed power of relations of subjects. A teacher of penmanship cannot use

writing as a potent means of thought expression. A teacher of art alone, cannot understand its intimate relations to geography, science, and history. A special teacher of arithmetic cannot use numbers as a mode of reasoning upon all subjects. A teacher of reading has few opportunities to use oral expression as a means of intensifying thought in all-sided expression of all subjects. It is not easy for a teacher of history to relate that subject to geography as a basis for reasoning and memory. How many teachers of science see in nature-study the best possible means of teaching, reading, writing, number, and art? Often a teacher of literature does not readily understand that literature is the mirror of the highest thought of the age in which it was written, and therefore does not turn to advantage its reflected rays upon historical epochs. A director of physical training cannot well appreciate that the end and aim of all physical exercise is to make the body a more efficient instrument of attention, expression, and reflection. A teacher of vocal music may fail to use the potent influence of cadenced rhythm to harmonize body, mind, and soul. In fact, from the very nature of things, it is practically impossible for a special teacher to use all subjects of study and modes of skill for the purpose of concentrating them upon one subject.[3]

(3) Throughout the elementary school, a teacher needs every subject as direct means of individual development. To take away any one subject is practically to rob the teacher of a potent means of education.

(4) Whatever a special teacher manages, the regular teacher is very apt to omit from his list of studies, and a failure of interest is the inevitable result.

It is argued that specialists give their entire time to one subject—and therefore can best teach that subject. This argument falls under the quality ideal. A regular teacher who understands his pupils, and whose sole aim is quality of mental action, will use a subject which he imperfectly knows with far greater effect than a specialist though comparatively master of his subject. Knowledge of subjects is of immense importance—indeed, ignorance of subject-matter is a fundamental weakness in teaching; but great as is its importance, lack of insight and knowledge of personal character is the prime reason why the efforts of many highly educated teachers are wholly ineffective. It should be added that a teacher who studies personal character needs must be, from the very nature of things, a persistent student. The most encouraging feature of the theory of concentration is that it demands persistent study of all subjects, and practice in all modes of expresison on the part of the regular teacher; indeed I venture to predict that the last teachers to study and adopt this theory will be the teachers of special subjects.

The preëminent virtue of concentration is the economy of mental power, the path to freedom by the shortest line of resistance. It proposes that the action of the mind shall be concentrated from first to last upon intrinsic educative thought; that all modes of expression and attention shall be auxiliaries, and acquired as auxiliaries. It means that the famous "3 R's" of antiquity may be learned—nay, are learned—far better, far more effectually and efficiently, used as means to an end, rather than as ends in themselves. It means that a child during the habit-forming and curiosity-seeking period of life shall be led directly to the sources of truth, and shall lay sure foundations for all future growth. It means the early establishment of the habits of self-effort, attention, and observation. It means the habit of using and applying that which is acquired. It means the cultivation of judgment and the power to generalize; the establishment of the true relation between life and school.

The quantity ideal defeats itself, is stultified in piles and heaps of mere formal acquisitions. The right of choice, the glories of the imagination, the curiosity for knowledge, are crushed and maimed by ignorant teaching. When the child comes to its own through the mediation of the artist-teacher, the power, the knowledge, the skill acquired will immeasurably exceed that of the few genuises who have blessed the earth. A genius is an unsuppressed soul with strength enough to overcome all difficulties and reach its own. "Seek first the kingdom of heaven and all things shall be added unto you." "Eternity is quality," says Hegel. "Time is the false-reply," affirms Emerson. The child will come to his own when he has the liberty and conditions of becoming free.

Concentration demands the continual revision of courses of study; revisions comprehending progressive movement in the art of teaching. An ideal course consists of the presentation and arrangement of all conditions adapted to the steps and stages of individual development. Such a course in the hands of poor teachers is like an intricate and complex piece of machinery in the hands of a tinker. The more meager the course, the better for inferior teachers whose mechanical drudgery is fixed in the Procrustean bed of formal monthly tests, and inspired by *en bloc* promotions. An effective course of study must be adapted to circumstances; circumstances involve the knowledge and skill of teachers, the art of supervision, and the intelligence of communities. Such a course of study bends upward under the energy of progressive teachers, and downward to meet the scanty wants of the artisan; it moves onward toward the ideal; it is constantly receiving new additions as skill advances. The theory of concentration suggests the line of progress, and the direction of courses of study.

Germany offers us several expositions of the science of education; undoubtedly the best is the Herbartian theory of concentration; it is certainly well worth the careful and profound study of all educators. But, however good and sound a theory may be, its adaptation to conditions must be considered; form of government, relation of classes, and social customs have a powerful influence over it. The Herbartian theory stops short of the demand for complete individual freedom through personal effort.

For one hundred and eighteen years the greatest experiment in the world's history has been tried in our republic—the attempt of society to rule itself. With the progress and partial success of this experiment dangerous complications appear which imperil its final triumph. Character, whose essence is love for God and man, alone can save us, and lead us to the time when obedience to divine law shall be the one rule of action. In a democracy only, can the theory of personal freedom be translated into action; the doctrine of personal freedom and of concentration are one and the same. With a profound belief in God and man and faith in democracy as the path to universal freedom, I present this theory to you, my fellow teachers, as a suggestion *(eine Ahnung)* of the truth.

1 John Dewey, *How We Think* (D. C. Heath), Chap. VIII concerning "Judgment."

2 John Dewey, *How We Think* (D. C. Heath), Chap. VII concerning "systematic Inference."

8 Colonel Parker early introduced special teachers into his school in Chicago. They were experts in the various fields of education who taught the students in the Normal School, the members of Colonel Parker's own faculty, and they also supervised the work done in each grade.

In later years Colonel Parker under this experience somewhat modified his views and practice from those states above. Since no one person can be efficient in all modes of expression; special teachers of art, music, physical training, shop, science, history, literature, and dramatics, assisted the grade heads in teaching, working in close coöperation with them to the great advantage of the children. The gifted child was helped to express himself to his own satisfaction, and those handicapped in coördination or powers of observation had special attention. However, the educational principal stated above was not violated. The various modes of expression were not taught in *isolation* but the special teachers *helped the grade teachers give each child his best opportunity for adequate expression, in whatever study or activity he was carrying on in the classroom.*

XVI

DEMOCRACY AND EDUCATION

THROUGHOUT the ages mankind has moved on under two great controlling ideals of government: the predominating one, the rule of the many by the few, the artisocratic ideal; the other, embryonic, unformed, glimmering and flickering down the centuries, an ideal at times almost disappearing from view, again flaming, lurid with portentous light—a belief that society should rule itself.

I need not pause to define the ideal of aristocracy. History is full of its types in every form from the beginning. The fundamental motive of this ideal is selfishness, the desire for domination, power, ease, luxury. It posits that a few human beings are born to rule, are God's anointed; that the rest are subjects, foreordained and predestined to obey and to serve without question. Its design is the complete subjugation of the masses to the domination of the few; its methods, to prevent human souls from seeking and finding the truth.

The motive of aristocracy is one and the same everywhere, whatever its guise, phase, and method; all for one purpose, to one end—complete domination and subserviency of the majority to the unquestioned will of the small minority. Aristocracy watches with keen eyes every potent influence and captures it for its own behests. Whenever and wherever an organization of state, church, or society acquires great influence over the masses, no matter how good and pure the principles or creed that brings it into power, it is seized, bound hand and foot, and made to serve the governing power. Selfishness masquerades in the garb of purity when there is no other way to reach its ends.

Every religion in itself has been the initiation of something better for man. The great founders and reformers of religions have, almost without exception, discovered divine truths, have brought into the world some great good for humanity, inspirations and revelations for the elevation of humanity. They and their immediate followers were ready to endure torture and death so that new truth and new life might touch the souls of men. The better the religion, the more it appealed to the divine principle in man, the more heroically self-sacrificing the deeds of its disciples, the greater its influence over the people, the greater its power for evil became when controlled and wielded by selfishness. In the history of every great movement for good there comes the time when, seeing its influence, the dominant few grasp it and use it as a means of control. This rule has been without exception in the past, and is just as true to-day as it was centuries ago; no matter what the party or what the sect, predominating influence makes it the prey of sordid gain; thus religion suffers under a burden of reproach and recrimination due entirely to the greed of selfish man. A believer in democracy and perfect toleration, I shall criticize no religion, nor religious sect; I shall confine my discussion to those methods which keep man from a personal knowledge of divine truth.

It is my purpose to trace the methods by which selfishness has managed to rule the people, in order to understand their mighty traditional effect upon a nation which proposes to rule itself.

The first method is that of mystery. The early savage was terrified by the forces of nature; his more cunning brother having solved a few of the simpler mysteries used the acquired knowledge to overawe and enslave the souls of his brethren. Ever since, mystery has been one of the most effective means to control the masses. That knowledge of nature's laws which should be a common heritage, has been shut up in temples and caves, and used by astute priests and rulers to keep the masses in terrified subjection. Anathemas, promising woes unbearable to those who dared to doubt self-constituted authorities, were thundered in the ears of crouching vassals. The most repulsive and repugnant doctrines that have brooded like a nightmare over a suffering world had their origin in this motive of selfishness and absolute domination.

The presumption that certain divinely anointed persons are the favored recipients of revelation, from which the ignorant masses are rigidly excluded, and that a human soul is not capable of finding truth for itself, have thus been the effective means of its utter subjection. Astrology, alchemy, and the so-called occult sciences have been in turn used to blind the eyes of the ignorant, to make them tremble before facts exceedingly simple, and which should have been used as means of education. The stream of life has been poisoned at its source.

The second method is that of physical force—of prisons, torture, police, and standing armies. It may not be fair to say that all crime is the result of oppression, but this statement is not far from the truth. There are crimes which are virtues: the crime of disobedience to soul-degrading laws—laws that forbid the personal search for truth; the crime of rebellion against injustice and oppression; against inhuman laws that have filled dungeons with countless thousands, and covered battle-fields with the slain whose one fault was a desire for liberty. The plan under the method of physical force was to keep the masses in the total darkness of ignorance, and hold them in abject subserviency by fear of punishment. This enforced ignorance is the prolific cause of nearly all genuine crimes; it is the direct and inherited outcome of that abuse of power which has one aim—the complete domination of the masses by a small minority.

The mighty standing armies of to-day, which eat out the hearts of nations and make misery and poverty the burdens of society, are kept more as a means of suppressing the personal right of choice than of defending the nation against foreign foes.

Isolation of a people into classes is a powerful method of selfishness. Isolation of society into classes and castes is the sowing of the dragon's teeth, from which spring misunderstanding, mistrust, suspicion, contempt, and hate. A homogeneous people is, from its very nature, a strong people. Up to the time of the Savior, each nation had its own gods; everything outside of the nation was wrong and wicked; the gods of other nations were devils; the national god forbade intercourse and commanded extirpation of all peoples not under his immediate control.

The forms of isolation are many, but the effects are the same; they are well illustrated by China, which is the example of geographical or natural isolation: having the oldest civilization in the world, making the greatest progress in its earliest civilization, but separated by great mountains and deserts from other nations, it shut itself up within its borders and longest resisted the modifying influence of other peoples. The result was a fixed form of government, fixed ideas, and stagnation. The people of China had an utter contempt for what to them were the outer barbarians. People must mingle with each other in order to know each other; nations must have immediate contact with each other. Nations must obtain that knowledge of other nations which the exigencies of growth demand.

Class and caste isolation has been, and is to-day, the strongest means of reducing the essential power of a nation, by making its lower classes weak and uninfluential. An illustration of this is found in India. We are told by the Hindus that caste in its origin was a necessity, but for it India is suffering to-day. It prevents all homogeneity of action. That which is true of India is true of all the nations of the old world. Separation of peoples into classes is the most effectual means of keeping the common people from any notion of their rights.

Class isolation is strongly supplemented by class education. It is a well-known fact that no nation in the world other than the United States has common schools; that is, common to all the people. The splendid schools of Germany, for instance, are class schools. The only free school, *Volkschule,* is for poor people. This isolation of classes and sects in education is a potent means of holding society in its stratifications, the permanent basis of thrones. Any feeling of personal rights on the part of the common people is in the highest degree dangerous to the rule of the few; therefore the entire machinery of suppression is used to stifle human reason, or render its results abortive. Class separation of children in schools is the only safety of central governments. Common schools in any monarchy would threaten its form of government.

Equally influential is church or sectarian isolation, the education of children of adherents of one sect in separate schools. No one can disclaim the right of parents to educate their children; but the effect of sectarian isolation in school, no matter what the religion taught may be, is mistrust, contempt, and too often, hatred, of all other sects. The creed does not rely upon its intrinsic value, but upon its method of isolation; upon the keeping of the children of its peculiar sect separate, that they may be inoculated with prejudices, instead of being filled with love for all mankind. It is true that a few come together from all schools into the universities, but there is no actual union. The class or the sectarian feeling by this time has become so strong, that mutual sympathy is well-nigh impossible.

Isolation is the most effective method of aristocracy. If the people of the North and the South had known each other in 1861 as they do now, if they had been bound together by railroads and telegraphs as to-day, no power on earth would have led them to drench the land in fratricidal blood. The foundation of most evil is misunderstanding, distrust, repulsion, or hate, the baneful products of isolation. People in order to love each other, and work for each other, must live together in communities, must be bound together by common interests.

The next method of aristocracy to which I allude is bribery. All the machinery and methods of oppression and suppression possible cannot effectually keep the human spirit from struggling to become free; and so there have been in all ages children of the people, with a vague sense of inalienable rights, reaching upward to the light. In war, in inventions, in learning, no matter how great the difficulties, a few pertinacious, persevering souls have made their power and influence felt. One effective method has been used upon such persons; the moment their influence was needed for the rule of the few, it was bought—paid for by office, or by direct gifts of money, if that were possible. Aristocracy is ever on the watch for these dangerous individuals, who break down the barriers and reach heights from which they can look down upon "God's anointed."

We all recall the early republics of Greece and Rome that were changed into tyrannies by buying the franchise of the masses. Bossism in politics is the survival of this powerful means of suppressing freedom of thought.

But one cannot fail to see in history that in spite of all opposition the human spirit has moved on; there are ever new necessities creating new demands. The primitive method that has dominated up to within a few years was to keep the masses of people in utter ignorance, controlling them by mystery, force, and bribery. But there came a time when the demands for education were too strong; when a ruler, for instance, would see that the subjects of his nation would be better servants with some education. Or it may be that a glimmer of the truth would come into the brain of a king, and he would hear the command, "Let my people go." At all events, a movement toward popular education has marked this and the latter part of the eighteenth century.

But here arose a great difficulty—how to make useful subjects, and at the same time prevent them from thinking and reasoning for themselves. The most dangerous thing absolute authority can have is a born leader in the lower classes with some glimmer of his own rights—some belief that he, no matter how poor his condition, is equal to the highest in the land. This specter, which has ever haunted absolute power, is the "perturbed spirit" of all centuries, and will not down.

The problem was how to give the people education and keep them from exercising the divine gift of choice; to make them believe that they were educated and at the same time to prevent free action of the mind. This problem was effectively solved in the method of quantity teaching. I need not describe at any great length what the method of quantity is, it is the prevailing method of to-day—of textbooks, pages, word-cramming and word-recitation; of learning, believing, and conforming; the method of pedantry; the method that liimits the mental horizon; the method that keeps the mind from looking outside of a certain definite circle; the method of implicit belief. It is the last ditch of the rule of the few—forced by necessity to give the people education, but still acting to keep the people from the highway of freedom. The method of quantity teaching is almost absolute in its influence; not quite so, for there have been in every age geniuses who, given a stone, would transform it into the bread of life.

In order to explain this method, I must contrast it with the true method, the method of quality—quality of mental action. I have said that education is self-effort toward freedom by the shortest line of resistance; it is self-effort in finding and applying the truth; and this is what I mean by quality of mental action—that action of the mind which makes original inferences, which goes through consecutive reasoning processes based upon exact data. The most precious gift of God to man is choice; free choice is the dividing line between man and the brute and between man and man. All progress consists in the discovery and application of truth; man was created to contribute his personal mite of self-choice to the great body of discovered truth. Education consists in presenting the right conditions for personal choice.

If the quality of mental action is right, the quantity will take care of itself. The reason why most students have, after long years of painful, arduous drudgery, so little mental power, is that their whole ideal is the acquisition of a quantity of facts; they have never had any exercise in quality of action; their minds are simply passive receptacles, taking without resistance that which comes from supposed authorities. Self-reliance has become buried past all resurrection by sixteen years of persistent word-cram.

The products of this method of quantity may be so-called scholars, learned savants, pedants, talking encyclopedias; but always the inventions of the ages, the newer discoveries of truth have been met by the opposition of just this class of pedants. The common people have always heard the truth gladly; but the pedant, whose belief in himself is absolute, whose imagination never catches a glimpse beyond the fixed barrier of his own fixed belief, has ever rejected it. Pedants and bigots are the worst outcome of quantity teaching. They have stood as the mighty barriers of progress in all ages; they drove Galileo to prison. It was not one sect alone, but all the learned men, both Protestant and Catholic, of Europe who opposed him, because they had not the power to investigate the truth he presented.[1]

The most striking example of this quantity learning is found in the annals of the little kingdom of Prussia, than which no nation has ever had a more wonderful history.

The kingdom of Prussia, consisting of swamp and sand, in the cold north, is surrounded, aside from the icy waters of the North Sea, on all sides by opposing nations: on the East, Russia; on the South, Austria and the rest of the German states; close by, France and Great Britain. In the early part of the eighteenth century the common people of Germany were boors, just emerging from barbarism, with a language which Frederick the Great, himself, said was not fit to be spoken by gentlemen. The great problem of Frederick the Great, a born warrior and a born king, was to make his kingdom a power in Europe. Like all the members of the Hohenzollern family, he had great insight and a profound knowledge of conditions. His first movement was to train soldiers—a work begun by his rough and energetic father. The first soldiers to stand firmly in line and be shot down were the soldiers of Frederick the Great in Silesia. The next step in progress was to train workmen—laborers to cultivate the farms and work in the shops. And for this purpose Frederick the Great founded, in 1735, the first industrial school in Berlin.

Frederick the Great's design—a dangerous one for a monarch —was to make his subjects a great power in the nation; it was not his purpose to raise the lower classes or to increase their political influence, but to give them the skill necessary to essential assistance in the government. He did not understand the potency of better environment upon the awaiting soul.

Yet there have always been men who have pierced the darkness; who have felt the glimmer of the light of freedom; who have had a glimpse of the path of liberty; who, divinely appointed, belong to no age and to no one set of people. In Prussia the pregnant discussions in philosophy by Wolff and Leibnitz came with awakening force; but a still greater influence came from the republic of Switzerland, when a man inspired to save mankind sought and found means to educate the children. That means was quality of action, and the conditions were to bring the children close to the great teacher, nature. Pestalozzi translated into action his fundamental precept, "Education is the generation of power." Generation of individual power is what monarch, kings, nobles, and princes have everlastingly denied. This hero of education, this divinely inspired man, was indeed a voice crying in the wilderness, "Prepare ye the way,"—give to each human soul the liberty to work out its own salvation.

Fichte, the great German philosopher, heard of the work of Pestalozzi, and he persuaded William III to send ambassadors across the mountains to sit at the feet of this teacher of new truth; and when he learned how the wonderful teacher brought little children around him and awakened them to sermons in stones and good in everything, he said, "I await the regeneration of Germany from the teaching of Pestalozzi." This was the first glimmer in Prussia of quality teaching, of the teaching of self-effort, the first opening of the path to freedom. It came into the Prussian schools, and for the time controlled them; but then came fear and trembling upon the king and nobles. The smothered rights of the people in France broke, with volcanic horrors, the crust of ages of oppression, destroying artificial society, threatening all Europe with the same fate. The advisers of the king were quick to see the cause: "The people are thinking; they believe that they are our equals. This is the fundamental cause of the difficulty in France, and this is what you are doing in the schools of Prussia; you are teaching the children to think for themselves; you must stop it or you are lost."

In Prussia a minister of education was given complete control of educational affairs, and to him the king issued his command bidding him to go back to the catechism, to page-learning, to belief in implicit authority; go back to that which keeps the soul from becoming free; return to the methods of quantity. And back they went; then followed years of retrogression.

That minister of wrath against oppression, the great Napoleon, himself the incarnation of selfishness, proved the inherent weakness of aristocracy by hurling thrones to earth, and crumbling in the dust governments supported by oppression. He laid his heavy hand upon Prussia, and crushed it like an eggshell. Hope seemed gone, and the mighty power developed by the genius of Frederick was, to all appearances, annihilated. At this critical moment appeared a statesman with the vision of future centuries—Von Stein. The great minister said to the king: "You have feared the masses and separated them from you; let them feel your sympathy; let us change our method from quantity to quality; bring back into the school the spirit of Pestalozzi." It was done; a new cultus-minister was appointed, and the breath of liberty swept over the land. The people felt its saving power, and came *en masse* at the king's call. Under Blucher, at Belle Alliance, the conqueror of Europe met his final overthrow.

Indeed, Prussia seemed to have set itself particularly to solving the problem of just how far it was safe to allow a people to think for themselves. Her tentacles, never cut, recoiled quickly at the first suspicion of danger. In 1848, at the time of the general uprising in Europe, the first movement of Prussia was to suppress quality teaching, object teaching, science teaching, everything, in fact, which led in the direction of freedom. Diesterweg, the devoted follower of Pestalozzi, and one of the fine teachers of Germany, was dismissed from his position as principal of the normal school in Berlin, and Froebel's kindergarten was interdicted; the flame of liberty was blazing too brightly under their fostering care.

I will cite one more instance. The great statesman, Bismarck, had the all-absorbing ambition to reunite into one great empire the German states, which had been separated ever since the days of Frederick Barbarossa. How did he do it? Though an absolute monarchist himself, he knew how to touch the hearts of the people; he knew how to bring them together as one. The people were sensitive of their own rights, and they must be made to feel that the purpose of the king was the recognition of these rights. A new cultus-minister, Von Falk, was appointed, and the teaching of quality again begun in the schools—object-lessons, investigations, experiments, liberty to think, liberty to become free. The people, as ever, responded generously and heroically: Prussia, at the head of the German nation, conquered France, and reëstablished in its pristine glory an ancient empire. Thus, from first to last, the education of Prussia has wavered between autocracy and democracy, between quantity and quality.

There is one more method to which I wish to allude briefly, and this I may call the method of charity. I would speak of it with many qualifications, and would first define as clearly as possible what I mean by the method of charity. There is a genuine charity which cares for incompetents and unfortunates, for imbeciles, for the deaf and the blind, which needs no commendation; it is intrinsically ethical. There is another form of charity, which keeps people from helping themselves, lessens self-effort, and creates paupers—a charity which has given Europe millions of beggars, who hover around the church portals and crowd the streets; millions whose regular and ostensible business is begging; a method of charity which, to-day in America, is creating droves of tramps that infest the land. What is the cause of this widespread and baneful method of charity? It can with safety be said that nine-tenths of all money given in the name of benevolence has for its lasting effect the suppression of honest self-effort. When a nation does not give its people the means of education, the liberty to become free, the genuine means of self-help, there must result, from the very nature of things, a great mass of poor and wretched people, who are thus rendered unable to help themselves. They say: "The world owes me a living, and must give it to me." From this class springs much of real crime, for it is but a step from beggary to burglary. Persistent charity to people who could and should be led to help themselves promotes crime and vice, and creates a class of incapables.

There is money enough, land enough, food enough, and work enough, for all mankind, and the problem of charity is the problem of justice—the problem of the right distribution of labor, the right distribution of effort. There is no religion or government worthy the name which does not give to each individual the means of self-effort, the means of self-support, the means of gaining food and a livelihood, happiness, and freedom. This is true charity.

There is another work of charity which is worthy of the most profound reverence and the greatest approbation: I speak of moral reforms that have swept over the civilized world during the present century; reforms in temperance and vice that fill the earth with wretchedness, poverty, and crime, sapping the very foundations of society. Millions of money have been spent and millions of lives have been sacrificed to this sacred cause of remedying—what? That which never should have existed and never would have existed if the nation took proper care of its children. The deadly virus of centralized and absolute government has inoculated humanity-loving people with the predominating disbelief in the possibility of developing moral character out of the divinity born in every child.

Eager thousands will crowd around enthusiastic orators describing the alarming dangers that threaten society and pointing out a one and only remedy. When shall we have the same kind of conventions of the people thoughtfully to consider the ample means of saving every child? Give one tithe of the earnestness and enthusiasm to child education (prevention) that is given to reform, and the blessed work will be done.

Moral reforms are necessities caused by false and sordid systems of government. Reforms must gravitate toward the child; when the exhaustless, loving energy of reform is concentrated there, truth will surely make His children free.

The rule of the few over the many has been universal, because a lack of faith in the people has been universal: men have taught that the human soul cannot find the truth for itself; that it must have a sure and certain guide, and that this guide and this authority reside in certain divinely anointed powers, who reign by virtue of special grace; that the masses must follow these guides implicitly, unquestioningly. The inevitable result of this method, under the ideal which suppresses human action and crushes the divine instinct in the human soul, has been poverty, vice and crime. It is the cause of untold miseries under which we suffer to-day in America. Anarchy and nihilism, in their worst forms, are not natural outgrowths from the common people: They are the sure and deadly products of the methods of the rule of the few over the many, of the minority suppressing the rights of the majority. Let us put the blame where it belongs.

The main buttress of aristocracies is lack of faith in the masses. "The masses," is the cry, "have not the intelligence and moral power to rule themselves." The methods of aristocracy have to all appearances abundantly proved this proposition. That which they have most feared is the success of any attempts toward a democratic form of government. Such success would overthrow all the canons of their logic. When brother met brother in deadly strife in "the greatest civil war that ever darkened the earth," the aristocracies of the Old World gazed from palace and castle upon battle-fields with satisfaction. They cared not a fig for either party—what they believed had at last come, *the destruction of the one great trial of the new form of government,* which, once destroyed, meant peace and comfort for the few—continued wretchedness for the many.

The universal movement, that had its beginning when the morning stars first sang together, was the tendency of the soul toward freedom. The form of government it took was democracy founded upon the principle that society can rule itself; that each member of society contributes to the good of all, lives for all, and receives from all that which all can give. Democracy is the shortest line of resistance to human development. A fundamental principle of democracy is the responsibility of each for all, and all for each. If one is weak in the government, if one is weak who has the ballot, who has a choosing power, it means the weakness of all; and it becomes the imperative duty of all to present the needed conditions to awaken the feeling of responsibility.

The goal of humanity is freedom. Freedom comprehends the aim and direction of progress and the personal education of man. Liberty is the right of all men, but freedom is an individual acquirement through search for God's laws and obedience to them. The possession of freedom includes every possible good to the possessor—happiness, citizenship, personal development, and ethical action. The highest personal right a community can accord to an individual is the liberty and the means to become free. Liberty is accorded by laws, written and unwritten, which restrict the way of freedom entirely to personal effort, which place nothing between the individual and freedom but the inherent limitations of personality. The means of acquiring freedom may be summed up in one word—education. True education is the presentation of the conditions necessary for the evolution of personality into freedom. Democracy is the only form of government under which the methods of freedom can be fostered. The great central principle of democracy is mutual responsibility. Democracy in its essence gives to each individual the liberty of becoming free; raises no artificial barriers, political or social, between him and his goal. This is the ideal of democracy.

Pure democracy does not exist to-day since more than one-half of the people of the United States are excluded from franchise.[2]

The highest outcome, and, I say with the greatest reverence, the divinest outcome, of all the ages of human progress is the common school. Like democracy, it is still an ideal; it has not come into its own. The common school is the antipodes of isolation, the antipodes of that method so efficiently used by monarchy and hierarchy to keep the people from loving each other and helping each other.

The public school means that in their early life children of all classes, of all nationalities, of all sects, of rich and poor alike, children of both sexes, shall work together under the highest and best conditions in one community for from eight to twelve years; that they shall have teachers who are trained in the art of all arts—the art of teaching; that in the school, before prejudice has entered their childish souls, before hate has become fixed, before mistrust has become a habit, they shall have influence surrounding them that shall lead to the best work with the best motive of mutual assistance.

Why should boys and girls be taught together from the kindergarten through the university? Because they are to live together, to help each other throughout life, and must understand each other. The isolation of sexes in school has begotten mistrust, misunderstanding, false—nay even impure—fancies. The separation of sexes in school is a crime against nature. It is often argued that the sexes differ in intellectual capacity and moral power, and therefore should be separated in education; if this be true, it is all the more reason why they should be together. The strongest factor in education is the reflected light of character upon character.

The social factor in school is the greatest factor of all; it stands higher than subjects of learning, than methods of teaching, or than the teacher. That which children learn from each other in play and work is the highest that is ever learned. The young man in the university learns from his mates, of good or bad, than from his professors. This mingling, fusing, and blending give personal power, and make the public school a tremendous force for the upbuilding of democracy.

Let us now turn for a moment to the problem of America. We who are in the thick of the fight, in the midst of a struggle which is almost overwhelming, do not appreciate the tremendous trend of human affairs; the danger signals which fly before us are unwatched and unheeded. What are we proposing to do? That which had never yet been done in the world's history. Foreign colonies have settled in the other nations to be ostracized, persecuted, opposed, and downtrodden; but here in America we are bringing together all peoples from all parts of the known world, with all their prejudices born of centuries, each naturally having its own customs, rooted in earliest times and growing with the national growth; the Germans and the French, the Italians and the Russians, the Poles and the Irish, each with their prejudices, with their views of life, producing different customs, political, social, and religious, opposed as earth and heaven. Here they come into our broad continent, and we propose to have them live together, and legislate together for the best good of the whole. No dream of the past, no vision of the progress of humanity, could ever propose such a tremendous problem as this—this blending and fusing of the people of the whole earth in one crucible of common interests and brotherly love. Amalgamation of interests and ideas is the keynote of the situation: If any people or sect, no matter what, comes to America, lives by itself, speaks its own language, refuses to learn the genius of American citizenship, it is weakness to all, and if not arrested, threatens destruction to all.

Peoples come with their prejudices; for instance, the prejudice of separate and class education. I have in mind a nation that has given us the best discussions and investigations of education of any people on earth; has given more for the study of education than any and all the rest of the world together; still, they come to this country bitterly opposed to coeducation, and would legislate and use every influence to keep boys and girls separate from beginning to end. Peoples come with their ideas of class education, and above all, of sectarian education. They hold that children must be kept apart in their own sectarian schools during the first eight or ten years of their lives, in order that they may be indoctrinated; and all these peoples are honest in their beliefs, and as fixed as they are honest. Fancy the antipodal ideas of a pious New Englander and an equally pious German on the use of Sunday, or on the prohibition question. How shall they ever learn to know each other? When and where? If society is cut into classes following the old plan, they will never meet there; nor in the church, no matter how pious they may be, for the conflict there is as strongly marked. There is but one place where children of all nations and sects can come together, sit together, play together, live together, work together, know each other, and that place is the common school. The mission of the common school is to dissolve the prejudices that have been inculcated under methods of oppression.

It is a mistake to suppose that our forefathers came to the new continent with even the faintest glimmer of a purpose to found a republic, or that this idea took definite shape before the Revolution. The republic grew out of circumstances, and these circumstances were favorable: fixed traditions were uprooted; the early settlers left their material surroundings of tradition; they were transplanted into new conditions, where the conflicts and struggles of pioneer life, the subduing of virgin forests, the contests with the aborigines, and friction of different nationalities, brought out new necessities and developed new ideas.

It is even more of a mistake to surmise that the dimmest outline of a common-school system was in the minds of the founders of America. When the proposition was under way that society should rule itself, thoughtful men made up their minds that society must be intelligent, and that the state must furnish the means of intelligence. This idea took shadowy form in Massachusetts after the Revolution.

Yet the common-school system of Massachusetts owes its origin to no well-defined purpose that the community or state should assume the responsibility of the education of each individual. The methods of the ragged, the hedgerow, and the dame schools were transplanted from England. Rural communities found it less expensive to establish free schools at the public expense. Boston, taking the plan, in general, of the great schools of England, early started a limited system of free schools for boys. The plan of a free-school system was initiated in Massachusetts directly after the Revolution, but its early life was extremely feeble. Private institutions and academies were founded everywhere by religious sects, and in these schools most of the children were educated. The free schools sank to the level of charity schools, to which only poor people sent their children. Those who were well enough off sent their sons to the academies.

In 1837, to all appearances, the common-school system of Massachusetts was a failure; the country schools were taught by the spiritual descendants of the hedgerow and dame school teachers of Great Britain, or by uneducated and untrained girls. The terms were short, and the teaching miserable. The academies predominated and controlled education and bitterly opposed anything that looked to the improvement of the common-school system. As I have already said, our forefathers had no plan, no ideal, of a system of universal education, the great apostle of democracy, Thomas Jefferson, excepted. He is the one man who saw clearly the absolute conditions necessary for the success of democracy; he drew an outline of a system which included the primary school and the university, supported by the state. His great plans fell to the ground for a time, throttled by slavery; but the doctrine of universal education lived. Thoughtful men were at work everywhere—men who felt the immense responsibility under the new ideal of democracy.

In Connecticut, previous to 1837, educational reformers appeared who were strong advocates of a common-school system. The most prominent of these men was Dr. Henry Barnard, of Hartford. To this man the common school owes much. He was a pioneer in education before Horace Mann began his work and has published much upon education. He was ably supported in his efforts in Connecticut by Dr. Gallaudet, the renowned teacher of deaf-mutes, by William C. Woodbridge, and others.

In Concord, Vt., Rev. S. R. Hall had started the idea of training teachers for their work. S. G. Carter, of Massachusetts, vigorously seconded this movement.

But the whole system of common schools was in a state of collapse, and in danger of utter failure, when a great man grasped the situation, and gave his life to the work of promoting the interest of the common school. Horace Mann, born in 1796, in the little town of Franklin, Mass., was a typical New England boy; raised in poverty upon a rough farm, he heard what every boy of that time had ringing in his soul—"Get knowledge; knowledge is power." He worked upon the farm, braided hats, and studied by the light of pitch-pine knots; made use of the scanty means of the common school; prepared for college; taught school; went through Brown University, and then studied law—he did all this unaided. By indomitable will he struggled toward the tempting goal, and at last found himself on the high-road to success. No man in Massachusetts at that time had such a future. He was the peer of Charles Sumner, his contemporary. Great statesmen were needed; Horace Mann made a success at the bar, a success in politics, he was honored and respected by the most intelligent of his fellow citizens. He was gifted, like all inspired men, with a deep insight into the future; he comprehended the tremendous responsibility of citizenship; he felt the imminent danger in the outworking of the new plan of democracy; without intelligence among the people he knew that democracy would be a failure.

Horace Mann was a thorough democrat; he believed in the people; he believed in the new form of government; and he knew that the plan was certain of failure unless it was supported by intelligent people. The success of the common school was to him the one hope of democracy. He aroused some enthusiasm among educated people in regard to the common-schools, and was influential in having a board of education appointed by the General Court. This board of education was appointed to investigate the public-school system, and see what could be done to promote its welfare. A man was needed to guide the investigations. Horace Mann, as I have said, had every prospect of a famous career—everything that the state and nation could give was open to him—a high place as a legislator and statesman. But he knew in his soul that something must be done, that something must be done which could not be done in legislative halls, which must be done with the people. The board of education, of which Horace Mann was a member, selected him as its secretary, and begged him, with a full comprehension of the sacrifice demanded, to give his life to the work. In doing so he must renounce all ideas of fame and honor; he must give up his chosen path; he must go into a fight in which there was no glory, in which he must sacrifice every personal ambition.

He accepted the office at the meager pittance of $1000 a year, and in 1837 began his work.

He found in Massachusetts what has been found in every state—the idea of the responsibility of communities for each child was repugnant to the people. An echo of that ancient cry, "Am I my brother's keeper?" finds easy lodgment in the hearts of unthinking people. There was in their minds little sense of responsibility. Most of them were farmers, hard at work at the problem of self-preservation. The light of the common school, as I have said, was just flickering, ready to expire.

I cannot in a few words give you an adequate idea of the self-sacrifice and devotion of this hero of education. He went all over the state of Massachusetts, and though an incomparable orator, with great magnetic power, he was met by the people with sullen indifference; he talked in schoolhouses, many times, to audiences of a half-dozen people. He strove with all his eloquence to convince them of their responsibility in education. Horace Mann painfully realized his own limitations, his own lack of knowledge in the direction of education. He sought everywhere for books, but found few. He visited schools, and found less to assist him. "Is there," he thought, "any place in the wide world where I can get help for the children?" He had heard of the schools of Europe, of Germany and Scotland in particular. There were no means of paying his expenses; he sold his precious law library, took the money, and visited the schools of the Old World; went from schoolhouse to schoolhouse, observing and studying. He returned, and in his famous Seventh Annual Report told the people of Massachusetts what he had found.

(1) He found that corporal punishment could be greatly diminished. The essence of method in Massachusetts consisted of the ferule and the strap, without which, it was believed, there could be no education.

(2) He found that the children could learn to spell better by writing words than by the common method of oral spelling.

(3) That there were improved methods for teaching reading; that it was unscientific and wrong to learn the names of letters as a means of taking the first steps.

He presented definite propositions for reform in his famous Seventh Annual Report. He had discovered something better for the children. His advocacy of "newfangled notions" met the usual fate; the pedants, the disciples of quantity teaching, were there to meet him and to deny every proposition.

One would fancy that the school-teachers of Massachusetts, especially of the intelligent city of Boston, would have received him and his discoveries with open arms; far from it. They denied *in toto* every proposition he made; they proved to their own satisfaction that that which he brought was nonsense; that their ways were the best ways.

Fortunately there stood at the back of Horace Mann a few of the most intelligent people in Massachusetts. He had one great advantage—he commanded the profound respect of thoughtful men of the time. From the opposition to his simple and reasonable propositions he learned a valuable lesson: without intelligent, trained teachers there could be no progress in schools; and to this end he worked for years against the fiercest opposition. The believers in isolated education opposed as they have always opposed, the common-school system; the bitterest opposition came in organized form from the academies.

When Horace Mann proposed that teaching should be a profession, and that teachers must be educated like ministers, lawyers, and doctors, a howl of derision, of profound contempt, went up from the private schools, was echoed by the colleges, and sustained by the people. Quantity teaching needed no preparation except firmness and brutality, supported by the ferule and the strap. The "new idea" would spoil the "business," as it did that of the Ephesian artisans.

After a heroic struggle against pedantry on one hand and stinginess on the other, this leader of democracy founded, near the old battle-ground of Lexington, the first normal school in America in 1839, and put it into the hands of Father Pierce, another hero in education. Then, one normal school after another was established in Massachusetts.

The pioneer work of Massachusetts had a great influence over the other states, notably New York, and after a prolonged struggle a normal school was established in Albany, N. Y., in 1843,[3] with David P. Page as principal. Three hundred academies in the Empire State fought tooth and nail against the founding of this school; their cry was: "We are sufficient for all these things; we can train teachers." But in spite of all opposition the new idea grew; people began to believe that the establishment of the common-school meant the perpetuity of the republic.

The establishment of normal schools was the first great step in the forward movement of the common-school system; it meant better teaching. All the normal schools of the United States took their pattern from the schools established by Horace Mann. The first normal school of which a woman was principal was founded in St. Louis, and Anna C. Brackett, graduate of the Framingham Normal School, was made its efficient head. The early period of the common schools was one of chaos, of dim ideas, of glimmerings, of flickerings; the people had to be convinced of the necessity for common schools. The idea of expense frightened the people; the opposition of private institutions was great, and colleges and universities, with some notable exceptions, had little or no sympathy for them.

The second period of the common schools may be called the period of organization, the building of schoolhouses, organizing systems of education, making courses of study, grading schools, getting all the machinery necessary for effective school-work.

Then followed a period of groping after means and methods of teaching; a strong suspicion of something better was aroused in the minds of people and teachers. The evolution of the common-school system covers a relatively short period; in Illinois, less than forty years; and in the South it was organized after the Civil War.

The rapid growth and development of the common-school system of the United States has no equal in all history: born of the people, supported and nourished by the people, it has steadily made its way into the hearts of the people, and has become an absolute necessity in the growth and perpetuity of our political institutions.

In the Old World, where public schools, not common schools, have been established, the system is entirely controlled by central power, by the minister of education, by one intelligence to which everything is subordinate. There are great advantages in the matter of organization, and a great saving of time, to appearances, in such a plan of central power. The authority, for instance, of the cultus-minister reaches every school in Prussia; he can determine the textbooks, and course of study, and the method; but in our country we have no central system. The citizens of each school-district, the citizens of a city, have absolute control over their schools; there is no domination from the center; even the State assumes very little control of the schools, outside of enabling acts, and limitations in the matter of time and general subjects of study. This is probably the best illustration in all history of true democratic growth. What the schools are, their value in education in the district, is determined by the people themselves. In the case of two adjacent districts, one may have excellent schools and the schools of the other may be in a very inferior condition. This, superficially considered, would argue the superiority of a central system; but the democratic mode of growth is from within, and admits greater possibilities than any other plan.

A central system of government easily becomes fixed. For instance, to-day schools of Germany pedagogically speaking are far better than the schools of the United States. In fifty years the schools of the United States will exceed in value the schools of any centralized system of government because the United States' plan tends to originality and research. It brings out the best in all. With all its defects the common-school of the United States in idea is incomparably the noblest and best institution on earth. It has accomplished vast results; the common-school system is the heart of the republic.

The high accomplishment of the common-school has not been through methods of teaching or subjects taught; it has consisted principally in the great social factor—the mingling, blending, and fusing of all classes of society.

It is, then, for every thoughtful person to consider with the greatest care the present situation of the common-school system, and what can be done to make it better. To this subject I invite your attention. What has been done and what remains to be done? Viewing it from the standpoint of the growth of a great central idea, of the partial realization of a divine inspiration, the common-school system of the United States is exalted to the highest degree. But when we consider what is to be done, we can see plainly that we have made small beginning; that the common-school is still in its swaddling-clothes; that it has only been well started; that it must be made better; that it is not equal to the demand—the salvation of all the children.

Democracy means the responsibility of all for each; the common school is the direct exposition of this fundamental principle; common education is the means of freedom. The children of to-day are in our hands; whatever we do for them will determine the future. Our lack of faith in this direction is the greatest infidelity. To use a common illustration: A Kentucky farmer will look at a hundred colts and say, "I will train every one of them to become a useful horse." We look at the children and decide that we can save but a few of them; that many of them must become criminals, many of them a burden upon society; that many of them will enhance vice, and put barriers in the way of our political institutions. We must know that we can save every child. The citizen should say in his heart: "I await the regeneration of the world from the teaching of the common schools of America."

The foundations of the great American system of education into democracy have been laid by devoted patriots. The people believe in the common school. The necessary organizations are now ready for a great advance; the line of progress is plainly before us; that line is parallel with the great lines of progress in this century that have been marked by searching, prolonged investigation, and profound study—study that has compelled the natural forces to yield themselves to the service of man.

The same kind of study, the same wisdom, earnestness, and zeal, must be given to the study of the child. Already careful investigations in child-life are being made by scientists all over the civilized world; wonderful results are at hand.

The conditions must be discovered and applied, by which every child may be developed into the full stature of manhood or womanhood. All sciences have been improved, and some, revolutionized within a few years; means for the genuine study of history have been multiplied; great literature is made accessible to every child; art with its treasures stands ready to help. Compared with the paucity of means of even fifty years ago, the supply is unlimited.

The conditions of knowledge and action must be adapted to the development of the whole being. This adaptation, general and individual, is called method, the essential factor in the art of educating.

No subject of inquiry, study, and investigation is comparable to the science of the soul and the laws of its development. This is the science of education, the science that comprehends all sciences. Like all other sciences, if we except mathematics, there is an infinity of knowledge yet to be found in this comprehensive science. Progress means a knowledge of the science of education and its application; it means that teachers must be educated, cultured, and trained into the most important of all professions.

What stands in the way of the one precious thing on earth— the freedom of the soul, the advancement of civilization, the happiness of man? I answer, first of all, tradition and its methods. It is impossible to measure the tremendous influence of tradition. It is very difficult to draw the line between education and heredity, but it is far more difficult to draw it between tradition and original personal power. We are at best creatures of tradition, controlled by the past, often bound hand and foot by the fixed habits of mankind; and this influence is dominant to-day in our public schools.

The methods of the few, in their control of the many, still govern our public schools, and to a great degree determine their management: the method of the prison, torture, and standing army survives in corporal punishment; the method of bribery— in reward- and prize-giving. Both of these immoral methods are absolutely useless; they are the outcome of quantity teaching and the makeshifts of unskilled teachers. Given devoted trained teachers, together with right surroundings and the right educative work, there is absolutely no necessity for either corparal punishment or the bribery of rewards.

The method of mystery still exercises its fearful power—the inoculated belief that there is something occult and mysterious in knowledge. The height of art is its simplicity, and the same can be said of the art of teaching. What I mean by the control of mystery is illustrated by the attitude of the people toward education. Let a teacher in a country school teach that which a farmer most needs upon the farm—practical chemistry; let him teach soil, physics, meteorology, zoölogy of the insects that infest his crops; let him teach arithmetic sensibly by measuring and weighing—and the farmers would call an indignation meeting and put out a man holding and teaching such newfangled notions. By learning they mean some mysterious process foreign to them. It does not readily enter their minds that that which is most practical is most logical, and that the old teaching of quantity, the mysterious pedantry of the school-teacher, who is supposed to know so much, is a relic of barbarism, and should hold the same place in the world of affairs as the sickle and the scythe.

I have used the farmer simply as an illustration; the same false ideas prevade all society to the detriment of education. The chemistry needed in the kitchen, the physiology that pertains to health, the physical training that develops a sound body, and history and civics essential to citizenship, the necessity of practical ethics, the relation of handwork to the brain and to true success, are little appreciated; while memorizing a jumble of words, grammar that will scarcely be used for lack of thought, a mastery of that incubus upon English education—the intricacies of unphonetic spelling, are the idols of the people, and, alas! of the majority of teachers.

The aristocratic idea of charity is still a potent influence in education. Our school system began as charity schools—charity schools such as the *Volksschule* of Germany. Many wealthy people have the traditional or *parvenu* feeling of class distinction look to-day upon the common-school system as a charity, and hold that there should be one education for rich children and another for the poor; that the children of the rich should not mingle with, and be contaminated by, the children of the poor.

No child, no citizen of a republic, can be educated into citizenship outside of the common school; the common school is not a charity; it is the inalienable right of every child, and common education is the imperative duty of every community. On a lower plane we may look at universal intelligence as the one means for the preservation of the republic; society, in order to preserve itself, must develop the highest character in every child.

The charity idea obtains largely among people who depend upon laborers and servants. I once talked with a gentleman upon a religious subject; he seemed to be imbued, or thought he was, with the spirit of Christ; he was a nail-manufacturer. When I spoke to him about the education of his employees, suggesting that they should have better opportunities for personal improvement, he said: "But that would spoil them as laborers. I must have employees; there must be a class of workers." This Christian gentleman was entirely willing to suppress human souls in the interest of nails.

The method of quantity teaching is without doubt the most prominent. You will remember what I have said of this method—that its means are the most effective in keeping children from anything like a search for the truth, and from a realization of their own liberty—the method of textbooks, page learning, per-cent examinations, with all the countless devices and means which serve to make quantity learning the end and aim of education.

When the common-school was founded there was little or no knowledge of, or belief in, a science of education. Most of our teachers took their patterns from England, where at that time the discoveries of Comenius and Pestalozzi had kindled no life. The old methods naturally took the field, and held their ground. The great majority of people are still firm believers in quantity: they insist that their children shall "go over," "go through," but particularly shall "finish." They measure education by the yard and weigh it by the pound. The people of to-day are the people of yesterday, their fixed ideas the inheritance of their teachers' teachers.

Most colleges demand quantity; they do not ask applicants, "Who are you? What have you done? What can you do?" But, "How many pages have you learned? Have you read Virgil? Xenophon? Homer? Come in and learn some more words."

The strongest indication that quantity teaching is in the ascendancy is the profound disbelief of the people in anything like a science of education. I cannot prove that there is a science of education. If, however, there is no such science, then all the other sciences are delusions. Science is organized knowledge of law; and to deny that there is a science of education is to deny that the development of human beings is governed by law.

The substantial disbelief in a science of education, and the almost universal indifference in regard to it, has one cause, and that cause is quantity teaching; the stimulus to the drudgery is the strap, or, worse, rewards and prizes. A teacher with a conscience, an artist-teacher, cannot do such menial service: it would be like requiring a Raphael to paint a board fence. If quantity teaching is ideal teaching, then the plainest deduction is, there is no science of education.

By far the greatest barrier to making the common school what it should and can be, springs by no means from active opposition to the system or from the patronage and pulls of pothouse politicians; the greatest barrier is the profound indifference of the most intelligent people in regard to the possibilities of radical improvement. This indifference has been enhanced until within a few years by the influence of colleges and universities, in which quantity instruction has had full swing. The average member of a school board often fancies that he knows all there is to be known about teaching; his measure is the quantity standard, acquired in his own education, which he rigidly enforces, crushing every effort toward quality work.

The social and political standing of teachers indicates the general depreciation of anything like a science of education or an art of teaching.

The people generally have never felt the quickening power of scientific teaching; they believe that their children must submit to the same process that they have endured; they judge teachers by their power to go over the most ground thoroughly. To them there is no need of a science of education, and from the quantity standpoint this judgment is perfectly logical. Scientific teaching means quality of mental action; it means the shortest line of resistance in the advance toward truth; it means the development of mental and moral power—a power that comprehends conditions and overcomes obstacles. I repeat, profound public indifference and an alarming ignorance in regard to the possibilities of education are the greatest obstacles to progress.

Quality is freedom. Let the quality of mental action be right, quantity will take care of itself. The principal cause of so many dullards is quantity teaching. Quantity teaching is strongly intrenched by incompetency. An imperative demand for scientific teaching would throw large numbers of present school incumbents out of business, or make them burn the midnight oil to an extent hitherto unheard of.

The quantity plan is the politician's opportunity. The state pays more money for schools than for any other purpose, except prisons, penitentiaries, poorhouses, and criminal courts; the schools present the most places to fill with "friends," whose acquirements, as a rule, are of the lowest order. Thousands of girls without culture, with very deficient education, manage, after repeated trials, to pass cram examinations met by quantity drills—examinations that are no tests whatever of ability to teach. These same girls, the daughters, friends, and relatives of ward politicians with a pull, are put in charge of fifty or more immortal souls, to repeat as best they may the wretched process of quantity teaching. Very few men remain in the profession on account of the low salaries, the precariousness of positions, the catering to public opinion, and, worst of all, the demand for fawning vassalage by corrupt or ignorant political bosses.

Although the initial battle for the common school has been fought and won, still it has many open and secret enemies. Who are they? First, the opponents of the common school are those who were born and bred outside of the atmosphere of liberty, who have had environment and traditions that compel them to believe as they do. It would be strange indeed if the most influential newcomers, whose education has been received in surroundings entirely opposed to the spirit of liberty, of which the common school is the main buttress, did believe in our system of schools. They are honestly opposed to the system, and should be respected for their honesty and met by honest argument.

The fundamental method of the Old World education is isolation; it is supported by no particular party nor sect; the people educated in this method believe in it from their habit of life and the tradition of ages. Why should they understand the genius of American Liberty? Why should those who have become habituated to class education believe that the stratification of American society into fixed classes means sure death to the republic and the future hopes of democracy? Public school education means that the children of one class would become indoctrinated with the opinions, political and religious, of other classes; that fixed beliefs would become unsettled.

So far as the destruction of these fixed ideas is concerned, the argument is logical: The common-school destroys caste, makes democrats, annihilates the domination of the few. Of all the places in the world where children can practice religion, the common school is the most favorable. School is the place for doing, not preaching, righteousness. No, the purpose of the opponents of the common school is not to teach religion, but to preserve the integrity of aristocratic power, by isolation and the consequent maintenance of distinct classes.

The marvelous growth of the fundamental democratic idea —the common-school—is unparalleled in history. The traditional plan of private, class, and sectarian education has been over-turned. The proposition to give every child a good education at the expense of the community and state has been established upon a permanent basis by the votes of the people. Millions of dollars are freely given every year for common education; open and direct opposition, that marked the early stages, is becoming less and less. Glorious as this work is, it is but the foundation for the superstructure, the initial step to improvements infinitely better.

The progress of the common school imperatively demands the application of the science of education. The methods of quantity instruction have reached their utmost limits; the time for quality teaching has fully come. What stands in the way? First of all, the profound indifference of intelligent people in regard to better teachers and teaching, and indifference resting upon an obstinate disbelief in the possibilities of the art of teaching. It is a product of quantity teaching, from which are derived the prevailing standards of intellectual mensuration. The results of this indifference are: withdrawal of large numbers of children of the so-called better classes from the common-school, and a growing tendency to put it into the category of eleemosynary institutions. We hear much adverse criticism in regard to private sectarian schools, while little or nothing is said about the still greater number of children isolated from the masses in education by rich parents.[4] The reason for withdrawing children from the common schools is that they are not good enough; this reason seems valid. It would be so indeed if the sole cause of the defects in the common schools was not the indifference of the very people who want better schools than the public affords.

Further, whatever duties the body politic neglects, become the prey and spoil of the pot-house politician. Many of the common-schools in this republic are managed and controlled by a class of spoilmongers who do not have the faintest idea of education, who indeed do not care what becomes of the schools if their patronage is not touched. Their prey is the innocent children; they strike at the very heart of the republic.

If any business in the world, any railroad, bank, store, or manufactory were conducted upon the same principles that obtain in the management of schools in most of our large cities and in many small districts, hopeless bankruptcy would be the inevitable result. Superintendents are too seldom chosen for professional skill or executive ability, and when they are, the school boards often take away from them every vital influence that would make them efficient managers. The vast majority of teachers have not the slightest professional training or the faintest idea of the science of education; thus quantity cram is the rule, and quality teaching the exception. Every other business in the world except the care of immortal souls, requires experts!!

The great-hearted city of Chicago pours out six millions of dollars yearly for its school; but there is little or no question of whether the money shall be spent for education or patronage, for one per-cent dividend or a thousand. Let teachers move in the direction of the divine art of teaching, and a commanding halt is heard from authority. Let experts examine the cramming methods that form the bulk of most school-work and condemn them, the result is a prolonged howl of indignation from the school boards, public teachers, and often from school periodicals.

The greatest popular satisfaction is often evinced for the poorest school system.

Whether from design or not, the indifference of the people, the patronage of politicians, the weakness of supervision, and the inefficiency of teachers, furnish the best possible means of degrading the common school, putting it upon a charity basis, weaning intelligent people from all active interest and sympathy and leading to the downfall of the most precious institution which was ever established by a free people.

I have not overdrawn the indictment. There are beautiful streaks of light everywhere amid the general darkness of unprofessional teaching, proving beyond all doubt that the people can make every common-school a perfect means of developing true manhood and womanhood. An effective school means an educated, cultured, trained, devoted teacher. To-day in most communities there is very little discrimination between an excellent teacher and a poor one; too often the latter has a marked advantage. There is not a coin small enough, ever stamped by the hand of man, to pay the salary of a poor teacher; there is not gold enough in the mines of the world to measure the value of a teacher who lifts the souls of children to the true dignity of life and living. Put such teachers in the slums of our great cities, supply them with every necessary means, and we would soon find that "an ounce of prevention is worth a ton of cure." The right teaching, the possible teaching, would diminish the attendance upon bridewells, prisons, reformatories, almshouses, lunatic asylums; would lessen the number of voters that can be bought and take away the following of corrupt politicians; would insure the perpetuity of the republic, the hope of humanity. What stands in the way? The indifference, the lethargy, the lack of active interest even on the part of the good, noble men and women.

Nothing will reach the hearts of fathers and mothers like the prospect of better things for their precious children; yet many a mother, who would die for the sum of her earthly treasures—her little ones—never gives a thought to the possibilities of an exalted life for children by means of better education.

The time has come, the hour is here, when the loving sympathy that so richly abounds for charity, for the saving of beings who are lost from neglect, must be turned upon the infinite possibilities of child nurture and growth.

I have argued that the inefficiency of our common schools is owing to the traditional methods that have been the effective means of keeping the masses in subjection through the long ages of human history. America could be made an educational center of the world; to our land have come a vast multitude, marred and scarred by the selfishness of the few; here they have brought the wounds of tyranny. They have come to be healed; let them come. But we must heal these wounds, must quicken stagnant blood, and revive despairing hearts by the breath of liberty. We must do it, I say, else our republic dies, and with it the hopes of freedom for centuries.

Let us welcome all religions; let us freely accord to all believers the right to worship God as they see fit, and, disbelievers, to deny His existence; but we dare not, must not, allow the methods of aristocracy to ruin all we hold dear.

"Who possesses the youth, possesses the future," sounds in our ears. Who should possess the youth? Not the aristocracy, with its long record in human subjection and slavery. No party, no creed, should possess the future. The truth, and the truth alone, should possess the youth. Who possesses the truth in its richness and fullness? None in the past. Who have applied it? Let prisons, dungeons, torture, poverty, woe, misery, and the outer darkness of ignorance answer. We may hold a satisfying

religion, we may respect each other's opinions, we may have the
perfect tolerance of universal love, but while we know that the
path of progress has been strewn with the wrecks of theories, we
dare not fetter the souls of children with a fixed and implicit
belief in any theory. We must believe that there is truth enough
and power enough and love enough to carry the bread of life
to every hungry and needy soul. The methods of aristocracy
have not done this, and cannot do it; but when it is applied
the perfect love, born into the world upon the hills of Palestine,
can do it—the love that is filled with the gospel of the Father-
hood of God and the brotherhood of man.

The spirit of democracy respects all rights of parents as sacred
except the right to deprive a child of a good education. Attractive education is far more powerful than compulsory education.
The common school can be made the best school in the world.
Everything is ready except scientific teaching and the method
of democracy—that education which shall set the souls of children free.

It is no dream or illusion, the realization of a common school,
perfect in its appointments, with the means for the highest and
best education at hand. All is ready when the people are ready
to move, to demand that the methods of quantity shall go, and
the methods of quality shall come in. Unrealized possibilities
of human growth are the infinite line of march.

A school should be a model home, a complete community
and embryonic democracy. How? you ask. I answer by putting
into every schoolroom an educated, cultured, trained, devoted,
child-loving teacher, a teacher imbued with a knowledge of the
science of education, and a zealous, enthusiastic applicant of its
principles. Where shall we find such teachers? They will spring
from the earth and drop from the clouds when they hear the
demand. We have asked for quantity teachers, and they have

come by the tens of thousands. Now let us demand the artist-teacher, the teacher trained and skilled in the science of education.

Nothing that is good is too good for the child—no thought too deep, no toil too great, no work too arduous,—for the welfare of the child means happier homes, better society, a pure ballot and the perpetuity of republican institutions. Not only must the people demand the artist-teacher with an authority which will admit no denial, but they must also demand that the methods of aristocracy, which have degraded and debased mankind, be totally eliminated from the training of citizens. Let us have a doctrine of education which means freedom to every child. I commend to your careful study the Theory of Concentration, a theory that makes personal liberty the path to universal freedom.

I have said these words "with malice toward none, and charity for all." Fighting for four years in the Civil War, as best I could, for the preservation of the democractic ideal, a teacher of little children for nearly forty years, I believe four things, as I believe in God—that democracy is the one hope of the world; that democracy without efficient common schools is impossible; that every school in the land should be made a home and a heaven for children; fourth, that when the ideal of the public school is realized, "the blood shed by the blessed martyrs for freedom will not have been shed in vain."

---

[1] Wm. H. Kilpatrick, *Education for a Changing Civilization,* Chap. I.

[2] This statement shows Colonel Parker's attitude toward woman's suffrage which had not been accomplished in the U. S. at the time he wrote this book.

[3] Horace Mann founded Antioch College in the year 1836.

[4] While Colonel Parker believed that a private school for wealthy children only, had no place in a democracy—he thought that there was definite need for private laboratory schools including children from all economic levels, all races and creeds who would live, work, and play together through their growing years.

In these laboratory schools educational experiments might be tried out for the benefit of public school practice, which would be impractical in an unwieldy large school system. Indeed, Colonel Parker himself more reluctantly left the Chicago Public School system in 1899. He had struggled valiantly and unremittently for eighteen years against great odds and obstacles imposed by a politically controlled School Board. He believed he could work faster and most effectively for the children of the Chicago schools—for all children—in a private laboratory —a Normal and Demonstration School—where he could be free to put to the test the Social Philosophy of Education in whi h he ardently believed.

XVII

EXAMINATIONS[1]

By Francis W. Parker

I BELIEVE that the greatest obstacle in the way of real teaching today, is the standard of examinations. The cause is not far to seek. The standard for the work has a powerful influence on the work itself. What should examinations be? The test of real teaching–of genuine work. What is teaching? Teaching is the evolution of thought, and thought is the mind's mode of action. Teaching arouses mental activity, so as to develop the mind in the best possible way, and at the same time, leads to the acquisition of that knowledge which is most useful to the mind and its development. There is one other important factor to be considered, and that is, the training of that skill which leads to the proper expression of the thought evolved. This factor in teaching, is usually called training, the results of which are correct modes of expression, such as talking, writing, drawing, making, and building. All school work, then, is comprehended in thought and its expression. It must be understood at every step, that expression is only necessary when thought is evolved. Train expression at the expense of thought, and we have the body without the living soul.

Real teaching, meaning by this the evolution of thought, and the training of its expression, does not aim at the learning of disconnected facts. Real teaching leads to the systematic, symmetrical, all-sided upbuilding of a compact

[1]Chapter reprinted from Patridge, Lelila E. *Notes of Talks on Teaching, Given by Francis W. Parker, at the Martha's Vineyard Summer Institute, July 17 to August 19, 1882.* New York and Chicago: E.L. Kellogg & Co., (1889): 150-155.

body of knowledge in the mind. Every faculty of the mind-perception, judgment, classification, reason, imagination, and memory–is brought into action in this upbuilding or instruction; and the foundations are laid broad and deep, in sense-products. Words and all other means of expression, are simply indications of thought-building, and its complicated processes. Examinations, then, should test the conditions and progress, of mind in its development. The means of examination are found in language, oral and written, in drawing, and all other forms of expression.

If I am not mistaken, the examinations usually given, simply test the pupil's power of memorizing disconnected facts. Take, for illustration, the innumerable facts in history; of these, that which a child can learn in a course of four or five years' vigorous study would be as a drop of water to the ocean. It would be an easy matter, to set an examination of ten seemingly simple questions in history, for Mommsen, Curtius, Droysen, Bancroft, and other eminent historians, which they would utterly fail to pass. How, then, can we judge of a child's knowledge by asking ten questions? The same can be said of geography and the natural sciences. The fact is, the only just way to examine pupils is, to find out what the teacher has taught, and her manner and method of teaching. Examination should find out what a child does know, and not what he does not know. Suppose, then, that in the example just mentioned, the pupils have been under the guidance of a skillful teacher, who has given out, one after another, the most interesting subjects to be found in history, and had her pupils read all they could find in various books about them, and after taking these acquired treasures of knowledge, and arranging the events in logical order, had finally had the children write out in good English the whole story. The test of such work would simply be, to request the pupils to tell orally, or on paper, all they knew about Columbus, Walter Raleigh, Bunker Hill, or any other interesting subject they have studied.

It is very easy, for one accustomed to such examinations, to judge of the true teaching power of the teacher by the written papers. If meaningless words have been memorized, if there is a lack of research, investigation, and original thought, the results will be painfully apparent. Whatever the teacher has done, or failed to do, can be readily comprehended by an expert in examination. In the same way geography and the sciences may be examined. The test of spelling, penmanship, composition, punctuation, and the power to use correct language, can be tested in no better way than by the writings of such compositions as these.

Examinations should not be made the test of fitness for promotion. If the teacher really teaches, and faithfully watches the mental growth of her pupils, through the work of one or two years, she alone is the best judge of the fitness of her pupils to do the work of the next grade. If she does not teach, it is impossible for her to prepare her pupils for advanced work. The great question for the supervisor to decide is, Has the teacher the ability to instruct the children in the proper manner and by the best methods? Is it possible for a supervisor to find out in one hour, by a series of set questions, more than the teacher, who watches carefully the development of her pupils for one or two years?

Those who understand children, will readily appreciate the excitement and strain under which they labor, when their fate depends upon the correct answering of ten disconnected questions. It is well known to you, that some of the best pupils, generally do their worst in the confusion that attends such highly-wrought nervous states. How much better, then, is it to take the entire work of the pupil for the whole year, than the results of one hour, under such adverse conditions?

Again, examinations demand more than the children can perform. What teacher ever received a class from a lower grade, fully prepared for the work fixed by the examination for her grade? I have never found one. Supposing children have been in the school three or four years under poor teaching, and do not know anything thoroughly–cannot read, write, reckon, or think. Now the teacher who takes such poorly prepared pupils, must choose one of two courses. She must do the children under her charge the greatest possible good, by teaching them thoroughly what they have failed to learn, and then have them fail entirely of passing the uniform examinations; or by sheer force of verbal memory, the paragraphs, pages, and propositions necessary for the test, may be put into their minds. "Having," says Spencer, "by our method induced helplessness, we straightway make helplessness the reason for our method."

Perfect freedom should be given the teacher to do the best work in her own way. That is, the highest good of the child should be the sole aim of the teacher, without the slightest regard for false standards. The teacher who strives for examinations and promotions, can never really teach. The only true motive that should govern the teacher, must spring from the truth, found in the nature of the child's mind and the subject taught.

The purpose of the superintendent's examination should be, to ascertain whether the principals under his charge, have the requisite ability and knowledge to organize, supervise, and teach a large school. The examinations of the principal, should test the teaching power of his teachers; and lastly, the teacher should test, by examinations, the mental growth of her pupils. This is the true economical system of responsibility. First, ascertain whether superintendent, principal, and teacher can be trusted, and then trust them.

The answer to this proposition, I have heard a thousand times. "Your plan would be good enough, if we had good teachers. The fault is, that the teachers are so poor we cannot trust them. If we did not examine them in this way, they would absolutely do nothing." The fallacy of this answer may be exposed in two ways. First, a uniform examination of disconnected questions, prevents the good teacher from exercising her art; second, the poor teacher will never be able to see the wide margin between good work and that which she does, until the true test of real teaching is placed before her. There has been legislation enough for poor teachers and poor teaching. Give the good teachers a chance! The testimony of countless good teachers has been uniform in this respect. When asked, "Why don't you do better work?" "Why don't you use the methods taught in normal schools, and advocated by educational periodicals and books?" The answer is, "We cannot do it. Look at our

course of study. In three weeks, or months, these children
will be examined. We have not one moment of time to
spend in real teaching!" No wonder that teaching is a trade
and not an art! No wonder there is little or no demand for
books upon the science and art of teaching, such as
"Payne's Lectures," etc. The demand fixed by examiners is
for cram, and not for an art; and so long as the demand
exists, so long will the teacher's mind shrivel and dwarf, in
the everlasting treadmill that has no beginning or end, and
the more it turns the more it creaks! So long, too, will this
tinkering of immortal souls go on! Teachers often complain
of their social position, their salaries, and the lack of sympathy in the public. "The fault," dear teachers, "is not in our
stars, but in ourselves, that we are underlings." Instead of
stubbornly standing, and obstinately denying that there is
no need of reform, and that all so-called new methods are
worthless; let us honestly, earnestly, prayerfully study the
great science of teaching. Let us learn, and courageously
apply the truths that shall set us free; and the day will soon
come when the teacher will lead society, and mould opinion.

XVIII

INTRODUCTION[1]

to *Notes on Talks on Teaching*

By Lelila W. Patridge

THERE is, perhaps, no name more widely known among the teachers of this country, that that of Col. Francis W. Parker. The results of his supervision of the Quincy schools have made him the most talked of, if not the most popular educator of our time. Whatever may be thought of him or his work–and it would be idle to deny that opinions differ regarding both–he is acknowledged, even by his opponents, to be one of those who are destined to mould public opinion. Concerning such the world is always curious. We desire to know their history, their environment, that we may judge their power.

Remembering this, I have thought that something of the man, as well as his methods, might prove interesting to the readers of the "Notes." I have, therefore, persuaded Col. Parker to give me the salient points of his life, more especially those that bear upon his career as a teacher, and these I have thrown into shape and order in the sketch which follows.

Francis Wayland Parker, born October 9th, 1837, in the town of Bedford (now Manchester), N.H., came of a race of scholars and teachers. His great-grandfather on his mother's side was Librarian of Harvard College, and a class-mate of Hancock. His mother taught for several years before her marriage, showing marked originality in her

[1]Chapter reprinted from Patridge, Lelila E. *Notes of Talks on Teaching, Given by Francis W. Parker, at the Martha's Vineyard Summer Institute, July 17 to August 19, 1882.* New York and Chicago: E.L. Kellogg & Co., (1889): xi-xxi.

methods; and all her children were born teachers.

From earliest childhood he thought and talked of being a teacher. It was always his dream, and his one ambition. His father dying when Francis was but six years old, at eight the boy was bound out, according to New England phrase, that is, apprenticed to a farmer till he was twenty-one. But nature was too strong for circumstance. A farmer he could not, would not be, and at the age of thirteen he broke his bonds, and started out into the world for himself. Without money, influence or friends, for he had angered his relatives by this move, he struggled on for the next four years, doing whatever he could find to do, and going to school whenever opportunity offered. The he put his foot on the first round of the ladder; he obtained his first school. It was at Corser Hill, Boscawen (now Webster), and he was paid fifteen dollars per month.

This venture proved successful, though many of his pupils were older than their teacher, and some (he says) knew more. The next winter he taught at Over-the-Brook in the town of Auburn, for seventeen dollars a month, and "boarded around." From this time his services were in such demand in the town, that he taught, not only the winter schools for the next three years, but opened a "select school" on his own account during the autumn months. One term of teaching in Hinsdale, and one in the grammar school of his native village, ended his work in New England for several years.

In the fall of 1859 he received a call to the Principalship of the graded school at Carrollton, Ill., and there he remained till the breaking out of war in the spring of 1861. Finding, then, that loyalty to the Union was the one qualification in a school-master for which they had no use in that vicinity, he resigned his position before his committee had fully decided that they wished for it, and was immediately offered a better one with a higher salary at Alton, Ill. This he declined and started for the East, where he at once enrolled as a private in the Fourth New Hampshire Regiment just forming. He fought all through the war, became lieutenant, captain, lieutenant-colonel, and brevet-colonel. He was wounded in the throat and chin at the battle of Deep Bottom, August 16th, 1864, was taken prisoner by the confederates at Magnolia, N.C., and released just as peace was declared. Then with the remnant of his regiment he returned to New Hampshire, and was mustered out of service August, 1865.

At the call of his country he had left the schoolroom; now she required his services in the field no longer. Where next? Many ways were open to his choice. Military preferment, political office, excellent business positions were offered to him at this time, but he declined them all. His passion for teaching was too strong for these to tempt him. He never wavered for a moment, not even when his best worldly interests seemed to be at stake. A teacher he was born, a teacher he would live and die. He accepted the Principalship of the North Grammar School of Manchester, N.H., at a salary of eleven hundred dollars, and held the position for three years. From there he went to Dayton, Ohio, in 1869, to take charge of the school in District No. I. Here he had the supervision not only of the grammar grades, but of the primary; and now his primary work began. He had all along had his own way of doing things, and had from the very first his conception of how teaching should be done. Indeed, he tells with some amusement at his own audacity, that when only eight years old, he rose in school one day and informed the teacher that he didn't know how to teach! Even war, with all its horrors, did not wholly absorb his mind from its favorite theme. Often, as he sat before the camp fire, or lay in his tent at night, he studied how the mind grows, and planned many of the methods which have since made him famous. It was in Manchester where he used to work all day, and then spend half the night preparing for the next, that he first began to apply his theories. But in the primary schools of Dayton, he felt for the first time that he had begun at the beginning of the great work of mind development. At the end of the year he became Principal of the Dayton Normal School, a position he held for two years, being then elected Assistant Superintendent of the City Schools.

No one who steps out of the beaten track can walk long in his new path unchallenged. To desert the old, to fail in respect for the traditional, to imply that customary ways of doing things might not be the best ways, is treason, and high treason. This Col. Parker was made to feel, and feel keenly. Though a soldier, he loved peace better than war, but he began to see, as time went on, that his fighting days were not yet over. More and more he found himself antagonizing the convictions of his fellow-teachers, as day by day he grew away from the time-honored traditions of his vocation. They would not agree to his views, he could not agree to theirs; and one party must be in the wrong-which was it? Where did truth lie? It would seem with the majority. But he would not give up what seemed to him so clearly right without reasons. He would consult the highest authorities in the art of teaching, and learn if he were wrong. Accordingly, in the fall of 1872, he went to Germany, and entered King William's University, at Berlin, for a two years' course in philosophy, history, and pedagogics.

It need not be said that his opinions found confirmation strong in that centre of intellectual development; and he returned to his native land eager for an opportunity to put his theories, now fully fledged, into practice. When it comes to pass in this world that the right man finds the right place, we have a way of saying, "How very providential!" as if affairs were only occasionally under the care of Providence. But it was certainly a singularly happy coincidence that just about this time one of the most intelligent school committees of these United States, located at Quincy, Mass., made a discovery which forced them to a conclusion, and that in turn decided them to make an experiment. Their discovery was, that after eight years of attendance in the public schools, "the children could neither write with facility nor read fluently; nor could they speak or spell their own language very perfectly." Their conclusion was, "that the whole existing system was wrong-a system from which the life had gone out. The school year had become one long period of diffusion and cram, and smatter had become the order of the day."

[It is not to be understood by this that the Quincy schools were any worse than the average, but merely that they had a committee intelligent enough to comprehend their true condition.]

Acting on this conclusion, they had decided to try to remedy matters. But they were busy men, not specialists in education, and wise enough to know that they were unequal to this difficult and delicate work. Thus they had come to the decision to find some one to do it for them. They would try the experiment of having a Superintendent of Schools. That committee found the man they sought, in Francis W. Parker. So Col. Parker went to Quincy, and nothing since the time of Horace Mann has created such a sensation as his five years' supervision of those schools.

Said his committee in their report after he had left them, "For five years the town had the benefit of his faithful, intelligent and enthusiastic services. In these years he transformed our public schools. He found them machines, he left them living organisms; drill gave way to growth, and the weary prison became a pleasure house. His dominant intelligence as a master, and his pervasive magnetism as a man, informed his school-work. He breathed life, growth and happiness into our school-rooms. The results are plain to see before the eyes of every one, solid, substantial, unmistakable. They cannot be gainsaid, or successfully questioned." Said Charles Francis Adams, Jr., in his paper on the "New Departure in the Common Schools of Quincy," "The revolution was all-pervading. Nothing escaped its influence; it began with the alphabet, and extended into the latest effort of the grammar-school course. So daring an experiment as this can, however, be tested in but one way –by its practical results, as proven by the experience of a number of years, and testified to by parents and teachers. Out of five hundred grammar-school children, taken promiscuously from all the schools, no less than four hundred showed results which were either excellent or satisfactory, while its advantages are questioned by none, least of all by teachers and parents... The quality of the instruction given has been immeasurably improved."

Such a success as this, heralded abroad by the thousand who visited the Quincy schools, could not fail to bring advancement in its train. Accordingly, when in 1880 Boston gave the country Superintendent a call to "come up higher," and be one of its supervisors, he accepted, and at the expiration of his time of service (two years) was re-elected for a second term. In October, 1882, Col. Parker received an urgent call to the Principalship of the Cook County Normal School (just outside Chicago), at a salary of five thousand dollars; and later, the same year, was offered the Superintendency of the city of Philadelphia, at a still higher salary. In December he resigned his position in Boston, and yielding to his overmastering desire to teach, declined the office of Superintendent, which Philadelphia would gladly have given him, and accepted instead the charge of the Normal School in Illinois. The first day of January, 1883, he entered upon his duties as Principal of the Cook County Normal School, where he is now working with all his characteristic force and spirit.

With greater opportunities than have ever been granted to him before, with an experience broadened and deepened by the failures and successes of the past, with his old-time energy and enthusiasm no whit abated, we have faith to believe that the future will show results, which shall make what he has done in the past seem but the crudest of beginnings.

THE MARTHA'S VINEYARD LECTURES

The first of the year, 1881, Col. Parker received an urgent request from the Directors of the Martha's Vineyard Summer Institute that he should become the head of the Department of Didactics, at their next session, beginning in July of the same year. Although working already to his utmost, it was a great temptation to have a few weeks of his favorite pursuit thus offered him in the midst of so much supervisory work. Consequently, he decided to give three weeks of his much needed summer rest for this purpose. The matter being decided hastily, and at the last moment, was not properly advertised, and the Class in Didactics that first year was small to what it would otherwise have been, numbering only fifty members.

The following year, feeling that here was an opportunity for wide-spread influence, and much good to be done, he returned to the Vineyard. He found that his small beginning of the summer before had been a true beginning, for not only did many of the class of '81 return, but they showed that they had been making a study of the great art of teaching, and came back better prepared for the lectures, by their year's experience and observation. This season the Class in Didactics numbered nearly one hundred and fifty members, representing twenty-three States and Nova Scotia. Of this number there were forty-seven Principals or Heads of Departments, seven Superintendents, eleven Kindergartners, and two Institute Lecturers. The course extended through five weeks, and the following were the Lecturers and Teachers:

PRINCIPAL, COL. FRANCIS W. PARKER,
"Art of Teaching."

DR. WILLIAM T. HARRIS,
"History and Science of Education."

DR. LARKIN DUNTON, Head Master of the Boston Normal School.
"Principles of Teaching."

PROF. MOSES TRUE BROWN, Professor of Oratory in Tuft's College.
"Reading in Grammar and High Schools."

PROF. H. E. HOLT, Supervisor of Music in Public Schools, Boston.
"Teaching Music to Little Children."

PROF. HERMANN B. BOISEN, Author of Boisen's
New German Course.
"Principles of Teaching Modern Languages."

H. P. WARREN, Principal of the N. H. State Normal School.
"Teaching History."

PROF L. ALONZO BUTTERFIELD, Teacher of Elocution at the Newton
Theological Institution, and Associate Principal with Alex. Graham Bell,
in School of Vocal Physiology, Boston, Mass.
"Phonics."

MISS RUTH R. BURRITT, Principal
Kindergarten Training School, Phila.
"How to Teach Form by Moulding Clay"

MISS HETTA CLEMENT, First Assistant, Coddington School, Quincy.
"Moulding Geographical Forms."

MRS. MARY D. HICKS, Late Supervisor of Drawing, Syracuse, N. Y.
"Lessons on Drawing."

MRS. M. FRANK STUART, Boston School of Oratory.
"The Delsarte Method–Its Uses and Abuses."

MISS LELILA E. PATRIDGE, Instructor at Teachers' Institutes, Penn.
"Gymnastic Drill."

358

Col. Parker, yielding to the strongly expressed desire of his pupils and fellow-teachers, has consented to resume his work at the Institute the coming season; but it will be his last year at the Vineyard. His regular work in the West is too arduous and absorbing to permit of any outside interests. Besides, he cannot afford to fall before the fight is ended; and not even his splendid vitality could long endure the strain of such exhausting and continuous labor. However much we of the East may regret the loss of his inspiring lessons on the great art of teaching, we must be willing to forego them after this season, not only for his own sake —that his days may be long, but for the sake of the little children of the land; for when he dies they lose their warmest friend, ablest champion, and wisest benefactor.

PHILADELPHIA, March, 1883.
L.E.P.

XIX

In Memoriam

COLONEL FRANCIS WAYLAND PARKER
LATE DIRECTOR OF THE SCHOOL OF EDUCATION,
UNIVERSITY OF CHICAGO.

ADDRESSES DELIVERED AT THE SERVICES HELD
AT THE UNIVERSITY, MARCH 6, 1902.[1]

By President William R. Harper

MANY lives contain tragedies greater and sadder than the tragedy which marks the end; but in the life that has just closed, so far as I know it, the greatest tragedy has been that in which it ended.

The life of our friend was never a smooth one, as lives go. With his temperament, it could not have been expected to be smooth; but, on the other hand, it was not an unhappy life, nor was it one devoid of meaning to himself and to his friends. Few men, probably, have found greater satisfaction in life; for it was his determined purpose to make of it as much as possible–a purpose the execution of which assisted many and injured none.

The Colonel's life was a varied one. As soldier, student, teacher, as leader, administrator, and thinker, he filled at various times positions of high responsibility. There was a certain brusqueness in his voice and manner which some, perhaps, did not understand, and with which they were not in sympathy; but even those who were in the outer circle of his acquaintanceship knew that this was only an external physical expression which did not represent his heart.

[1]Chapter reprinted from "In Memoriam. Colonel Francis Wayland Parker." *The Elementary School Teacher and Course of Study* 2 (1902): 699-715.

To me he seems to have been rather a prophet than a philosopher. The courage and strength which he expended in fighting for the highest ideals of educational work, against opposition and in the midst of difficulties, marked the prophetic character. His singleness of purpose and his devotion to the cause he held so dear were most striking; but to those who knew him they were only natural. His mind was alert and always vigorous, widely interested and full of vision. His greatest strength lay in the wonderful power given him to sympathize with others; to enter into and to appreciate the experiences of others.

His love for children was extraordinary, and this single factor controlled his thinking and his life. Nor was it love for children in the abstract. The satisfaction with which he studied the growth and development of a particular child, the interest manifested in each individual, were the truest expression of the joy and gladness which seemed to fill his soul in its close communion with child-life. These, at all events, were some of the strong peculiarities of this, our friend, who has been taken from us.

I can see him now, as he sits with his hands crossed, listening with supreme delight to the expressions of child-thought, one following the other, each illustrating some phase of the child-nature. I can hear him now, speaking strongly and enthusiastically of the possibilities of child-work; of the greatness and the nobility of the profession of child-culture. And I remember how, during the last months, his whole soul seemed to be centered on the thought and the conception of the buildings for the School of Education. How he waited; so long and so patiently; always ready to sacrifice the present for the sake of a higher ideal to be realized in the future.

He was a man of superb idealism, unmindful of the present, provided that there seemed to be promise of a greater future; never moved by motives of expediency, but holding out before himself, as well as those associated with him, a high and splendid ideal toward the realization of which he made the most earnest effort; and in this is found the tragedy of the situation.

It was the realization of his most extravagant hopes when a broad-minded woman came to his assistance and placed within his reach the means with which to carry out his long-cherished plans. How unexpected, how generous; what possibilities it furnished! And then came the union with the University, which, to him, signified broader lines and still greater possibilities. The building plans revised and enlarged–his interest in it all, and his devotion to it all; through these months–the tender and sympathetic regard of the old trustees–every care being taken to secure for him and his work the most favorable environment; and, at the same time, his peculiar and deep appreciation of the favor and courtesy thus extended to him; and now he is gone, while the work is hardly begun. Three more years and he could have died in peace, with all his efforts rewarded, his ideas formulated, himself seeing the walls of the magnificent group of buildings which are to be the outgrowth of his thinking and his work. Could anything be more sad? And yet he turned the soil for these buildings last June, and he spoke the first words uttered upon the grounds of the great school which through all the years will bear the stamp of his influence. Could we have known that day what was to be, how even more solemn and significant this occasion would have seemed!

In Memoriam

COLONEL FRANCIS WAYLAND PARKER
LATE DIRECTOR OF THE SCHOOL OF EDUCATION, UNIVERSITY OF CHICAGO.

ADDRESSES DELIVERED AT THE SERVICES HELD AT THE UNIVERSITY, MARCH 6, 1902.

By Albert G. Lane,
District Superintendent, Public Schools, Chicago.

COLONEL PARKER came to the Cook County Normal School at a time when there was a rapid growth in this city and county, and when about three hundred teachers were needed annually to supply the increased demand and to take the places of those who retired from the service. This demand brought many experienced teachers here who availed themselves of the privilege of attending the normal school and of acquiring a knowledge of the principles and practices of the "new education" as enunciated by Colonel Parker. The high-school graduates who desired to teach in the county were required to take one year of professional training before they could become teachers. From the beginning of his work in this county he strongly molded and influenced the ideas, the motives, plans, and methods of all who came under his instruction. Nearly every graduate of his school commenced teaching with high ideals of the teacher's mission and a quickened power to arouse in children a keen, natural interest in any work which was undertaken. His graduates became observers and students of child-nature. They sought to lead the unfolding powers of childhood into channels of activity that would make them observant of things, their relations and uses. They gave new life to the child's efforts by opening up various forms of constructive work, by making drawing a delight to children as a language for expressing thought. They made the study of geography full of intense interest by the lessons in science, by visiting and observing the surrounding country, by examining and studying the products of the soil, their growth, and the changes necessary to convert them to man's use.

His graduates learned to make reading a great means of growth and culture, relating it to some subject or object which was of attractive interest, something which the child was anxious to know. Many books furnishing information were brought into the schoolroom, and the children learned to use them. History, no longer memorized by the page, was made a delight to children as they read stories of the children of other lands, their dress, customs, and homes; of men's travels and achievements; of their struggles to build a nation where each citizen should have a chance to develop all that was highest and best in him.

Colonel Parker impressed his graduates with the value of each life as a factor in building up and maintaining the social well-being of any community. The central thought of all his teaching was mutual responsibility and freedom of the individual to come to a knowledge of truth. Truth frees from bondage. His graduates were trained to ally themselves to all public movements for the common good in the places where they taught. The people were brought to feel that they had a part in the life of the school Old and young were frequently brought together and made conscious of the necessity of unity in all true growth and advancement.

I will not attempt to enumerate all the changes that have grown into our educational work as the result of Colonel Parker's labors during the last seventeen years. During that time about twelve hundred teachers have been graduated, and many others have taken partial courses, have studied his principles of education, and adapted many of his methods. The schools of Chicago and Cook county bear the evidences of more rational developing and inspiring work with the children. Their lives have been made brighter by the transforming influences of wiser, better teaching.

Colonel Parker's work and influence have not been confined to this vicinity. In those great annual institutes which were held, averaging for several years from five to six hundred teachers, he found opportunities to set forth higher standards of education. His writings on education have been read and studied, and their suggestions put into practice. Text-books for children have been modified to meet his thought, and that of others who have stood with him or followed his educational theories and practice. There is scarcely a state in this union where he has not lectured and aroused people to consider more carefully and intelligently the marvelous possibilities in the training of children.

During these years he has changed in many respects his methods of work, although holding firmly to fundamental principles. His conception of education is expressed in these words, spoken by him last summer at the meeting of the National Educational Association at Detroit:

"We are marching along the endless pathway of unrealized possibilities of human growth. We believe that all that education has yet done, with its principles and methods, its reformers and its organization, is but a crude step toward that which must be. We believe that the inner development of the human soul in righteousness is the one purpose of education."

It must be left to a coming generation to perceive clearly how great a work Colonel Parker has accomplished. We see some of the defects which are naturally allied to new movements. Time will sift the dross and leave the pure gold. He gave his life freely to the cause of elementary education. His own life unfolded to higher and better things. I recall that stanza which Mrs. Parker loved to repeat:

> Build thee more stately mansions, O my soul,
> As the swift seasons roll!
> Leave thy low-vaulted past!
> Let each new temple, nobler than the last,
> Shut thee from heaven with a dome more vast,
> Till thou at length art free,
> Leaving thine outgrown shell by life's unresting sea!

If Colonel Parker could speak now, I think he would say: "Remember the words which I spake unto you while I was yet with you."

In Memoriam

COLONEL FRANCIS WAYLAND PARKER
LATE DIRECTOR OF THE SCHOOL OF EDUCATION,
UNIVERSITY OF CHICAGO.

By Dr. John Dewey[1]

THIS is neither the time nor the place to attempt a review of the educational philosophy or the educational work of Colonel Parker. But our noble and single-minded friend obeyed above most men the scriptural injunction; he loved and did with his whole mind and his whole soul. Hence it is as impossible to speak of his personality apart from his educational work as it is to speak of his educational work apart from his personality. He was fortunate in the complete identification of his whole being, his whole personality, with the work to which he devoted himself.

Thus there are three things in his educational work which come to me because they are characteristic of his personality, because they belong to the man. Colonel Parker was upon the program of the educational meeting which was held in the city last week, but was kept away by his sickness. The title of his speech was "Education into Citizenship." If there could have been anything more characteristic than this of Colonel Parker's attitude toward education, it was the sub-title: "Relating Especially to Dependent and Defective and Backward Children." His last address sums up the man, his recognition of the social element in education, of that which makes it a real force in community life; and the outgoing of his heart to all those who, being helpless, needed peculiarly tender care. Much as

[1] From stenographic report.

he did for education in the way of improving and reforming its methods of teaching and its administration, the essence of what he did was greater than any specific contribution; it was to inspire the teacher and the child in the schoolroom with his own affectionate and sympathetic personality. He renewed the old lesson as to the shortcomings of all instruction until it adds devotion and love to intellectuality: "The greatest of these is love." He was accustomed to say that the social spirit of the schoolroom does more for the child than the formal instruction given; that what the children learn from contact with one another and the teacher is more than what they learn from the text-book and the lecture. If this be true, then the atmosphere and spirit of the schoolroom must be that of freedom, of confidence, of mutual interest in a common life of work and play. He was accustomed to say that all the resources of the schoolroom should be centered upon the "bad" child-resources of helpfulness and sympathy. That was most needed in the schoolroom. That which to the pedant and formalist is a barrier was to him an appeal. What he did in breaking down the despotism, formalism and the rigidity of the old-fashioned school he did, not just because of abstract theory, but because he insisted that the love and faith, which are the tokens of the highest character everywhere, find a peculiarly appropriate place in the contact of the learned and the mature with the little and the feeble.

The second thing that comes to me in the connection of his personality with his educational work is that he believed there is absolutely nothing too good for the children. Many of you, doubtless, have heard him give a talk entitled "Nature and the Child," in which he gave a poetic and idealized sketch (which I supposed to be autobiographical, although he did not say so) of a boy on a farm and his contact with nature. On that farm he studied, without being aware of it, mineralogy, geography, geology, botany, and zoölogy, and came in contact with nature in all her forms. He believed that what he did there himself in that undirected and casual way every child should be allowed to do, should be encouraged to do, through an educational system. Thus he did much for what is termed the enrichment of the elementary-school curriculum; not, again, just as an intellectual matter of putting in this and that study, but because he believed that whatever there is of value in the history of man and in the world of nature is the true birthright of every child born among us. To do anything by any method, by any system of administration which keeps the child from full and complete contact with these things, is a wrong against human nature and against the human spirit.

The third point in which his educational faith and his personality came together was his faith in the professional training of teachers, and in the science of education. I once heard him say that it was this thing that induced him to come out here. He gave up a position which, judged by a conventional standard, was one of superior dignity and importance. But in the position which he occupied he felt that he was getting away from the children. The more he had to do with such a position, the more also he realized that the future of education depends upon the training of the teacher. His belief in the unrealized possibilities of the art of teaching was sublime. It is an inspiration to all teachers everywhere–just as it has been to those have come immediately under his personality. Just as he believed that there was nothing in the world of nature or art too good for the child, so he believed that there was nothing in the personality of another, no element of the human spirit, which should not be called forth in the art of educating, of developing the latent possibilities of the human soul. It was that moral goal, that moral ideal, the possibility of a fuller development, which inspired him in the work he did with teachers.

The great lesson that comes home to me from Colonel Parker's life, the great lesson that I feel that I ought to call especially to the attention of the younger people here present, is what it means really to attain success in life. Colonel Parker never temporized, he never used little expediencies or policies. He never got lost in the smaller things of life; he kept his eyes steadily on the great things, and he fought onward with all the vigor of his personality for those things which are enduring, invisible, and worth while. He waged warfare against opposition; the opposition that came from those who could not get beyond the things they could see and touch, and who, consequently, had attached themselves to the mechanical and formal. The opposition was sometimes active and virulent; more often that of indifference and inertia—harder to face than the active sort. But he never wavered a moment; he never compromised; he never sacrificed the spirit to the letter. As a result, more than the usual measure of success came to him.

Twenty-five years ago, in Quincy, Massachusetts, the work he undertook was an object of derision, as well as of sympathy, all over the country. He was a pioneer, and to many he seemed a faddist, a fanatic. It was only twenty-five years ago; and yet the things for which he then stood are taken today almost as a matter of course, without debate, in all the best schools of this country. Afterward, in Chicago, he waged, against untoward influences, the battle of the professional training of teachers; he fought to keep away every political and personal influence that might in any way lower the standard of the school. Every year he had to wage the battle over again, and every year he simply made his appeal to the people, to the democracy, in which was his trust. His faith in human nature was rewarded. Every year forces rallied about him, and, working with him, won his battles against the combined ranks of political and personal enemies. He gave years of struggle to the elevation of the education of the child and of the teacher; and in his last years, with full poetic justice, with more than the recognition that comes to most pioneers and apostles in this world, his beneficent friend crowned his work with that generous gift which brought within sight–alas, not within grasp–a realization of his lifelong dreams. These things came to him not because he sought them, but because he sought the things which he considered permanently worthy and desirable. And with these other successes came to him the love and loyalty of devoted and attached friends. He was fortunate above most in winning to himself the loyal assistance and unflinching confidence of others.

When a great life has passed away, we get a better perspective of the things that are really worth while; the smaller things, the temporary things, drop back where they belong; and the qualities that ennoble life–faith, courage, devotion to ideals, an end to fight for and to live for–stand out in their supreme significance. Our friend's physical presence has left us, but his spirit remains, reinforced and multiplied. It abides not only in this university community and in this city community, but it lives on in the heart and in the work of every teacher throughout this broad land who has been touched by a truer perception of the high ideal and calling of the teacher.

In Memoriam

COLONEL FRANCIS WAYLAND PARKER LATE DIRECTOR OF THE SCHOOL OF EDUCATION, UNIVERSITY OF CHICAGO.

By Emil G. Hirsch[1]

FETICHES are not always or exclusively cut into stone or carved into wood. Notions and conceits, prejudices, venerable on account of their age and errors, parading in the habiliments of truth, have had their altars at which as intent worship was paid them as ever was to stock and star by untutored savage. They who refuse to bend the knee before the idol built of hasty or false conclusions must expect to meet with ill-will. Walking their own and often lonely paths, they are judged by others as bent upon undermining the very foundations of the social structure. The penalty paid by the bold thinker has often been the forfeiture of his life. Socrates was accused of atheism, and was sentenced to drink the fatal cup, by idol-worshipers whose soul was too dull to comprehend that he whom they hounded into death had seen the face of the true God. Some pioneers had to mount the funeral pyre, while others expired on the cross, purchasing by their life the freedom denied them to think, to prophesy, to teach concerning the vital things. Idolatry works mischief in whatever field its shrines be erected. Politics, economics, and what not, have been under its baneful influences. The fumes rising from censers swung before the image often intercept the rays from a clearer sky. They have kept men in darkness long after the sun has risen. The astrologer receded unwillingly before the astronomer. The

---

[1] Revised from stenographic report.

alchemist would not welcome the chemist. They who searched for the elixir of life would not be hospitable to the botanist. Now, in no field of human endeavor is slavery to the fetich of routine and dogma more dangerous and harmful than in that of education. The pedant fears the advent of the pedagogue. He insists upon the right of his fetiches to receive tribute and to be revered. He denounces as impious the prophet who would destroy the temple of his Baal. Yet, for all his opposition, his deities are tottering to their doom. Elijah, declaring the true God, puts to confusion the howling dervishes.

Among the Elijahs, accused of troubling Israel while announcing the gathering of clouds bringing in their folds the refreshing rain of a new knowledge and a deeper wisdom, he, around whose bier we have assembled, will be numbered. If his end was more merciful than that of Bruno; if his disciples were not forced to hold last converse with him while the jailer prepared for him the draught of hemlock, he, like Socrates of old, like Galileo, escaped not in life the worry and anxiety, the mistrust and suspicions, that are the steady companions of the reformer who heralds a new revelation. In the rabbinical amplifications of Abraham's biography we are told that to him it fell with ax to destroy the idols of his fathers, when reasoning and reflection had impressed upon him that vain was their power and degrading their continued worship. So came to Colonel Parker the duty to splinter the idols that in undisturbed autocracy had exacted their tithes from blind devotees in the schools of this country. We, who have crossed the noon-line of our life, remember well that routine, mechanical reciting, deadening, soulless, devitalized memorizing, ruled in unquestioned regal state in the schoolroom when we were young. A mighty change has been wrought since we were forced to submit to this paralyzing torture of the primer and speller. Then the teacher was regarded as a machine, so constructed as to measure off, in accurately determined quantities, intellectual electuaries which the pupil was to swallow. Education, so-called, consisted in transmitting, in well-regulated flow, from a large barrel containing information, to the memory of the child, the daily doses. And the pupil's part in this process was restricted to parroting, with prescribed sing-song, the text-book. History was a jungle of unconnected and bewildering dates and names. Stress was laid on ability to rattle off, at a given signal, forward or backward, as whim pleased, the catalogue of battles or of presidents. He who could mumble off the names without tripping, and at the highest speed, was crowned with distinction. Arithmetic was a series of tricks, never the application of general and well-comprehended principles to concrete instances. Imitation, not initiative, was the keyword to the educational creed. The eye and the ear were not called into play for the purpose of mastering the inconsistencies and intricacies of English orthography. That the historical development of our language had no place in the scheme goes without saying. But even the natural instruments at the disposal of every child were neglected. Spelling was a drudgery–another tax on the memory. Words jumbled together, for no other reason than that they were of the same number of syllables, were pumped into the mind of the hapless victim of the system. Interest was rigidly banished. Rough and ready utility was invoked to figleaf the nudity. Today air, sunshine, life, flood the schoolroom.

Pupil and teacher alike have been freed from the house of bondage. Whose is the credit? It is his whose mortal remains will soon be consigned, by loving hands, to the grave. It was not an easy task to arouse men and women to a better understanding of the implications of education. The old way, just because it was rigidly mechanical, was the easiest way. It ran along the line of the least resistance. The daily program could without much thought and trouble be arranged. The standards of promotion from one grade to another could without difficulty be fixed. Teachers could be held inflexibly to finishing a certain amount of work. They could be rated successful or the reverse without much labor. Why, then, should this convenient scheme be replaced by another? Colonel Parker put the trumpet to his mouth and declared to American educational idol-worshipers their transgression. Prophet he, he sounded the alarm in no uncertain notes. Bel and Dagon toppled over. The walls of Jericho crumbled before his blast. Routine had to give room to reason. Reception and transmission of knowledge were relegated to the rear. In their stead America learned to put emphasis on thought, on observation, on objects. Books were made subsidiary. The manual was almost branded an intolerable intruder. The appeal of the teacher went out to the creative energy of the pupil's soul. Learning was discovered to be, in very truth, construction and combination, not repetition and imitation.

And another Moloch, to which children had been offered, was destroyed. The old routine had invited the spirit of rivalry to an important function. Competition was encouraged and stimulated. School work was twisted into an end lying beyond. Prizes, marks, honors, were deemed incentives and ultimate objective points. Unholy passions were aroused and played upon. Envy, jealousy, opening the door to dishonesty and favoritism, followed in the wake of the competitive zeal. Another Ruskin, our departed friend saw the pernicious influence of the plan. He understood the injustice inseparably connected with its much-lauded philosophy. That it resulted in injustice to the honest pupils he could not conceal from himself. Who won the distinctions? Not the conscientious boy; but he that nature had most lavishly gifted. Medals and the best marks fell to him who, richly remembered at birth, could without pain absorb what fragment of knowledge constituted the test, and easily rattle off or write down the answer to the decisive question. But the painstaking boy of nervous organization, the timid lad, or he of less quick reaction who had to work hard to master the problem, or, rather, to remember the trick shown to lead to the solution, because of slower temper and of more limited capacity, was not rewarded. Effort counted for nothing. Results only were considered. Colonel Parker could not compromise with such fundamental immorality. Co-operation, not competition; altruism, not selfishness, he held to be the sacramental terms of consecrated pedagogy. Justice he would have reign wherever teachers and pupils met. What to him that the world also follows the haphazard plan of distributing its prizes not in accordance with merit but with results? The school for him had all the more urgently the duty to construe its world on ideal lines. Merit, not result; effort, not attainment, was his polestar.

Again, because he had so high a conception of the function of education, he was among the first to preach in this country a gospel long before heard and accepted in other lands. He insisted that teaching was noble enough, was exhausting and encompassing enough, to be a profession, meant to fill out the life of him who would embrace it. It is not so long ago that teaching was regarded as a sort of stepping-stone to something ulterior and more profitable. The schoolroom was looked upon as a convenient wayside station where one might get off and while away one's time, "hearing lessons," before an express train came along to rush one on to the ultimate destination. Teachers were almost Micawbers, "waiting for something to turn up." In consequence, everybody that was equipped with a moderate amount of information, disjointed and inaccurate though it was, was thought fit to be a teacher. To teaching turned those who had not yet made up their mind what to become, those that had no mind to decide in what field their vocation lay, as well as the thousand and one that had suffered shipwreck on the ocean of life, the sad "misfits" that had been found incompetent in other pursuits. That the teacher's dignity suffered as much as did the school under this hallucination is plain. Acknowledgement of the social service the teacher renders, and adequate compensation therefor, was not meted out to the small, noble fraternity of true and devoted pedagogues that even at that time here and there had made their work tell under these most trying circumstances. But the teacher's profession finally won recognition, and then largely through the persistent efforts of Francis W. Parker. His normal school sounded the deathknell to the ridiculous pretension that everybody that chose to be could be a teacher. It emphasized the truth that knowledge is the least part of the teacher's qualifications. Teaching is both a science and an art. Few are they who can wear the miter of its priesthood. And they that minister in the temple of elementary or other education must pass many years in self-searching preparation before they can be admitted to the diaconate and the higher orders. The old assumption that teaching was a convenient refuge for the waifs of fortune, and waiters for larger opportunities, played into the hands of politicians. Appointments and emoluments in the schools were welcome crumbs for ward-heelers and committeemen to wrangle over. The whole administration of the public schools was, as a rule, in the hands of men with political ambitions or political influence, the parasites of our free institutions. Men were named or elected to serve on boards on education not because they had shown particular fitness for or understanding of the responsibility of the post. They had to be rewarded for contributions to the campaign fund, or cajoled into good humor by the appointment or nomination, lest they might at another election not be as liberal or as active. Men were empowered to decide upon pedagogical methods that had shown eminent skill in organizing primaries or bringing out the "boys." Such conditions Parker had to face when he first came among us. And almost every year the fight had to be renewed against Amalek. We had come to his aid every twelvemonth and, like Hur and Aaron in the biblical story, support the arms of this our Moses, until the Amalekites were defeated. We felt that this support on our part was not for his sake. The world was open to him. But we could not spare him. Cook county had to be spared the shame to have him leave his normal school because petty politicians and malicious meddlers with a "pull" in high quarters would not give his genius the liberty to be true to itself. They said that his pupils were not proficient in the three R's. Someone discovered that their spelling was not above reproach. They labeled him faddist. They talked long about the taxpayer's rights. They would not appropriate funds for luxuries and fanciful notions. So ran the threadbare argument to cover the hunger of the politician for influence and patronage which the Colonel had never stooped and would never stoop to pander to. Faddist indeed! he, the great pedagogue. He had, indeed, not stitched to the worn rag of mechanical routine a few patches of newer color. His was not a crazy–quilt of all sorts of curious novelties. A faddist is he who, to quote Isaiah, adds "*Saw lesaw, kaw lekaw; zeir sham, zeir sham*": "Precept upon precept, law upon law; a little here, a little there." Not such was Parker's method. In his scheme there is organic unity, there is interdependence, there is correlation. From the kindergarten to the highest and last rung of the ladder, one step follows from the preceding. No part may be missed; for every part has its place in the economy of the whole. If this be faddism, may God grant us more of it.

The ultimate goal of his educational purpose was to emancipate the child and the teacher both. He was a host in our fight against pernicious politics in the administration of the schools. But still more vital was his combat for the freedom of the child, his right to be himself, and to learn to know himself. What is the highest in man? Personality. In the personal lies power. Through personality principles become effective. None of the teachings of Jesus, perhaps, was new. But in him principles and precepts known before assumed the vital force of a personal life. The word became flesh. Education is exploration. It would lead the child to discover himself. Every human individual is intended for service. What that service is for which this particular child is called, the school must have a concern to find out. This is the gist of the philosophy of the new education. Hence the school shall not be a preparation for society, but be society. The social aspects of life are in the foreground of its interests. Altruism, co-ordination, interdependence of the component factors and forces–these, the moralities and the humanities, for very sooth, are the focal solicitudes of the school. But to awaken personality, the teacher himself must be a personality. Goethe says somewhere that if the eye were not of solar affinity it could not respond to the sun. So, if the teacher is not a beautiful personality, he cannot hope to awaken it in others. Parker's was this, the supreme gift of the teacher.

Thus armored in the consciousness and consecration of his mission, our departed friend could well scorn derision and be indifferent to the whirlwind of opposition. A soldier he when his country called, a soldier was he when the school was in danger. He would not forsake the flag of his beloved nation when it was assailed. He would not lower his flag before the less brave enemies of the emancipated and redeemed school.

To him was appointed the disappointment that, in God's providence, appears to be the pathos of the life of all true leaders. Moses does not enter the promised land. From afar he may behold its entrancing beauty; but another must lead the host across the dividing river. Another Moses, Parker, from the heights of Pisgah beheld the land of his larger hope and richer harvest. A few months ago he turned the first shovel of sod in the plot where soon will rise the buildings of the school for the coming of which he had struggled and waited these long years of circumscribed activity. That vision of the laughing plains and towering mountain ranges, of the Jordan and the Lebanon, the Carmel and the Sharon of his educational Palestine, will take on real form. It will be his monument *aere perennius*. More loudly even than the walls of the stately group of halls soon to be reared, will proclaim his fame and the gratitude of his disciples the spirit of the activities which will find a home under the roofs of this University. He will be honored by every teacher throughout this broad land. He was the emancipator of the profession. Every American school child will have cause to bless his memory. The young will bring, every day, flowers to his grave. Yea, of him we may say, in the words of the Psalm, "*Mipi Yonkim weollalim yisadta oz*": "Out of the mouth of children and babes Thou hast well established strength and victory." Enter into peace, thou, prophet and priest, pioneer and pathfinder, exemplar and emancipator!

WORKS REFERENCED

"In Memoriam. Colonel Francis Wayland Parker." *The Elementary School Teacher and Course of Study* 2 (1902): 699-715.

Heffron, Ida C. *Francis Wayland Parker: An Interpretive Biography*. Los Angeles: Ivan Deach Jr., 1934.

Parker, Francis W. *Talks on Pedagogics: An Outline of the Theory of Concentration*. New York: The John Day Company, 1937.

Patridge, Lelila E. *Notes of Talks on Teaching, Given by Francis W. Parker, at the Martha's Vineyard Summer Institute, July 17 to August 19, 1882*. New York and Chicago: E.L. Kellogg & Co., 1889.

Stone, Marie K. *The Progressive Legacy: Chicago's Francis W. Parker School (1901-2001)*. New York: Peter Lang, 2001.